CHILDHOOD VICTIMIZATION

INTERPERSONAL*VIOLENCE*

Series Editors

Claire Renzetti, Ph.D.
Jeffrey L. Edleson, Ph.D.

Parenting by Men Who Batter: New Directions for Assessment and Intervention
Edited by Jeffrey L. Edleson and Oliver J. Williams

Coercive Control: How Men Entrap Women in Personal Life
Evan Stark

Childhood Victimization: Violence, Crime, and Abuse in the Lives of Young People
David Finkelhor

Restorative Justice and Violence Against Women
Edited by James Ptacek

Familicidal Hearts: The Emotional Styles of 211 Killers
Neil Websdale

Childhood Victimization

Violence, Crime, and Abuse in the Lives of Young People

David Finkelhor

with contributors

Oxford University Press is a department of the University of Oxford.
It furthers the University's objective of excellence in research, scholarship,
and education by publishing worldwide.

Oxford New York
Auckland Cape Town Dar es Salaam Hong Kong Karachi
Kuala Lumpur Madrid Melbourne Mexico City Nairobi
New Delhi Shanghai Taipei Toronto

With offices in
Argentina Austria Brazil Chile Czech Republic France Greece
Guatemala Hungary Italy Japan Poland Portugal Singapore
South Korea Switzerland Thailand Turkey Ukraine Vietnam

Published in the United States of America by
Oxford University Press
198 Madison Avenue, New York, NY 10016

First issued as an Oxford University Press paperback, 2014.

Library of Congress Cataloging-in-Publication Data
Finkelhor, David.
Childhood victimization : violence, crime, and abuse in the lives of young people /
David Finkelhor, with contributors.
p. cm.—(Interpersonal violence series)
Includes bibliographical references and index.
ISBN 978-0-19-534285-7 (hardcover : alk. paper); 978-0-19-935915-8 (paperback : alk. paper)
1. Abused children—United States. 2. Abused children—Services for—
United States. 3. Children—Crimes against—United States.
4. Child abuse—United States. I. Title.
HV741.F55 2008
362.88083'0973—dc22 2007031636

For Misha and Christine.

—DF

Preface

We have no shortage of books describing threats to childhood in general and to children in particular. Many are calls to alarm. Many are critiques of current public policy and professional practice. A few are dissenting voices pointing out tendencies to exaggerate or overreact when it comes to child welfare. This book takes a different tack from all of those. It is an effort to reconceptualize one particular domain of child welfare concern: the victimization of children. It tries to take some of the conventional ideas about child victims and compact, refine, and mold them into a more integrated and holistic, and also complex, view of the problem.

The central contention is that we have missed the bigger picture. People have been too intensely focused on particular threats such as sexual abuse, bullying, or exposure to domestic violence. This has led to competition for public attention among advocates and scholars who really are concerned about a common problem. This fragmentation has had some unfortunate fallout. It has diminished awareness of the true scope, seriousness, and complexity of child victimization. It has inhibited more systematic and theoretically useful conceptualizations of the problem. It has spawned partial and inadequate policies and response systems. This book is intended to be an illustration of the benefits of looking at these problems in a more integrated fashion.

The first chapter presents the argument that childhood victimization has been neglected as a topic and underestimated as a phenomenon in part because it has been approached in such a fragmented way. The fragmented approaches to child victimization are contrasted with more unified approaches employed in a related field, the study of juvenile offenders and juvenile delinquents, which has left a considerably larger footprint in public policy and academic scholarship.

The second chapter sketches the outlines of the integrated approach we propose as a solution to this fragmentation: a field we have dubbed *developmental victimology*, or the comprehensive study of all forms of child victimization across all stages of childhood. This chapter grapples with some of the definitional issues in this field and illustrates how some valuable conceptual ideas, typologies, and developmental propositions can be fostered by this more comprehensive perspective. It introduces the important concept of the *poly-victim*, a term that highlights the intersection of various forms of victimization.

The third chapter integrates the differing approaches taken by various juvenile victimization subfields to the matter of risk. It poses the question of which children are most likely to experience victimization and why. It moves toward promoting an integrated and comprehensive perspective on victimization risk through a critique and elaboration of the often used *routine activities theory* approach to crime vulnerability.

The fourth chapter addresses the impact of victimization on children and, in addition to arguing for a more comprehensive perspective, proposes two important corrections to current formulations about victimization impact. One correction is to move beyond some of the conceptual restrictions imposed by the heritage of influence from the field of traumatic stress research, which has dominated much of the scholarly and clinical work on child victimization. The other is to think more systematically about how developmental differences influence responses to child victimization. Toward that end, the chapter introduces a model that illustrates how developmental factors such as appraisals, developmental tasks, coping strategies, and environmental buffers influence responses to victimization.

The fifth chapter illustrates how naïve developmental ideas actually can be an impediment to a scientifically based understanding of child victimization. It takes on the assumption that peer victimization is less "serious" when it occurs between younger children.

The sixth chapter looks at the aftermath of child victimization in a more comprehensive way and examines what barriers prevent child victims from getting more assistance from the criminal justice and mental health systems. It presents a conceptual framework for thinking about the complex factors that affect access to these systems and, once again, illustrates the utility of combining perspectives from criminology, social service, and mental health.

The seventh chapter takes a comprehensive look at recent historical trends in various forms of child victimization and also some related child welfare indicators (such as suicide and teen pregnancy). It attempts to explain a relatively unheralded but remarkable development: since the mid-1990s, various forms of child victimization have simultaneously declined. The chapter reviews a variety of sociological factors that may be responsible for the widespread trend, illustrating again how interconnected the various forms of victimization are.

The eighth chapter proposes a comprehensive and systemic framework for understanding the agencies and institutions that respond to child victimization—something we term the *juvenile victim justice system*. The chapter offers a diagram that illustrates the interrelationships among the parts of this system and reviews what is known about how these different parts interact.

A final chapter makes some proposals for preventing and intervening in child victimization; these proposals draw together the various themes examined this book.

These various topics do not begin to do justice to the many complex issues in the field. They also skirt many of the matters most familiar to researchers and practitioners, and staples of many textbooks on the subject. But it is my hope that the unfamiliarity of some of the terrain and the attempt to bring together topics that aren't always associated with one another will inspire readers to think about child victimization in a fresh light.

Acknowledgments

I am not a person who works well in isolation. I found this out early in my scholarly career, when I reached a dead end while working on my dissertation and almost abandoned the effort. But later, when I turned my attention to the topic of child maltreatment and found a congenial community of scholars and practitioners, suddenly 25 years went by with hardly a moment when my enthusiasm balked or my creative energy flagged.

I am very grateful to the many, many colleagues who have been part of this community and who have supported me along the way. A number of the particularly important colleagues who have directly collaborated on the work presented here include Ted Cross, Kathy Kendall-Tackett, Lisa Jones, Dick Ormrod, Heather Turner, and Janis Wolak. Other present and former members of our research group at the University of New Hampshire, including Kim Mitchell, Glenda Kaufman Kantor, Wendy Walsh, Melissa Holt, and Linda Williams, have also provided invaluable ideas and commentary. I am very appreciative of the roster of NIMH-sponsored postdoctoral fellows who spent time with our program during the past 30 years and who gave me many new things to think about.

Murray Straus, my one-time graduate advisor and then colleague for three decades, has been an unending source of inspiration and sage advice. A number of other colleagues have also been extremely influential in my professional and intellectual development in recent years, among them Lucy Berliner, Ben Saunders, John Leventhal, David Corwin, and Kim Oates. I have been the beneficiary of unusual institutional and financial support for my research activities, and for that I thank Senator Judd Gregg of New Hampshire, William Joslin, the Office of Juvenile Justice and Delinquency Prevention, and the National Center for Missing and Exploited Children. Regarding the preparation of this book I am incredibly indebted to my assistant, Kelly Foster, for her attention to so many important details, and to Jennifer Hagberg and Michelle Stransky for their excellent bibliographic help.

Then, of course, there is my life-support system. More than any publisher, editor, dean, or colleague, the person who most made the completion of this book a priority was my son, Misha, an aspiring young author himself, who encouraged me tremendously through his desire to witness firsthand the messy business of how books get written. To have his companionship in the magic world of words is a wonderful treasure. I am also blessed with my extraordinary life partner Christine, who has been a passionate advocate of my work from the moment we met. Her constant faith in the value of my thinking and writing are just a few of the many gifts with which she has so enriched my life. My good friend Chuck Morrison has been a devoted fan and creative interlocutor. Thanks to you all.

Contents

Contributors

David Finkelhor
Lucy Berliner
Ted Cross
Lisa Jones
Kathy Kendall-Tackett
Richard Ormrod
Elise N. Pepin
Heather Turner
Janis Wolak

CHILDHOOD VICTIMIZATION

Chapter 1

Child Victims: An Introduction

Children are arguably the most criminally victimized people in society. They suffer high rates of all the same crimes that adults do, plus a load of offenses specific to their status as children, such as child maltreatment. They are beaten by family members, bullied and attacked by schoolmates and peers, abused and raped by dating partners, and targeted by sex offenders in both physical and virtual realms. Childhood is indeed a gauntlet.

The claim that children are the most criminally victimized population is not one that requires definitional gerrymandering to prove. It is true even if we talk in the narrowest terms about conventional crime—police blotter crime—and leave out for the moment the special victimizations of childhood such as child abuse and neglect. For example, juveniles are two to three times more likely than adults in America to suffer a conventional rape, robbery, or aggravated assault—all serious violent crimes. They are three times more likely than adults to suffer what police call a "simple assault."

Such statistics, in case they come as a surprise, are from the most highly regarded source of crime-victimization information in the United States, the federal government's National Crime Victimization Survey (NCVS), derived from detailed interviews with over 100,000 citizens each year, conducted by the Bureau of Census for the U.S. Department of Justice. The NCVS uses a fairly careful and conservative measure of crime, one that tallies considerably fewer victimizations than many other victims surveys.[1] But the high vulnerability of children is clear-cut. For example, during the 1990s, the rate for aggravated assault against youths 12 to 17 years old was 15.5 per 1,000—over twice the rate for the general population (6.9 per 1,000). For rape, the comparison was 3.2 per 1,000 for youths to 1.3 per 1,000 for adults—almost 2.5 times higher. For violence overall, the rate was 2.6 times higher for youth.[2]

Arguments about the "Most Victimized" Claim

Nobody seriously questions the vulnerability of young people to crime. But the claim that they are the most criminally victimized sometimes provokes objections. The points at issue are worth addressing.

Some criminologists have contended that victimizations of young people, even those counted in the NCVS as crimes, although numerous, are not as serious as those of adults. Their view is that most victimizations of youth are squabbles and minor fights that do not qualify as "real crimes."[3] But this argument (taken up at greater length in Chapter 5) does not stand up to scrutiny. The strongest refutation is that young people in the NCVS interviews report considerably higher rates of *injury* than adults subsequent to victimization, and they also face more weapon-toting assailants than do other victims. So their rates of truly serious criminal victimization are clearly higher.

Another, more modest objection to the most victimized claim is the observation that certain statistics show that young adults, not juveniles, appear to be at the highest risk of criminal victimization. Indeed, some tabulations from the NCVS show higher rates for young adults 18 to 24 years old of rape, robbery, and aggravated assault (but not of simple assault or overall violent victimization). So even though "youth" are more victimized than "all adults," they are not, in this formal comparison, more victimized than "young adults." But a methodological idiosyncrasy in the way NCVS tabulates repeated victimizations turns the tables on this objection. The NCVS has a peculiar* way of undercounting what are called repeat victimizations (e.g., the abusive husband or neighborhood bully who attacks someone repeatedly over the course of a year), and this results in substantial undercounting of juvenile crime victims, who experience a disproportionate number of these repeat behaviors.[4] When that undercounting is corrected, juveniles are shown to be more frequently violently victimized than even young adults. (The only exception is sexual assault, for which the victimization rates for juveniles and young adults are statistically indistinguishable.)

Along similar lines, homicide statistics do not show juveniles to be the most victimized segment of the population. Young adults very clearly experience higher homicide victimization rates than do teenagers (e.g., 14.2 per 100,000 for 18- to 24-year-olds versus 4.6 for 14- to 17-year-olds[5]). While homicide is clearly the most tragic form of victimization, it is fortunately relatively rare. If the burden of crime is being tallied in terms of frequency rather than seriousness, homicide does not weigh much; it is a dimension that cannot claim children among its most victimized. There are nonetheless some grim homicide trophies that children can claim. For example, for female children, the first year of life holds one of the greatest risks for homicide.[6] Seventeen-year-old males also have one of the highest homicide rates of any population.

Another important question one might raise about the most-victimized claim is who, exactly, is considered a child. Some contend that the high crime vulnerability applies only to teens, not to younger children; they might insist that one say "teens" have the greatest vulnerability, rather than children in general.

Unfortunately, it is hard to assess the true vulnerability of younger children, for several reasons. First, the NCVS doesn't measure the criminal victimization rates of persons younger than age 12, so we do not have official data for all children. Second, there is considerable debate about how to define crimes against younger juveniles. If it is a violent crime when a 22-year-old man is punched by someone his own age, is it also a violent crime when a 5-year-old boy is punched by someone his own age? Nonetheless, studies of younger children do not offer much ammunition to those who might contend that younger children are considerably safer from violence and crime than are teenagers. While certain kinds of victimization may increase somewhat during the teenage years, the overall rate of violent victimization is already quite high for younger children (for more details, see Chapter 2).

Beyond Conventional Crime

As we have shown, the claim that children are "the most victimized" does bear up with respect to conventional crime, though it possibly has some weaknesses with respect to homicide, younger children, and in comparison with rates for young adults. But once we move beyond the confines of conventional crime and the NCVS and begin to factor in offenses such as child abuse, the arguments for children being the most victimized gain considerable heft.

The NCVS, which has been the basis for the discussion up until now, admittedly does its weakest job counting violence among family members—the kind of serious crimes that children are most vulnerable to. (For example, the NCVS does not require respondents to be interviewed in privacy, so it undercounts much intra-family violence.) Other studies that specifically look into family violence show that children suffer considerably more of this kind of crime than do other segments of the population. For example, according to the National Family Violence Survey, children experience three times as much serious violence at the hands of family members than do adults.[7] This comparison is between children living in families and adults living in families, but the reality is that nearly one in eight (13%) adults doesn't even live with family members, whereas virtually all children do. If the NCVS estimates better factored in family violence, the victimization disparity for children, even compared to young adults, might well be larger still.[†]

Another problem with the NCVS data is that they do not reflect some of the serious, special crimes and other victimizations that children alone suffer. For example, NCVS data count only forcible rape and sexual assault; none of the serious sexual abuses of children—crimes that have filled the paper in recent years—are counted by the NCVS unless they involve force or threat. And if we limit the survey to conventional crime, then we also miss most of the serious child neglect, treated by authorities as a major form of child victimization but rarely counted statistically as a crime. Over 50 percent of substantiated child maltreatment every year, some 500,000 cases nationally, involves child neglect.

The contribution of child abuse and neglect to the total burden of victimization affecting children is roughly apparent from official crime estimates. A crude estimate is that about 1.3 million violent crimes against children were reported to police in 2004, based on extrapolations from FBI data.[§] In comparison, there were approximately 872,000 cases of substantiated child abuse and neglect in 2004.[8] Not all of these would be considered crimes; 17% were physical abuse and 10% were sexual abuse—the latter the most clearly criminal of the child maltreatment types of crime. So most of this child abuse and neglect is not encompassed by the crime data,[9] and needs to be counted as an added victimization burden on children.

Moreover, whatever the data show—whatever the methodology, victim survey, or official crime statistics—offenses against children are more undercounted than other kinds of victimization. They are clearly the kind of victims least likely to make a report to the police. For example, in the NCVS, only 28% of crimes against children get reported to the police, compared to 44% of crimes against adults. Child victimizations are almost certainly underreported in surveys as well. With younger children, we often have to rely on parents and other caregivers to report abuse, and there is much that these caregivers may not know about or may be reluctant to disclose. Young people themselves are often reticent about abuse. The NCVS in particular was not designed with young people in mind as respondents. The interviews are not conducted in private, thereby affecting the willingness of children to disclose victimization at the hands of family members, or anything else they do not want their parents to know about. In addition, NCVS interviewers are allowed to conduct proxy interviews with caregivers instead of interviewing the youth involved. But those caregivers may not be aware of the extent of victimization. The fact that four times as many youth interviews as adult interviews involve use of a proxy (4.4% versus 0.9%) suggests considerable underestimation of youth victimization. So, the actual rates of child victimization in the NCVS, as well as in other surveys and official statistics, may be very underestimated.

Ultimately, however, the question of who is most victimized is largely rhetorical. Children are either the most crime-victimized or one of the most crime-victimized segments of the population; the answer depends in part on *which* children and *which* crimes we are most interested in. Children are an extremely crime-victimized segment of society; the crucial point is that this reality has not been sufficiently recognized or explored.

Why Children Are So Vulnerable

One sign that the extent of children's victimization is generally unrecognized is the fact that it has prompted so few attempts at an explanation. Theories abound on why young people commit crimes; the PhD dissertations on this topic are legion. Theories also abound on why certain demographic groups have high victimization rates, among them the poor, minorities, and city dwellers. But explanations for the high rate of juvenile victimization are scarce. Even child advocates have not often tried to formalize ideas on this subject.

Size and Strength

Perhaps people think that the explanations for high rates of juvenile victimization are self-evident. For example, children are young, small, and weak (at least some of them), and therefore easy victims. Features of physical vulnerability may be important in some kinds of victimization. For example, some studies, but not all, have shown that physically weaker children in the classroom are more likely to be victimized by bullies.[10] Older children are less likely to be hit by their parents, and this may have to do with their increased capacity to fight back or to intimidate their elders. But overall, physical smallness and weakness are not major and consistent risk factors, even though those conditions may create a subjective sense of vulnerability. The elderly, in spite of their weakness, have lower victimization rates than other adults. Women, who are on average smaller, have lower crime victimization rates than do men. In contrast, male teens, who are often big and strong, have a high victimization risk. So while they may be contributing factors, smallness and weakness are not sufficient criteria for increased risk.

Lack of Knowledge, Experience, and Self-Control

Children have other obvious disadvantages in terms of knowledge and experience, as well as in the ability to take action, and some of these may be associated with higher crime vulnerability. This notion is certainly implicit in the prevention strategy of providing young people with information to help them avoid becoming victims.

Children, at least at some ages, may be less able to identify dangerous people and places than adults. They may be less familiar with conflict-resolution strategies. In addition, some children engage in behaviors that almost certainly contribute to the increased risks that they experience. For example, some adolescents experiment with drugs and alcohol, participate in delinquent activities, join gangs, or put themselves into risky sexual situations. Some of this risky behavior reflects the lack of knowledge and experience that characterizes childhood, but some has other sources. The risky-behavior explanation is the one that has been emphasized most by the few criminologists who have looked at juvenile victimization.[11,12]

Indeed, there is good empirical evidence to support an association between risky activities and victimization. But some of the risky behavior may be a result of victimization rather than its cause. For example, youth may join gangs or drink or take drugs because they have been victimized and are using these strategies to cope, seeking protection in the case of gangs or solace in the case of alcohol or drugs. Ironically, these behaviors serve only to increase their vulnerability more.[13] Some longitudinal research shows the main sequence to be victimization first and risky behavior second, rather than vice versa. [14]

In any case, risky behavior has its limits in explaining the high risk for young children's victimization. It is better at explaining the victimization of teens and conventional crime victimization than at explaining children's maltreatment, for example. Also, the vulnerability of young children to homicide or physical assault by their parents is not well accounted for by this factor.

Rather than ascribing victimization to risky behavior, it may be better to formulate the point this way: young people, both children and teens, have more developmental difficulty controlling certain aspects of their behavior than do adults; this is part of being literally immature, and this lack of self-regulation can increase the risk of victimization by others. That is, the immaturity of self-regulation sometimes elicits or contributes to violence at the hands of family members, as well as aggressive and exploitative behaviors at the hands of peers and nonrelatives.

Although this argument may seem to be blaming young people for their own victimization, the truth of it is a reality that we must recognize in our prevention efforts. We caution new parents to expect it as developmentally normal, and not to take it as a sign of malice, when children have tantrums or lash out at their parents. We warn parents to expect teens to act as though they are invulnerable to danger. Adults are not supposed to be provoked by these youthful challenges, but the reality is that the actions of youth can be provoking. We recognize that we should not hold children responsible for their developmental immaturity; for this reason it seems to be better to talk about developmental immaturities in self-control rather than "risky behavior."

Weak Norms and Sanctions Against Victimization

Another probable reason for why children are at high risk of victimization is that our society has relatively weaker norms and sanctions about offenses against children. There are obvious exceptions—sex crimes against children are considered to be among the most heinous of sex crimes—but overall this is not the case. Acts considered serious offenses when their victims are adults are not taken so seriously when they are committed against children. Examples are everywhere. In most modern, civilized societies, hit your wife and you get arrested—at least if the police find out.

Hit your child, however, and little will happen if you make a reasonable argument that it was for disciplinary purposes and the child did not suffer physical injury. If a colleague punches you, the result will likely be a police investigation, followed by criminal charges and your colleague's almost certain loss of a job. If a child is punched by a schoolmate, the teacher may call it a fight and bring both children to the principal, but that will probably be the sternest official action taken.

The ambivalence toward child victimization is apparent in both societal norms and social sanctions. Some of this ambivalence stems from a reluctance to be harsh and punitive toward juveniles who commit offenses. Some stems from wanting to preserve a parent–child bond, even when parents mistreat their children. But some stems from the belief that these victimizations are different in nature from most others: that they are less serious, that they are simply an inevitable part of childhood or family life, and that they can even be educational or build character.

In particular, the reason it has taken so long to recognize problems like sexual harassment and bullying in childhood cannot be ascribed to a simple reluctance to be harsh or punitive with juvenile offenders. Rather, these experiences have just been considered a part of childhood, even when we stopped tolerating them among adults. In the case of other victimizations that have only recently been widely recognized, such as sexual abuse and child maltreatment, the barriers to recognition were the prerogatives and privileges that adults enjoyed with respect to their families. The protection of children simply did not weigh heavily enough on the scale of values to justify encroachments on these prerogatives. We still can't aggressively prosecute people who beat their children because those parents who want to be able to hit their children (but not injure them)—that is, those in favor of corporal punishment—insist on exculpatory criminal laws that end up protecting many abusers. Such laws allow parents charged with assaulting a child to counter that the act was in the service of disciplining the child, which generally constitutes a sufficient defense. Given the breadth of the disciplinary defense, police and prosecutors are unwilling to bring assault charges against parents except in instances of death or extreme bodily injury.

There is, however, considerable evidence that strengthened norms and sanctions play an important role in discouraging crime and offensive behavior. As norms have changed regarding spousal assault, evidence suggests that its incidence has declined.[15] As norms have changed with regard to corporal punishment, that has declined, too.[16] Community policing and the philosophy of intervention to restore community order are widely regarded as having contributed to the declining crime rates of the 1990s.[17] This is all evidence that when norms are clear and strict, offenses are discouraged. So it is quite possible that lax and unclear norms about offenses against children, and the view that such offenses are not very serious, play at least some role in the frequency of such victimization.

Lack of Choice over Associates

There is a final, generally overlooked but very important reason that children are at high risk for victimization, one that has to do with the conditions of children's social lives and their living arrangements: *children have comparatively little choice over whom they associate with.* Children do not choose the families they grow up with, they do not choose the neighborhoods they reside in, and they usually do not choose the schools they attend. This potentially puts them into more frequent involuntary contact with high-risk offenders and thus at greater jeopardy for victimization. For example, when children live in families whose members mistreat them, they are not free or able to just pick up and leave. When they live in dangerous neighborhoods, they cannot choose on their own to move elsewhere. If they attend a school with many hostile and delinquent peers, they cannot simply change schools or quit without adult assistance or consent. They are stuck. The absence of choice in associates and environments affects children's vulnerability to both intimate victimization and street crime, and it affects the vulnerability of both young children and teens.

Contrast this with the range of options generally available to adults who wish to gain protection from crime. Adults are able to seek divorces from dangerous family partners—and have increasingly opted to do so. Adults can change their residences in reaction to dangerous neighborhoods; indeed, concern about safety has been an important motive governing residential mobility in the United States for many generations. Adults also have other taken-for-granted lifestyle mechanisms they use to regulate whom they associate with. They have ready access to cars, an insular mode of transportation they have increasingly chosen over public conveyances, in part for safety reasons. Adults frequently live alone and work in the enclosed rooms of offices or factory complexes to which access is generally restricted, typically because of safety concerns.

Children, on the other hand, are obliged to live with other people. When they move about, they are more often in public conveyances or out on the streets, exposed to anyone who comes by. Children work in high-density, heterogeneous environments—for this is what almost all schools are—that are very different from adults' modern office and factory environments. As the stereotypical hallway encounter with the school bully well illustrates, it is very difficult to find protected space in most schools. The lack-of-control explanation for high juvenile victimization certainly has some support from other crime research. People such as convenience store clerks and deliverymen, to whom the general public has a lot of uncontrolled access, tend to experience more crime victimization. This lack of control also helps explain why children are more vulnerable to victimization than adults.

To summarize, children are at high risk of victimization compared to adults. That high risk is likely due to several factors: (1) children's developmental immaturity in controlling their own behavior, (2) society's tolerance for or weak sanctions concerning offenses against children, and (3) children's lesser ability to regulate and choose who they associate and interact with. These are all points that it will be useful to understand more broadly and deeply if we want to combat crimes against children.

Why Has High Vulnerability Not Been More Widely Recognized?

Although most Americans have a general sense that children are vulnerable, the fact that children are the most or among the most crime-victimized members of society is not a widely recognized fact. Compare it to other, better known sociological facts about crimes, for example: that minorities experience more crime, that women experience more sexual assaults, or that the elderly have the greatest fear of crime but in fact are at lower risk. Why hasn't the high vulnerability of children to crime received more formal and popular recognition? Several factors have probably contributed.

One factor is that the facts to support the conclusion of higher vulnerability have not been easy to obtain. Some of this is due to the inadequacies of current official statistics. For example, the FBI's well-known annual summary on crime, the Uniform Crime Report, does not break down crime victims by age, so it has not been easy to focus on the number of child crime victims. The other well-publicized national information about crime comes from the NCVS, but, curiously, until recently reports from this system have not considered juveniles under the age of 18 as a separate category. Moreover, since the NCVS information on crime victimization does not cover children under 12, it has not clearly reported on the situation for children in general.

Another barrier to recognizing the high vulnerability of children to crime is that statistics about juvenile victims are fragmented, as are the agencies that respond to them. The statistics on physically abused, sexually abused, and neglected children are collected and published by one organization, while another handles the statistics on crime.

But the largest problem has nothing to do with statistics. Rather, it has to do with competing stereotypes in the media and our culture about the problems of juveniles and crime. For the most part, when the topic of crime intersects with a concern about juveniles, the focus is on juvenile offenders, not juvenile victims. Indeed, juvenile offenders occupy a place of central notoriety in the media and in the public's awareness. Virtually every American knows that juveniles constitute a disproportionate share of offenders, even if they are unaware of the disproportion on the victims' side. In fact, polls typically show that the public overestimates the criminality of juveniles, seeing them as responsible for far more than the 18% of violent crimes that they commit.[18] A large majority of the public also continued to insist that juvenile offending was on the rise in the late 1990s, even as it fell to its lowest point in generations.[19] In a culture preoccupied with the notion of juveniles as offenders and that holds juveniles responsible for the general sense of societal insecurity, it may be hard to simultaneously become mobilized about the disproportionate number of victims in this same group.

It is curious how many realms show a similar, conspicuous disparity between the attention paid to juveniles as offenders versus juveniles as victims. The disparity is both historical and intellectual. The field of juvenile delinquency—the formal study of juveniles who commit crimes—extends back more than a century in the social sciences and public policy, all the way to the famous nineteenth-century social theorists and reformers.[20] In fact, the study of juvenile offenders is one of the most theoretically and empirically rich domains of social science, with many of the most famous social scientists of the twentieth century—Robert Merton, George Herbert Mead, Charles Cooley, and Marvin Wolfgang, to name a few—devoting considerable portions of their careers to the field.[21]

Juvenile victimization certainly has its history, too. Though cloaked to some degree in the concept of childhood sexual trauma, the topic certainly played a famous if somewhat obscure role in the development of Freudian psychoanalytic thinking.[22] The notion of parental maltreatment (although more concerned with emotional abuse and neglect) figured in early developmental thinking on the explanation of adult psychopathology. But child victimization has received considerably less attention than juvenile delinquency as a widespread social problem in need of public policy intervention. The establishment of juvenile courts and juvenile law as a response to juvenile offending dates to the nineteenth century; the legal framework and popular mobilization for child victims, however, is generally thought to have its modern origins in the 1960s and 1970s.[23]

The contrast in the treatments of children as victims and as offenders is apparent at the public-policy level, as well. The U.S. government agency dedicated to crime and children is the Office of Juvenile Justice and Delinquency Prevention. In spite of its name, the agency does concern itself to some extent with victims (a recent development) as well as offenders, but only the delinquents are noted in the agency's title, and they occupy the lion's share of the agency's funding and portfolio. The term "juvenile justice," interestingly, has come to refer almost exclusively to how juvenile offenders are dealt with by the legal system, in spite of the fact that, in colloquial terms, victims are very much in mind when we talk about "obtaining" or "receiving" justice. But the way in which the police or courts deal with juvenile victims is almost never a topic in treatises or within the agencies concerned with "juvenile justice."

Another stark contrast between the treatments of children's victimization and children's offending can be seen in the academic context. For example, virtually every college campus offers a course on juvenile delinquency and juvenile justice that is considered a staple of the introductory social science curriculum. Courses on juvenile victimization or child abuse, on the other hand, are much less common and often appear only in graduate-level curricula of those studying professional social work. The content of those courses on juvenile delinquency, juvenile justice, and juvenile crime—as reflected in the textbooks that are used—includes scant attention to juvenile victims, except, most commonly, in sections devoted to examining how offenders are formed; in some of the texts, there is no mention of juvenile victimization at all. It is not clear why American colleges feel their undergraduates have a greater need for exposure to thinking about juvenile offenders than about juvenile victims, given that their most frequent occupational destinations are education, social work, law enforcement, and medicine—fields in which they will deal with both of these problems. By contrast, courses on women and crime, to the extent that they exist, typically treat both women's victimization and offending.

The fact that juvenile offenders receive so much more attention than do juvenile victims might lead one to expect that juvenile delinquency is a much bigger problem than juvenile victimization—but that would be a mistake. Once again, the statistical comparison is not straightforward and is fraught with ambiguities; but almost any examination of comparative data suggests that juvenile delinquency and victimization are comparably huge problems affecting large segments of the child population.

To make a relatively evenhanded comparison, and one that is directly relevant to policy concerns, we can examine the number of juveniles who come to the attention of police as crime victims and the number who come to attention as offenders. Figure 1.1 traces by age the number of juvenile crime victims and offenders reported to police by anyone in any role according to the FBI's new comprehensive incident reporting system (National Incident Based Reporting System, or NIBRS). Overall, more juvenile victims come to police attention than juvenile offenders. The

FIGURE 1.1. Juvenile victims and juvenile offenders known to police, violent crimes, 2002. *Source*: U.S. Department of Justice, Federal Bureau of Investigation. (2004). *National Incident-Based Reporting System (NIBRS), 2002*. Ann Arbor, MI: Inter-University Consortium for Political and Social Research.

excess of victims over offenders occurs at every age up until age 15, when offenders overtake victims to a slight degree. Interestingly, for females and for white juveniles, the number of victims exceeds the number of offenders at every stage of childhood. Information coming from surveys of young people confirm a similar conclusion.[14] There are equivalently large numbers of juvenile victims and juvenile offenders, so it is not possible to make a convincing case that juvenile offending trumps juvenile victimization in any numerical sense.

Does Delinquency Encompass Victimization?

If it cannot be said that delinquents outnumber victims, why have delinquents received such disproportionate attention? One argument that is sometimes made for priority attention to offending over victimization is that attention to delinquents simultaneously grants attention to victims. That is, interest in delinquency does not obscure or ignore victimization but rather incorporates concern about victims. By studying and solving the delinquency problem, we are also understanding and remedying the victimization problem, since so much of juvenile victimization occurs at the hands of other juveniles. So, the thinking goes, victimization does not need to be a separate topic of concern, and even if it does, the charge that victims are neglected is exaggerated.

This argument has some truth in the abstract, but it is not convincing in its reality. In truth, very little of the research and writing on delinquency has much to say about victims. Likewise, very little of the policy response to delinquents has incorporated any mechanisms to help, treat, or rehabilitate victims. Similarly, few delinquency-prevention efforts consider how to mobilize and strengthen victims. Discussions of the juvenile justice system for offenders rarely highlight the role victims play or how they are treated. But victims are not simply indirect elements of the juvenile-offender problem, as perhaps family members are indirectly affected when a loved one contracts cancer or experiences mental illness. Indeed, the neglect of victims in the juvenile-delinquency area is telling.

Most important from a practical standpoint, much juvenile victimization does *not* occur at the hands of other juveniles. Adults are the perpetrators of almost half the crimes against children that come to the attention of the police. This part of the juvenile-victimization problem would not be solved even if juvenile offending were curbed. So, attention to juvenile offenders does not truly encompass juvenile victims, and it is justifiable to say that juvenile victims need equivalent attention.

Is Delinquency More Serious in its Effects?

The priority given to juvenile offenders compared to victims might be justified with claims that delinquency, even if not more common, is a more consequential problem. Indeed, people making this argument might point to the long careers of criminal behavior that sometimes follow juvenile delinquency. They may point to the tremendous social and personal costs of juvenile crime. They may add that short-circuiting a criminal career early in a person's life is cost-effective and socially progressive. These are valid arguments for why concern about delinquency is important. Unfortunately, these and almost all similar arguments apply in equal measure to juvenile victimization. Juvenile victims, according to the research, often go on to long careers of social disadvantage and behavioral problems, including delinquency.[23] Most of the costs of delinquent and criminal behavior are borne by individual victims. Short-circuiting these costs is also cost-effective and socially progressive, but that requires interventions beyond simply treating the delinquents. It is hard to mount any argument that says juvenile offending is consequential without simultaneously admitting that juvenile victimization is equivalently consequential.

Delinquency Prevention Represents the Priorities of Adults

If attention to juvenile delinquency takes policy priority over attention to juvenile victimization, this may indeed relate to differences in their consequences. But the difference may hinge on who bears the consequences, not their relative seriousness. Juvenile delinquency threatens everybody, including the adults who decide what issues receive priority attention. Juvenile victimization threatens mostly juveniles, who are not politically well positioned to argue their cause. Granted, juvenile victimization is of concern to adults as well, since many adults are parents and genuinely want to protect their children. But the direct impact of juvenile victimization is on juveniles. Ultimately, it might be said that *fear trumps empathy*—that the fear of the harm that juveniles might cause to adults is greater than the empathy adults might have for children who suffer victimization.

In rebuttal, it might be fairly argued that a focus on criminal offending of all sorts takes priority over concern for crime victims, and that the study of victimology is a relatively new field compared to the study of offending in general. In this sense, neglect of juvenile victims is a problem shared by neglect for victims in general. This circumstance may reflect a moral failure in public policy, but it is not one directed specifically at children.

But the neglect of child victims does seem somehow more specific, in light of children's extreme vulnerability to victimization and the disproportionate attention paid to juvenile offenders. It is interesting to note that, after generations of similar neglect, crimes against women have now achieved a very significant policy prominence. In fact, crimes against women receive considerably more attention from the U.S. government's Office of Victims of Crime than do juvenile victims. Women suffer from some particularly egregious and historically minimized kinds of crime, such as rape and domestic violence, but as a group they do not experience the enormously disproportionate levels of victimization that children do. If women's victimization is now a major policy priority, it is primarily due to the political mobilization of the women's movement and its lasting effects. This mobilization, in fact, illustrated well the special needs that a victim-oriented—as opposed to a conventional offender-oriented—crime policy promotes, emphasizing mechanisms such as victim advocates, protection orders, treatments, and compensation. It also highlights the disadvantages that children face because of their inability to advocate on their own behalf, a situation that has almost certainly delayed the mobilization of a victim-oriented crime policy targeted at the most criminally victimized segment of the population.

Child Victimization Is Sometimes Exaggerated

To claim that there has been a blanket minimization of and disregard for child victims in America's crime consciousness would be grossly unfair. At times, child victims have been very much in the limelight. In fact, there have been major mobilizations on behalf of child victims at several points in American history, including the sustained one that we are currently experiencing. Fears for children's safety in a world of abductors and rapists have been recurring themes for at least the last hundred years.[24] There were panics in the wake of the Lindbergh-baby abduction and related cases in the 1930s; child molestations and slayings prompted panics in the 1950s; a large national political mobilization for battered children occurred in the 1960s in response to efforts like those of pediatrician Henry Kempe and his colleagues; and child sexual abuse came into the spotlight in the late 1970s, as part of a larger women's-movement mobilization about rape and the vulnerability of women and girls.[25]

Perhaps the most blatant counter to the claim that child victims have been neglected is the child-abduction scare of the 1980s. In the wake of some very high-profile kidnappings and murders, both the general public and policymakers came to believe that tens of thousands of children were possibly being snatched every year by strangers. Yet it turned out that the number of "stereotypically kidnapped" children—those taken by strangers for a substantial distance or an extended period of time, murdered, or held for ransom—was in the low hundreds each year, not the thousands.[26,27] This episode is thought of as the archetypal example of how child victimization can be exaggerated, not minimized.[28] There have been some other recent examples of false child victimization "epidemics," including a child-abduction scare in the summer of 2003 and the school-shooter alarm of the 1990s. Although it is clear in retrospect that the spate of mass homicides by alienated youth is a somewhat new phenomenon, these highly publicized incidents did not signal a crime wave or a heightened vulnerability of children to murder in schools.[29,30]

Ultimately, the role of children in the greater picture of crime awareness is a complicated one. There are many aspects of child victimization that have been hard to draw attention to. Some of the realities that we take for granted today—the frequency of child abuse, the existence of intrafamilial sexual abuse, and considerable school bullying—are things that have only recently come to public awareness. Other aspects of child victimization remain controversial or hover outside of public awareness—for example, the very high rates of property crime that juveniles suffer and the reluctance to consider it a crime when parents assault children. At the same time, some examples of child victimization capture political and journalistic attention very readily, particularly sex crimes and child homicides.

Symbolic Versus Substantive Concern

These patterns of concern for child victims are characteristic of a protection orientation that is more symbolic than substantive, more proprietary than empathetic. In the days before domestic violence, date rape, and sexual harassment were acknowledged as crimes, other threats against symbolic womanhood mobilized anxiety—for example, worries about sexual overtures from blacks, immigrants, and other undesirables, or the generic threat to women from invading armies. These anxieties reigned at the same time that more frequent and more routine threats to women were generally unrecognized and often even denied.

In a similar vein, the criminal threats to symbolic childhood that have been most clearly recognized—for example, child molestation and kidnapping—seem also to be ones that emphasize the symbolic purity and innocence of youth, and perhaps even the ownership stake that adults wish to assert over children. The broader, more chronic threats, such as bullying, and the ones that implicate family and caregivers, such as child abuse and sibling violence, have taken longer to emerge into the daylight, and some still remain relatively unrecognized.

The Problem of Topic Fragmentation

If the subject of child victimization has had a checkered history and a somewhat diminutive status compared to juvenile delinquency, another culprit in this story might be the fragmented way the topic has been addressed. Indeed, the view of child victimization as an integrated concept is probably novel for most readers, who tend to think in more conventional terms of concepts such as child maltreatment, child abuse and neglect, or even "crimes against children."

It is interesting how many distinct forms of child victimization have become the focus of study and public policy in the last couple of decades. *Child abuse and neglect* grew up as a distinct field, with its own institutional framework, starting in the 1970s.[31] *Missing children*, which concerns children abducted by strangers or family members, coalesced as another distinct domain in the 1980s.[32] *Child exploitation*, including involvement of children in pornography, sex rings, and prostitution, has emerged with an identity clearly separate from the intrafamilial forms of sexual abuse that occupy the *child maltreatment* field.[33] *Bullying* has taken off recently as a topic of considerable independent focus.[34,35] *Adolescent dating violence* has its own researchers, curricula, and prevention strategies.[36] A separate field of interest, *exposure to community violence*, has emphasized the problems of children who witness and experience violence, particularly in the neighborhood but generally excluding intrafamilial offenses.[37] In a parallel track, a considerable bubble of interest has developed concerning *exposure to domestic violence*, which emphasizes the problems of children who witness their parents abusing each other.[38] This is not even an exhaustive list of fields.

One of the things demonstrated by this inventory of related fields is how ready researchers and advocates have been to "found" new fields rather than simply elaborate on or expand existing topics. This situation no doubt stems from a desire to generate new funding and new responses that might otherwise be less forthcoming if promoted as expansions of existing fields. But it is remarkable, as well, how little attention is generally paid to linking these topics, even when the theoretical and conceptual issues are similar. It seems as though these new-topic advocates have gone to great pains to differentiate themselves from existing field that actually are closely connected.

The fragmentation of the child victimization topic has led to many arbitrary and artificial distinctions. For example, children featured in child pornography and used for child prostitution are frequently abused, photographed, and sold by members of their own family, making this situation an elaboration of the field of intrafamily sex abuse. That is to say, the problems of sexual abuse and child exploitation frequently overlap and have more in common than not, yet often they are thought of as the separate domains of sexual abuse and child sexual exploitation. Similarly, the majority of children exposed to domestic violence are also subjected to violence by their caregivers, as well as to neglect and emotional abuse, so the distinction between the fields of child maltreatment and of children exposed to domestic violence is hardly tenable.

Is the Distinction Between Intrafamily and Extrafamily Victimization Important?

Interestingly, the biggest divide in fields with regard to child victims, and the one most enduringly observed, is between child maltreatment and extrafamily crime. The distinction is reinforced because two large, separate institutional complexes define their domains of operation in different ways. The child-protection system purports to deal with victimizations that implicate caregivers; this generally means family members but in practice often incorporates a wider network of caregivers, including babysitters and youth workers. The criminal-justice system, by contrast, purports to deal with crime and has traditionally been reluctant to become involved in intrafamily matters except when the violations are egregious.

Does this distinction have a strong conceptual and empirical basis? On the one hand, it does seem true, in the abstract, that threats to a child's well-being emanating from caregivers and family members have a different dynamic and require a different response. We want to preserve families and parent–child relationships as much as possible, so we respond to victimization in these environments differently. In short, sending abusive moms to jail is more complicated and less clearly in everybody's interest than is incarcerating strangers who abduct children.

On the other hand, there is much arbitrariness in the implementation of this distinction—arbitrariness that makes one wonder how important the distinction actually is. For example, the problem of family abduction has been dealt with largely by criminal justice authorities and generally ignored by child protection agencies, even though it is an intrafamily threat to a child's well-being.[32] In contrast, child protection authorities have frequently taken an interest in sexual abuse at the hands of noncaretakers. A good example of this is the way *sexual* crimes perpetrated by children and adolescents have been discovered and conceptually elaborated primarily within the child maltreatment field[39]; but the child maltreatment field has been uninterested in child- and adolescent-perpetrated *physical* assault, which has mostly been taken up by people concerned with bullying and exposure to community violence. So in practice, the crime/child maltreatment divide is less observed than the conceptual distinction might imply.

The Pitfalls of Fragmentation

A number of very strong arguments can be made against fragmentation of the child victimization field, including partitioning the activities between intrafamilial and extrafamilial spheres of intervention. These arguments imply a more holistic and integrative approach than has been practiced up until now.

First, fragmentation promotes a partial and isolated understanding of the problems that may get in the way of devising enduring solutions. There is considerable evidence that various child victimization problems overlap; just to cite two examples, children who suffer from child maltreatment also are more likely to be exposed to community violence,[40] and children who suffer from bullying are more likely to have been abused by someone within the family.[41]

Second, there is considerable evidence that common risk factors co-occur and create vulnerability for a wide variety of victimizations.[42] Children from disrupted family environments appear to be vulnerable to many different kinds of child victimization. Likewise, the symptoms that accompany a wide variety of victimizations appear to be similar. That is, features that are seen across victimizations include impairment of social skills, acquisition of defensive and overly reactive responses to threats, depression, and the use of substances to deal with unpleasant feelings.[23]

Failure to recognize these connections among risk factors and symptoms can lead to a variety of problematic responses. One such effect is the failure to respond to the children who are most in need of help and intervention. For example, the child who most needs help may not be the one who is sexually abused, but the one who is sexually abused, bullied, exposed to community violence, *and* who has witnessed domestic violence in the home. Screening for sexual abuse alone may not identify these children.

Third, the fragmented response may lead to misunderstandings about what is most damaging and deserving of priority treatment. Very few studies, for example, have controlled for other victimizations in trying to estimate the traumagenic impact of individual victimizations. So, in fact, the capacity of a single victimization to throw a child off developmental course may be overestimated; it may be the multiply-victimized or "poly-victimized" children who need help the most.

Fourth, the fragmented response may fail to get practitioners targeted on the problem that most needs to be addressed. The biggest problem for a victim of date rape may be the abuse she is suffering at home, but evaluating a child for the effects of date rape alone will not identify this other set of problems. In fact, there are signs that many of the current therapeutic interventions are overly narrow. The treatment of child victimization has been heavily dominated by the successful field of posttraumatic stress disorder (PTSD). Much of PTSD therapy focuses on desensitizing the victims to the details of their traumatic experience, but many of these victims may be suffering from multiple victimization occurrences. Their problems may be evidence of more of a victimization *condition* than a victimization *event*.

Fifth, fragmentation results in considerable inefficiency, duplication of effort, and unnecessary competition. Program developers, for example, vie for valuable classroom time, one with a program on sexual abuse, another with a program on bullying. The social worker who tries to help the family of a neglected child may not have the training and awareness to help that child reduce the bullying he or she is experiencing in school; that help has to be delegated to another professional.

Finally, fragmentation may contribute to a dilution of impact. The actual number of child victims is considerably larger than the number revealed by epidemiology concerning any one of these individual sub-problems.

The good news is that the institutional bifurcation between child protection and criminal justice appears to be eroding. Multidisciplinary approaches are increasingly regarded as best practice. Child protection workers, police, and mental health officials are working together to help children more often. These collaborations are able to titrate social control and therapeutic responses in flexible ways that respond to different situations and achieve maximal results.

A New, Holistic Approach: Developmental Victimology

What we need, and what we are moving to (albeit too slowly), is a holistic approach to child victimization. We need to overcome the fragmentation that allows professionals to study and assess children for school bullying without also factoring in whether they have been victimized at home or in the neighborhood. We need to understand how these different kinds of victimizations relate to one another. We need to have professionals who can identify and respond to a wider variety of victimizations, so that a child protective worker investigating a report of physical assault by a parent can also provide help if that child is being assaulted in the neighborhood or in school. We need police officers who, in responding to a sexually assaulted youth, can ascertain and help if that youth is also experiencing emotional abuse at the hands of a family member. We need researchers familiar with the literature and the dynamics of all these kinds of victimizations.

This holistic approach needs a name and a conceptualization. It could be called "child victimization" or "child maltreatment" or "crimes against children." But labels like "child maltreatment" or "crimes against children" already exist and refer to partial segments of the domain we are proposing to integrate. The word *child* in itself is sometimes taken to apply only to the younger half of the developmental spectrum, rather than all juveniles, so a more comprehensive word is needed.

We have proposed the term "developmental victimology" as the name for this new, holistic field. The word *victimology* applies to the study and understanding of the process of victimization, the effects of victimization, and the needs of victims. The word *developmental* qualifies victimology in two ways: it focuses on the aspect of victimology that applies specifically to children and youth, just as developmental psychology applies psychology to both children and youth and is not limited to young children alone; and it puts conceptual emphasis on how the issues of interest change and influence each other as children grow up.

This is not a static approach to how children and their victimization might be different. It is a dynamic approach, focusing on how the experiences and needs of victims evolve. Both victimology and developmental psychology are fields that have traditionally emphasized the importance of research, epidemiology, and, to some extent, program evaluation. It is important that developmental victimology, in its effort to integrate the various victimization domains, also aspire to that level of rigor. Some outlines of this approach are sketched in the next chapter.

Chapter 2

Developmental Victimology

In this chapter we sketch the outlines of the new field of developmental victimology. It is a field intended to promote interest in and understanding of the broad range of victimizations that children suffer and to suggest some specific lines of inquiry that such an interest should take. In promoting this holistic field, we contend that the problem of juvenile victimization can be addressed in many of the same comprehensive and conceptual ways that the field of juvenile delinquency has addressed the problem of juvenile offending.

The field of juvenile delinquency stands as a monument to social science as one of its most theoretically mature and empirically developed domains. By contrast, while there is substantial research on specific child-victimization topics such as child abuse or child sexual assault, there is no similarly integrated and theoretically articulated interest characterizing the field of juvenile victimization. In comparison with that of juvenile delinquency, the field of juvenile victimization involves much less theory about who gets victimized and why, much less solid data about the scope and nature of the problem, far fewer longitudinal and developmental studies looking at the "careers" of victimized children, and much less evaluation undertaken to ascertain the effectiveness of policies and programs intended to respond to juvenile victims.

These deficiencies are ironic, for a variety of reasons. For one thing, as we demonstrated in Chapter 1, children are one of the most highly victimized segments of the population. They suffer from high rates of the same crimes and violence as adults do, but they also suffer victimizations particular to childhood. Second, victimization has enormous consequences for children, derailing what would have been normal and healthy development. It can affect personality formation, have major mental health consequences, and impact academic performance, and it is strongly implicated in the development of delinquent and antisocial behaviors.[23] It is clear that, because of several factors such as children's special developmental vulnerability to victimization, its differential character during childhood, and the presence of specialized institutions to deal with it (such as child protection agencies), the victimization of children and youth deserves both more and specialized attention within the larger fields of criminology, justice studies, and even developmental psychology.

This chapter addresses a variety of issues, including how to define and categorize child and juvenile victimizations, what is known about the epidemiology of child victimization in broad terms, and how victimization changes across the developmental span of childhood.

Issues of Definition and Categorization

The interpersonal victimization that developmental victimology is concerned with is a kind of negative life experience that stands apart from other life events. This victimization can be defined as harm that comes to individuals because other *human actors* have behaved in ways that *violate social norms*. The human-agency and norm-violation components give victimization greater potential for traumatic impact. Victimization is different from other stresses and traumas, such as accidents, illnesses, bereavements, and natural disasters. Even though we sometimes refer to people as "victims of hurricanes," "cancer victims," or "accident victims," the more common reference for the term *victimization* is interpersonal victimization. In interpersonal victimization, the elements of malevolence, betrayal, injustice, and immorality are more likely to be factors than in accidents, diseases, and natural disasters. To a large extent, moreover, interpersonal victimizations engage a particular set of institutions and social responses that are often missing in other stresses and traumas: police, courts, agencies of social control, and efforts to reestablish justice and mete out punishment.

Although the area of interpersonal victimization is the traditional domain of criminology, one reason that criminologists have not fully explored its childhood dimensions may be that child victimizations do not fit neatly into conventional crime categories. While children suffer all the crimes that adults do, many of the violent and deviant behaviors engaged in by human actors to harm children have ambiguous status as crimes. The physical abuse of children, although technically criminal, is not frequently prosecuted and is generally handled by social-control agencies other than the police and criminal courts. Peer assaults, unless very serious or occurring among older children, are generally ignored by the criminal justice system.

To better define the new field of developmental victimology, we propose that the victimization of children embrace three categories: (1) conventional crimes in which children are victims (e.g., rape, robbery, assault), which we refer to as *crimes*; (2) acts that violate child welfare statutes, including some of the most serious and dangerous acts committed against children, such as abuse and neglect, but also some less frequently discussed topics such as the exploitation of child labor, which we refer to as *child maltreatment*; and (3) acts that would clearly be crimes if committed by adults against adults but which by convention are not generally of concern to the criminal justice system when they occur among or against children, such as sibling violence and assaults between pre-adolescent peers; we refer to these as *noncriminal juvenile crime equivalents*, or "noncrimes," for short.

Each of these categories is a complex domain, but each has its stereotypical forms, which sometimes help and at other times hinder thinking about the category. When the public thinks of crimes against children, what stands out are stranger abductions and extrafamily child molestations—situations in which adults threaten children and for which the proper protective and retributive actions originate with and are carried out by the police, courts, and criminal justice system. When the public hears of child maltreatment, they tend to think of parents abusing their children or neglecting their parental responsibilities, and they feel the appropriate domain of intervention comprises family courts, social workers, and mental health remedies. The public also is aware of noncriminal violence against children, and they think of peer assaults as offenses that would, and presumably should, be handled by parents or school authorities.

As different as their stereotypical forms may be, however, these are not neat and distinct categories; there is substantial overlap. Some forms of child victimization can have aspects of more than one type (Figure 2.1 shows various kinds of child victimization arranged in a space roughly defined by the three categories of crimes, child maltreatment, and noncrimes). Some kinds of child maltreatment are treated as crimes, some not. Child molestation is often considered both a crime and a child welfare violation. The same peer assault that might result in an arrest in one jurisdiction may be treated as a noncrime in another jurisdiction—something for parents or school authorities to sort out. Moreover, there are normative shifts in progress (illustrated by arrows in Fig. 2.1). Sibling sexual assaults once may have been viewed as neither crimes nor child maltreatment, but they are increasingly being handled by criminal-justice authorities. The abduction of children by family members is increasingly being viewed both as a crime and as child maltreatment.

The category of noncriminal juvenile crime equivalents often creates confusion or draws objections. Some see it as a watering down of the concept of "victim" or "crime" to include acts such as peer or sibling assault among children. But, for example, there is some equivalence between one adult hitting another in a bar and one child hitting another on a playground. To study victimization in a developmental fashion, we must look at equivalent acts across the life span, even if the social labels change as participants get older. The cultural assumption is that some acts are less serious or less criminal when they are engaged in at earlier ages, but whether and how these acts are different should be a matter of empirical

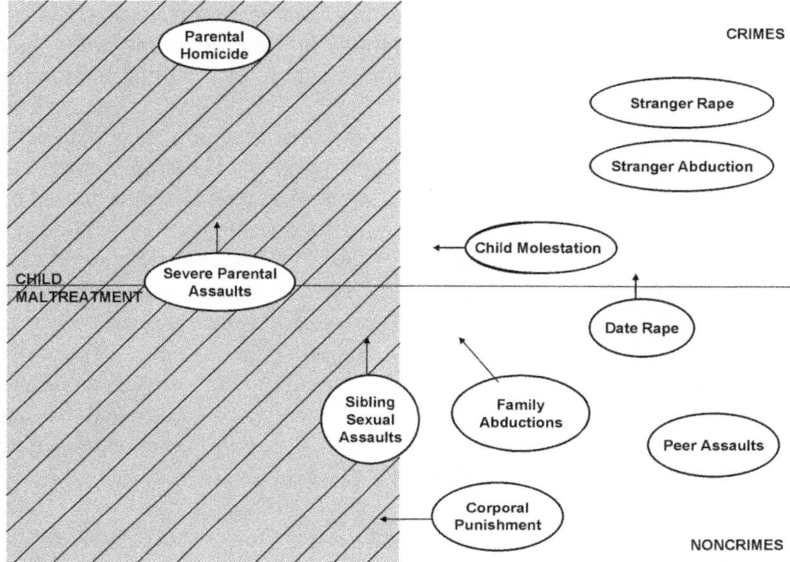

FIGURE 2.1. Conceptual geography of child victimization: Crimes, noncrimes, and child maltreatment.

investigation. In our research, we have not, for example, found that violence between younger children is less physically or psychologically injurious than that between adults.[43]

Understanding the basis for the social construction of victimization across the span of childhood should, in fact, be one of the key challenges for developmental victimology. For example, an even more problematic type of juvenile-crime equivalent is spanking or corporal punishment, which is a form of violence (*violence* defined as an act intended to cause physical pain) and would be considered assault if done to adults. But corporal punishment is not only typically viewed as minor victimization; it is actually considered salutary and educational by many segments of society. Since our definition of victimization requires the violation of social norms, some forms of normatively accepted corporal punishment may not qualify. However, there are signs that a normative transformation is in progress regarding corporal punishment.[44] A majority of states have banned all forms of corporal punishment in schools, many European countries have outlawed spanking even by parents, and the American Academy of Pediatrics has stated it is officially opposed to spanking. Social scientists have begun to study it as a form of victimization with short- and long-term negative consequences.[45,46] Some have argued that it is the foundation on which other violent behavior gets built. Clearly, developmental victimology needs to take account of corporal punishment, and spanking in particular, although it may deserve individualized theoretical and empirical treatment.

Another somewhat problematic category of developmental victimology is indirect victimization, or situations in which children witness or are closely affected by the criminal victimization of a family member or friend. These instances include children who are first-hand witnesses to spousal abuse,[47,48] who are deprived of a parent or sibling as a result of a homicide,[49] or who are present at but not injured in a playground massacre or the public killing of a teacher[50]—all situations that have been studied by researchers. While indirect victimization affects adults as well as children, the latter are particularly vulnerable owing to their dependency on those who have been victimized. Since most of the acts leading to indirect victimizations are crimes, these situations can readily be categorized as crimes, but some, such as witnessing a marital assault, also are treated as child welfare violations, in which the child is seen as a direct, not indirect, victim.

A new domain that falls within developmental victimology and that has garnered significant interest in recent years is Internet victimization. Three kinds of offenses fall within this rubric: (1) Internet sex crimes and solicitations for such crimes, (2) unwanted exposure to pornography, and (3) harassment and cyber-bullying.[51] When adults solicit underage youth for sexual activities, or even online interactions, it is considered a conventional crime. But while youth apparently receive a large quantity of online sexual solicitations, it is hard to assess how much of this cyber-activity originates with adults or individuals who are aware that their target is underage. The Internet has also exposed an enormous number of young people to inadvertent and unwanted sexual material, but, although offensive to many, such exposure has not yet been defined as a crime or a child welfare problem, in part because the element of harm to the children involved has not been clearly established. Harassment and cyber-bullying appear to be fairly straightforward extensions of conventional bullying behavior into the realm of electronic communication, and therefore they are the easiest to categorize. It is still too early to fully understand how the development of a widespread electronic-communications environment will alter the conception of or risk for victimization.

Another problematic category for developmental victimology is the domain of mass victimization, class victimization, and institutional and policy victimization. Warfare and generalized ethnic violence have a great impact on children. Since the main agent of this impact is violent or hurtful acts perpetrated by individuals, this does not stray far from the class of victimizations we are considering here. When we consider children's victimization by governmental or institutional policies, however, we are in a different arena. Children deprived of their rights or affected by budget cuts or land expropriations, or by even environmental policies, are often seen as victims of human agents who sometimes are acting outside of established norms. However, these victimizations fall far enough outside of the domain of the interpersonal actions we are considering here that they would best be the subject of their own unique specialized field.

An additional definitional complexity for developmental victimology is that, compared to adult victimization, specific victimization categories have been much less clearly drawn. Thus, for example, child sexual assault, child sexual abuse, and child molestation are often thought of as interchangeable, but these terms also refer to different aspects of sexual offenses involving children. Thus, child sexual abuse, when discussed in a child welfare context, often refers to sexual offenses committed against children by their caretakers and so might not include sexual assaults by strangers or peers. In colloquial terms, child molestation is thought of as sexual offenses committed against children by adults and thus might exclude date rapes and sexual assaults committed by other juveniles. Child sexual assault is sometimes taken literally to mean threatening and forceful sexual crimes committed against children, thus excluding sexual crimes against children not involving overt violence. All this ambiguity suggests that the field of developmental victimology can benefit from a great deal of definitional refinement and category organization.

The Differential Character of Child Victimization

The discussion of how developmental victimology should be defined highlights the fact that, in some important ways, child victimization does differ from the victimization of adults. Children, of course, suffer all the victimizations that adults do—homicides, robberies, sexual assault, and even economic crimes like extortion and fraud. But one salient difference is that children also suffer from offenses that are particular to their status. The main status characteristic of childhood is dependency, which is a function, at least in part, of social and psychological immaturity. The violation of this dependency status results in forms of victimization, such as physical neglect, that are not suffered by most adults (with the exception of the elderly or infirm, who often also become dependent).

Interestingly, the types of victimization that children suffer can be arrayed on a spectrum or continuum of dependency, according to the degree to which they violate a child's dependency status (see Fig. 2.2). At one

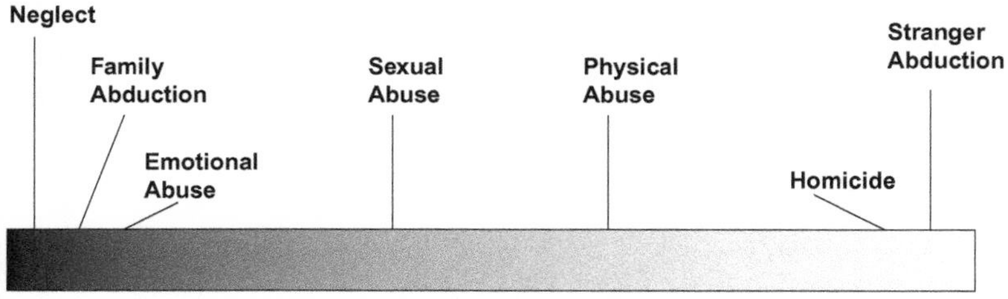

FIGURE 2.2. Dependence continuum for selected child victimization types.

extreme is physical neglect, which has practically no meaning as victimization except when a person is dependent and needs to be cared for by others, as is primarily the case for children. Similarly, family abduction is a dependency-specific victimization because it is the unlawful removal of a child from the person who is legally supposed to be caring for him or her.

At the other end of the continuum are forms of victimization defined largely without reference to dependency and that exist in similar forms for both children and adults. Stranger abduction is prototypical in this instance, since both children and adults can be taken against their will and imprisoned for ransom or sexual purposes. Homicide is similar—the dependency status of the victim does little to define the victimization. In some cases, to be sure, children's deaths result from extreme and willful cases of neglect, but there are parallel instances of adult deaths resulting from extreme and willful negligence.

One might think that most forms of child victimization are either dependency related or not. But in reality there are forms of child victimization located along the midsection of the dependency continuum. Sexual abuse falls here, for example, because it encompasses at least two different forms, one dependency related and one not. Some sexual abuse entails activities ordinarily acceptable between adults, like consensual sexual intercourse, that are deemed victimization when engaged in with children because of their immaturity and dependency. But other sexual abuse involves violence and coercion that would be victimizing even if aimed at a nondependent adult.

Other kinds of child victimization are a bit more ambiguous. Emotional abuse happens to both adults and children, but the sensitive psychological vulnerability of children in their dependent relationship to their caretakers is what makes society consider emotional abuse of children a form of victimization that warrants an institutional response. In the case of physical abuse, there also is some mixture of types. While most of the violent acts in the physical-abuse category would be considered victimization even between adults, some of them, such as shaken baby syndrome, develop almost exclusively in a caretaking relationship where there is enormous difference in size and physical control of the individuals involved.

The dependency continuum is a useful concept for thinking about some of the unique features of child victimizations. It also is helpful in generating hypotheses about the expected correlates of different types of victimization at different ages.

The Scope of Child Victimization

There is no single source for statistics on child victimization. The National Crime Victimization Survey (NCVS), which is the ultimate authority on crime victimization in general, has two unfortunate deficiencies when it comes to child victimization. First, as mentioned in Chapter 1, it does not gather information on victims younger than age 12. Second, it does not cover certain forms of child victimization, such as child abuse, sexual abuse, and kidnapping, that preoccupy public policy regarding children. But national estimates that compensate for these deficiencies of the NCVS are available from some other sources. Some of these other estimates are shown in Table 2.1.

Under some of the categories of victimization shown in Table 2.1, the estimates of several different studies have been listed, sometimes showing widely divergent rates. These differences stem from a variety of factors. For instance, some of the listed studies involve rates based on cases known to authorities (National Child Abuse and Neglect Data System, or NCANDS) or professionals (Third National Incidence Study of Child Abuse and Neglect, or NIS-3). Such studies are certain to count fewer cases than studies that obtain information directly from youth and their families. While it misses many cases, the advantage of information from authorities and professionals is that professional judgment is typically involved in assessing whether a legitimate qualifying victimization (e.g., physical abuse) occurred.

Other discrepancies are more complicated to account for. For a variety of victimizations covered in Table 2.1, estimates are available both from the NCVS and the Developmental Victimization Survey (DVS),[8] a study conducted by the author and colleagues. The NCVS is a highly rigorous survey conducted every year by the U.S. Bureau of the Census that involves interviews of nearly 10,000 youth ages 12 to 17. The DVS was a survey of both youth and caretakers regarding the experiences of 2,020 children from the ages of 2 to 17. The NCVS estimates are considerably lower than those from the DVS for every crime, and also lower than many other survey estimates of specific forms of juvenile victimization.[1] This is generally attributed to several factors. First, the NCVS uses a complex definition for each crime it measures, and respondents need to answer several sets of questions in specific ways in order to qualify. Second, the NCVS interviews respondents on several occasions over a period of 3 years to make sure that the reported incidents fall within and not outside the exact 1-year time period being asked about. Third, the NCVS clearly orients respondents to the topic of conventional crime, so incidents that respondents might not think of as crimes (for example, forced sex by a dating partner or being beaten by a parent) may not be reported. Fourth, the NCVS does not require that youth be interviewed confidentially, and so young people may fail to disclose incidents that they would not want their parents or family members to know about.

What this means is that the NCVS estimates are very conservative and count primarily incidents that would be considered conventional crimes in the narrow sense. The DVS estimates, by contrast, are probably inflated with minor incidents and incidents that some observers might dismiss as "not real crimes," such as sibling and peer assaults or disciplinary acts.

Table 2.1 reveals an enormous quantity and variety of child and youth victimizations. Based on the responses to the DVS, over half of all children

TABLE 2.1. Rates and Incidence of Various Childhood Victimizations

	Age (years)	Rate per 1000[a]	# Victimized	Year	Source[b]	Report Type	Notes
Assault, Any Physical	2 to 17	530	33,651,000	2002	DVS	Self/caretaker report	
	12 to 17	(72.8)	(1,686,842)	1993-2003	NCVS	Self-report	
Sibling Assault	2 to 17	355	22,481,000	2002	DVS	Self/caretaker report	
Robbery	2 to 17	40	2,543,000	2002	DVS	Self/caretaker report	Nonsibling
	12 to 17	7.8	(180,733)	1993-2003	NCVS	Self-report	
Theft	2 to 17	140	8,887,000	2002	DVS	Self/caretaker report	Nonsibling
	12 to 15	2.1	(35,874)	2004	NCVS 2003	Self-report	
Sexual Assault/Rape	2 to 17	32	2,053,000	2002	DVS	Self/caretaker report	
	12 to 17	3.2	(74,147)	1993-2003	NCVS	Self-report	
Sexual Abuse (sexual assault by known adult)	2 to 17	6	*	2002	DVS	Self/caretaker report	
	0 to 17	(1.2)	88,656	2002	NCANDS	Agency reports	
	0 to 17	4.5	300,200	1993	NIS-3	Agency reports	
Sexual Harassment	2 to 17	38	2,411,000	2002	DVS	Self/caretaker report	
	In 8th to 11th grade	(810)	(13,006,580)	2000	Hostile Hallways	Self-report	
Physical Abuse	2 to 17	37	2,320,000	2002	DVS	Self/caretaker report	
	0 to 17	(2.3)	166,920	2002	NCANDS	Agency reports	
	0 to 17	9.1	614,108	1993	NIS-3	Agency reports	
	0 to 17	49	(3,359,195)	1995	CTSPC-Gallup	Self-reports	
Neglect	2 to 17	14	909,000	2002	DVS	Self/caretaker report	

	0 to 17	(7.7)	541,832	2002	NCANDS	Agency reports	Includes medical neglect
	0 to 17	(19.9)	(1,355,100)	1993	NIS-3	Agency reports	
	0 to 17	270	(18,509,850)	1995	CTSPC-Gallup	Self-reports	
Psychological/ Emotional Abuse	2 to 17	103	6,498,000	2002	DVS	Self/caretaker report	
	0 to 17	(0.8)	58,022	2002	NCANDS	Agency reports	
Witnessing/ Domestic Violence	2 to 17	35	2,190,000	2002	DVS	Self/caretaker report	
	2 to 17	17	1,099,000	2002	DVS	Self/caretaker report	
Family Abductions (or custodial interference)	0 to 17	(2.9)	203,900	1999	NISMART-2	Caretaker reports	
Nonfamily Abductions	0 to 17	(0.8)	58,200	1999	NISMART-2	Caretaker reports	Legal definition, includes stereotypical kidnappings
	0 to 17	(0.0016)	115	1999	NISMART-2	Law enforcement	Stereotypical kidnapping
Homicide	0 to 17	(0.02)	1571	2002	SHR	Agency reports	
Bullying	In 6th to 10th grade	(168.8)	(3,245,904)	1998	HBSC	Self-report	Moderate and frequent bullying
	2 to 17	217	13,735,000	2002	DVS	Self/caretaker report	
Teasing or Emotional Bullying	0 to 17	614	42,092,770	1995	CTSPC-Gallup	Caretaker reports	
	2 to 17	249	15,745,000	2002	DVS	Self/caretaker report	

(continued)

TABLE 2.1. *(continued)*

	Age (years)	Rate per 1000[a]	# Victimized	Year	Source[b]	Report Type	Notes
Online Victimization							
Sexual Solicitations and Approaches	10 to 17	130	3,220,000	2005	YISS-2	Self-reports	
Unwanted Exposure to Sexual Material	10 to 17	340	8,430,000	2005	YISS-2	Self-reports	
Harassment	10 to 17	90	2,230,000	2005	YISS-2	Self-reports	
Corporal Punishment	0 to 17	(147.6)	(29,887,672)	1999	PCAA	Caretaker reports	
	0 to 17	(171.7)	34,800,000	2002	ABC News Poll	Caretaker reports	Spanked or hit ever

[a]Numbers given in parentheses did not appear in original source, but were derived from data presented therein. [b]Source acronyms: DVS: Developmental Victimization Survey,[8] NCVS: National Crime Victimization Survey,[2] NCVS 2003: National Crime Victimization Survey, 2003,[78] NCANDS: National Child Abuse & Neglect Data System, 2002,[79] NIS-3: Third National Incidence Study of Child Abuse and Neglect, 1993,[80] Hostile Hallways,[81] NISMART-2: Second National Incidence Study of Missing, Abducted, Runaway and Thrownaway Children, 1999,[228,82] SHR: Supplemental Homicide Reports,[83] HBSC: Health Behavior of School-aged Children,[84] CTSPC-Gallup,[85] YISS-2: Second Youth Internet Safety Survey,[51] PCAA: Prevent Child Abuse America,[86] ABC News Poll.[87]

experienced a physical assault in the course of the previous year, many of them perpetrated by siblings and peers. A fifth of them experienced physical bullying, and a quarter of them experienced emotional bullying. One in seven experienced a theft, and one in 20 a robbery. The NCVS rates are typically only a fraction—in some cases one-tenth or less—of the DVS estimates, which suggests how far we may still be from a consensus on the epidemiology of child victimization. But even the NCVS estimates suggest that conventional crime victimization rates for youth are at least three to four times greater than what is known to police[52] and two to three times the victimization rates for adults. [53]

A Typology of Child Victimization by Incidence

The formal estimates for various types of child victimization, in spite of their methodological limitations, definitional imprecision, and variability, can be broken down into three rough and broad categories according to their order of magnitude. First, there are the *pandemic* victimizations that appear to occur to a majority or near-majority of children at some time in the course of growing up. These include, at minimum, assault by siblings and theft, and probably also peer assault, vandalism, and robbery. Second, there are what might be called *acute* victimizations. These are less frequent and occur to a minority, though perhaps a sizable minority, of children, but are, on average, of generally greater severity These include physical abuse, neglect, and family abduction. Finally, there are the *extraordinary* victimizations that occur to only a very small number of children but which attract a great deal of attention. These include homicide, child abuse homicide, and nonfamily abduction.

Several observations follow from this typology. First, there has been much more public and professional attention paid to the extraordinary and acute victimizations compared to the pandemic ones. For example, sibling violence, the most frequent victimization, is conspicuous for how little it has been studied in proportion to how often it occurs. This neglect of pandemic victimizations needs to be rectified. For one thing, the situation fails to reflect the concerns of children themselves. In a survey of children, three times as many were concerned about the likelihood of their being beaten up by their peers as were concerned about being sexually abused.[54] The pandemic victimizations deserve greater attention if only for the alarming frequency with which they occur and the influence they have on children's everyday existence. It is a rule of public health that events having a small likelihood of negative consequences can be very serious in their total societal effects if they occur very frequently in a large population. So peer assaults could in principle, on a population basis, be responsible for more mental health problems than child abuse. Second, this typology can be useful in developing theories and methodology concerning child victimization. For example, different types of victimization may require different conceptual frameworks. Because pandemic victimizations are nearly normative occurrences, their impact may be very different from the extraordinary victimizations that children experience in relative isolation.

Finally, the typology helps illustrate the diversity and frequency of child victimization. Although homicide and child abuse have been widely studied, they are notable for how inadequately they convey the variety and true extent of other victimizations that children suffer. Almost all the data in Table 2.1 have been promoted in isolation at one time or another. When we view them together, we note that they are just part of the total environment of possible victimizations in which children live.

Poly-Victims

With so many children experiencing so many kinds of victimization, it is obvious that there must be considerable overlap. Unfortunately, the fragmentation of the field of child victimization (discussed in Chapter 1) has impeded inquiry into just how much overlap there is and why. Advocates and policymakers concerned about one form of child victimization, such as dating violence, tend to present estimates and studies about their chosen area as though it were the primary or only victimization that children suffer. They can do this because studies concentrating on one kind of victimization rarely ask about other kinds. Some studies might explore multiple forms of child maltreatment, such as physical and sexual abuse; other studies, like the NCVS, inquire about multiple forms of conventional crime, such as rape, robbery, and aggravated assault. But most studies never ask about a broad or comprehensive range of victimizations including child maltreatment, conventional crime, and exposure to family and community violence.

Yet it turns out that most juvenile victims do experience multiple victimizations. To ascertain whether this was the case, we developed a questionnaire that inquired about 34 different kinds of child victimization; we called it the Juvenile Victimization Questionnaire (JVQ).[55] This questionnaire asks about victimizations in five broad domains: conventional crime, child maltreatment, peer and sibling abuse, sexual victimization, and witnessing/indirect victimization. We used the questionnaire in a nationally representative sample survey of 2,020 American children ages 2 to 17. The families were recruited and interviewed by telephone in 2002 and 2003. Information on victimizations of youth ages 10 to 17 was obtained through direct interviews with the youth themselves (after gaining permission from parents), while information on the victimizations of younger children was obtained in interviews with the parent or adult who knew most about the child (which in about two-thirds of the cases was the mother). (Note: Children or parents who disclosed a situation of serious threat or ongoing victimization were re-contacted by a clinical member of the research team trained in telephone crisis counseling, whose responsibility was to stay in contact with the respondent until the situation was resolved or brought to the attention of appropriate authorities, with the cooperation of the respondent.) Some of the estimates from the survey are listed in Table 2.1, referenced there under the name of the Developmental Victimization Survey, or DVS.

We found that victimization was a frequent occurrence, with 71% of the children and youth surveyed experiencing at least one victimization in the previous year. But more important, we found that the experience of multiple victimization was very common as well. We defined *multiple victimization* as a child's experiencing different kinds of victimization in different episodes over the course of a year. This meant that an assault and a robbery on different occasions, even if by the same perpetrator, counted as multiple victimization, but two assaults by the same or even different perpetrators did not count as multiple victimization. We adopted this conservative way of defining the category in light of findings that different kinds of victimization appear to have more impact than repeated episodes of the same type of victimization.[56,57] Of the children experiencing any victimization in the previous year, two-thirds had experienced two or more victimizations. The *average* number of victimizations for a victimized child was three in the previous year, while the *total* number of victimizations ranged all the way up to 15.

Obviously, children who had experienced one kind of victimization were more likely to have suffered other victimizations as well. For example, if a child had been physically assaulted by a caretaker, he or she was 60% more likely than other children to also have been assaulted by a peer. Other studies have found similar transitivity of victimization risk. [58]

Children experiencing multiple victimizations should be of particular concern to professionals. In other fields, it is widely recognized that multiple, intersecting adversities frequently have impacts far beyond those of individual stressful events. So, for example, clients with several psychiatric diagnoses (co-morbidity) or who abuse different kinds of drugs (poly-drug users) pose particularly challenging treatment problems. There is every reason to believe that this is also the case with child victims.

We propose calling this group of multiply victimized children *poly-victims*. (We prefer the term *poly-victim* to *multiple victim* because "multiple victim" can mean a victimization in which there are several victims, rather than our intended meaning of a victim who has experienced several victimizations.) We expected that further research on poly-victims would show them to be particularly highly victimized, vulnerable, and distressed.

In fact, the DVS confirmed these predictions. We categorized the youth in our national survey who had experienced four or more victimizations over the course of a single year as poly-victims. Such youth constituted 31% of all victims and 22% of the full sample. But they were also the youth with the most serious kinds of victimization. Forty percent of the poly-victims had experienced a victimization injury, 42% had experienced a form of maltreatment, and 25% had been victimized by a weapon-toting assailant. Although the poly-victims were not that different from other youth in terms of their demographic profiles, they listed considerably more other lifetime adversities, such as major illnesses, accidents, or family problems. They were also clearly the most distressed youth. They were 5.8 times more likely than the other youth to be angry, 20.2 times more likely to be depressed, and 10.3 times more likely to be anxious as measured by symptom checklists. In fact, most of the clinically distressed kids were also poly-victims. A full 86% of the clinically depressed children also fit the poly-victim criteria.[56]

It increasingly appears that what professionals should be on the lookout for in children is poly-victimization, not just one type of victimization, even a serious one. Our analyses suggest that poly-victimization is the thing most closely associated with mental health problems and bad outcomes, and that poly-victims are harboring the greatest amount of distress. In fact, the associations between distress and individual victimizations often disappear when poly-victimization is taken into account.[56] That is, children who experience a single kind of victimization, such as bullying or even child maltreatment, appear able to recover from it, but youth who experience multiple kinds of victimization from multiple sources show signs that they are locked in a pattern or trapped in a downward spiral, and this should be of great concern to those trying to help.

As we come to better understand poly-victims, we may have to change some of the assumptions we have been making about victimization in general. Victimization has mostly been thought of as a stressful or traumatic *event*—this is partly a legacy of the field's close connection to the literature on posttraumatic stress. The earliest victimization experiences to be studied in detail were sexual assaults, which were considered to be highly threatening individual episodes happening to otherwise ordinary people who were often overwhelmed by the incident. But as victimization research has expanded, we have come to understand that many victims are subjected to repeated episodes of victimization over time; for example, the child who is bullied again and again on the playground or emotionally and physically abused repeatedly by a parent.

We are also now seeing that many children are subjected to a variety of victimizations, such as being beaten *and* sexually assaulted *and* robbed, over a relatively short period of time. This suggests that for some children victimization is more a *condition* than an event. A condition is a stable and ongoing process, while an event is time-limited—it is like the difference between failing a test and failing a course, or the difference between an acute medical condition such as appendicitis and a chronic one such as diabetes. Indeed, one of the most important diagnostic challenges facing professionals involved with child victimization is identifying those children for whom victimization has become a condition rather than just an event. We should expect these children to have different characteristics and a different prognosis.

Currently, what we know about poly-victims is that they experience a lot of victimization. Poly-victimization appears to occur equally among boys and girls, and it seems to be somewhat more common among older youth, although there certainly are a considerable number of very young poly-victims as well.[56] Existing evidence does not strongly suggest that poly-victims come from poor or minority backgrounds. On the other hand, such victimization does seem to have a connection with living in a family affected by divorce, separation, and/or remarriage. Obviously, considerably more study of these poly-victim youth is requred so that we can identify them and prevent or remediate their conditions as early as possible.

Some Developmental Propositions

Childhood is such an extremely heterogeneous category—4-year-olds and 17-year-olds have little in common—that it can be inherently misleading to discuss child victimization without reference to age. We would expect the nature, quantity, and impact of victimization to vary across periods of childhood and with the different capabilities, activities, and environments that are characteristic of different stages of development. This is the key principle of developmental victimology.

Unfortunately, the general culture is already full of assumptions about development and victimization, many of them questionable and sometimes even contradictory. Some victimizations are presumed to be worse for younger children, and others are thought to be worse for older children, mostly based on stereotype rather than evidence. We have already alluded to some of these assumptions. Peer violence is presumed to be more serious, injurious, traumatizing, and crime-like when it occurs to older children, for example. That is, a teenager punching another teenager is regarded as much more serious than a five-year-old punching another preschooler. But is there evidence that this is the case? In fact, when we examined these issues in a research study, we did *not* find less injury or psychological impact for younger children in instances of peer violence (see Chapter 5). Still, these are not entirely equivalent offenses, if only because we have different mechanisms for responding to them—police might want to arrest the teenage assailant but not the preschooler. It is important that we not assume, until we can study the matter more, that an act is more dangerous or the consequence more serious simply because the participants are older.

In contrast to common attitudes about peer violence, the colloquial assumption about child molestation is that it is more serious for younger children. Some people make the naïve assumption that because of their earlier developmental stage, they are more vulnerable to serious developmental disruption. For example, a child who has not yet been introduced to sex will be more affected by molestation than one who has developed some ideas and concepts about the act. But, here again, much of the available evidence casts doubt on colloquial assumptions. Some studies have found that sexual abuse and child molestation have greater consequences at younger ages, while others have found the opposite. One of the big problems we have is that victimization at an earlier age tends to go on for a longer period of time. It is clear that what developmental victimology needs is a rigorously empirical approach to these developmental issues, one that does not accept facile developmental assumptions at face value. Things are generally more complicated than most people, even experts, presume.

One good place to start an empirical examination in developmental victimology is with a proposition about how the types of victimization and types of perpetrators change over the course of childhood. The mix of victimization types is very likely to be different for younger children and older children. In considering one of the concepts introduced earlier, we would expect, for example, that victimizations stemming from the dependent status of children should be most common among the most dependent—hence, the youngest—children. A corollary is that as children get older, their victimization profile should come to increasingly resemble that of adults.

We can examine such propositions in a crude way with the data that are available. In fact, we do know that some dependency-related victimizations are most concentrated in the under-12 age group. For example, instances of physical neglect, or the failure to take care of the needs of a dependent child, are heavily concentrated among younger children. Family abduction is also heavily concentrated among younger children. When children are no longer so dependent, they tend to make their own choices about which parent to live with, and abduction is no longer a feasible strategy for disgruntled parents. By contrast, victimizations that we find grouped at the nondependency end of the continuum involve a greater percentage of teenagers. For example, homicide is a crime that is defined equivalently for minors and adults, and it is concentrated among teenagers.

Homicide is a particularly good crime to study to gain some additional insights about development and victimization, because fairly complete age data are available and because other efforts have been made to interpret the patterns.[59–63] Child homicide is also a complicated crime from a developmental point of view; it has a conspicuous bimodal frequency, with a high rate for the very youngest children under age 1 and another high rate for the oldest children ages 16 and 17 (see Fig. 2.3). But the two peaks represent very different phenomena. The homicides of young children are primarily committed by parents, by choking, smothering, and battering. In contrast, the homicides of older children are committed mostly by peers and acquaintances, primarily with firearms. Although the analysts do not agree entirely on the number and exact age span of the specific developmental categories for child homicides, a number of conclusions are clear.

1. There is a distinct group of neonaticides, or children killed within the first few weeks of life. The proportion of female and rural perpetrators is unusually high in this group.[63] Homicide at this age is generally considered to involve isolated parents dealing with unwanted children.

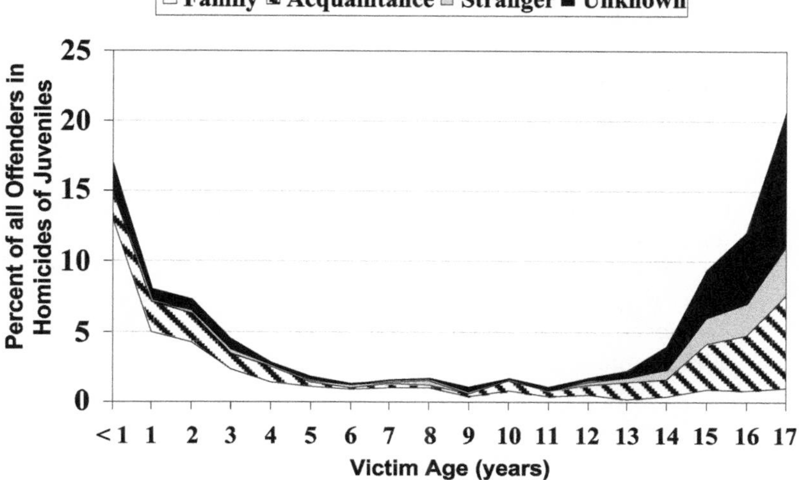

FIGURE 2.3. Juvenile victim homicide rates, by victim–offender relationship and victim age, 2003. *Source*: Fox, J. A. (2005). *Uniform Crime Reports [United States]: Supplementary Homicide Reports, 2003* [computer file]. Ann-Arbor, MI: Inter-University Consortium for Political and Societal Research.

2. After the neonatal period, there follows a period through about age 5 during which homicides are still primarily committed by caretakers using "personal weapons"—the criminologist's term for hands and feet—but the motives and circumstances are thought to be somewhat different from those pertaining to the neonatal period. These preschool-victim homicides appear to be mostly cases of fatal child abuse that occurs as a result of a parent's attempts to control a child or angry reactions to some of the young child's aversive behavior—uncontrollable crying, hitting parent or siblings, soiling himself or herself, or getting dirty, for example.[59,60] Such children are frequently thrown against hard surfaces, struck hard with a blow to the head or belly, or smothered. Because of their small size and physical vulnerability, many children at this age die from these acts of violence and force by adults—acts that would not be fatal to an older child.
3. As children approach school age, the rate of child homicide declines, and the nature of child homicides becomes somewhat different. Among school-age children, the number of killings by parents and caretakers gradually decreases, and that by peers and acquaintances rises. There are more firearm deaths. Children are murdered by suicidal parents bent on destroying their whole families. Children this age are also sometimes killed in child molestations, which begin to increase in this period (although

homicide is a rare accompaniment to child molestation). Some of the children in this age group die as innocent victims in robberies or arsons. There is a mixture here of the kinds of homicides that affect primarily younger children and those that affect older children, but the overall rate is low, and this is one of the safest times in the life of a child in terms of homicide risk.

4. At age 13, the homicide picture changes rapidly. The rate for boys diverges sharply from that for girls. Acquaintances become the predominant killers. Gangs and drugs are heavily implicated for this group, and the rate for minority groups—African Americans, Hispanic Americans, and Asian Americans—soars. The homicides for this group look a lot like the homicides for young adults, although, as we mentioned in the last chapter, this is one of the few forms of victimization that children suffer at lower rates.

These patterns of homicide victimization suggest some interesting conditions relevant to developmental victimology. First, they suggest at least three somewhat different "ecological niches" in which victimization occurs: (1) a preschool, family-based, early development niche (with a possible neonatal subenvironment); (2) a middle-childhood, somewhat protected, mixed school and family niche; and (3) and an adolescent, risk-exposed, transition-to-adulthood niche. The types of homicide suffered by children are related to the nature of their dependency and to the stage of their integration into the adult world. Among the factors that may well change across childhood and across these niches are the victim–offender relationship, the locale where the homicide occurs, the nature of the weapon, the motives involved, and the contribution the victim makes to the crime in terms of risk-taking and provocation. These homicide variations provide a good case for assuming the importance and utility of a developmental perspective on child victimizations and establish a model of how such an approach could be applied to other types of victimization.

Intrafamily Victimization

Unlike many adults, children do not live alone; they live mostly in families. Moreover, their involvement in their families wanes as they get older. So a plausible principle of developmental victimology is that younger children suffer a greater proportion of their victimizations at the hands of intimates, and correspondingly fewer at the hands of strangers, because they live more sheltered lives, spending more time in the home and around family. Figure 2.4(*A*) confirms this, with data on crimes against children known to the police, derived from the FBI's National Incident Based Reporting System (NIBRS). Family offenders are highest for the victims of youngest age, but the percentage for this group declines from nearly 70% to below 20% after age 12. At the same time, acquaintance victim-

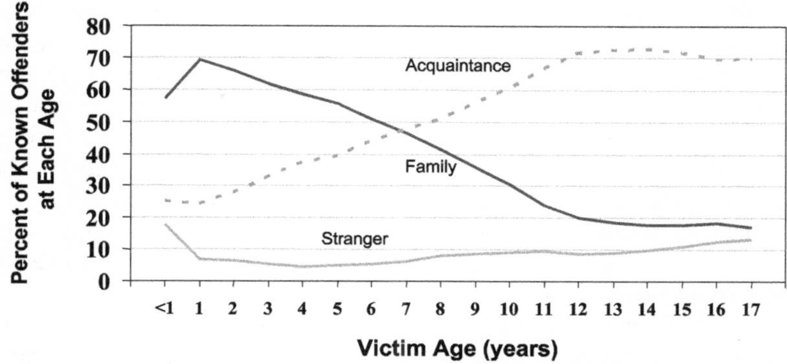

FIGURE 2.4(*A*). Juvenile victim relationship to offender by victim age: Police data for all crimes with a known offender. *Source*: U.S. Department of Justice, Federal Bureau of Investigation. (2004). *National Incident-Based Reporting System (NIBRS), 2002.* Ann Arbor, MI: Inter-University Consortium for Political and Social Research.

izations rise during childhood until adolescence, where they plateau at about 70%. Stranger victimizations remain low throughout childhood but start to increase a bit after age 15. The patterns are very similar for data on victimizations reported in the DVS, shown in Figure 2.4(*B*). Family offenders are highest for the youngest age victims, but between 8 and 11 years old children's vulnerability to family offenders drops off substantially. The homicide data also show a dramatic decline in family offenders after ages 7 and 8, but among homicides the family offenders continue to decline throughout adolescence.

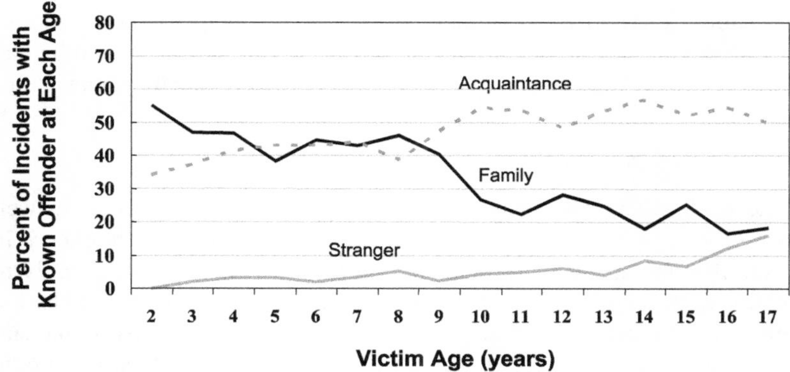

FIGURE 2.4(*B*). Juvenile victim relationship to offender by victim age: Survey data for 34 types of victimization. *Source*: Finkelhor, Ormrod, Turner, and Hamby, 2005.

Figure 2.4(*B*) shows that acquaintance victimizations rise during childhood until about mid-adolescence. It also shows that stranger victimizations remain low throughout childhood but start to increase in adolescence, particularly after age 15. These trends are consistent with what we know about children's social development. That is, social activities expand throughout childhood to include an increasingly large and more distant network of contacts. Overall, children have fewer of the characteristics that might make them suitable targets for strangers, such as money and valuable possessions. But in adolescence, they both acquire such valuables and begin to interact in more public arenas, so that increased victimization at the hands of strangers is logical.

An additional possible principle derived from these data is that the identity of perpetrators may vary according to the type of victimization and its place on the dependency continuum. Victimizations that are more dependency related should involve more parents and family members as perpetrators. Available data suggest that this is the case. Parents account for 100% of the perpetrators of neglect[64]—the most dependency-related victimization—but only 28% of the perpetrators of homicide.[65] This pattern exists because the responsibilities created by children's dependency status fall primarily on parents and family members; therefore, they are the main individuals in a position to violate those responsibilities in a way that creates victimization. Thus, when a sick child fails to receive medical attention, it is the parents who are charged with neglecting the child, even if the neighbors also did nothing.

In keeping with the developmental patterns in the victim–offender relationship and the dependency continuum, we would expect that more of the victimizations of younger children would take place in the home, and that victimizations would migrate farther from the home as children age and move into an ever-widening circle of social activity. We would also expect that, as the homicide data show, crimes against children involving firearms would increase along with child development. In fact, one explanation for why teens are murdered less than young adults, in spite of their equivalent or higher overall violent victimization rate, could be that teens and their associates have less access to firearms than do young adults.

Gender and Victimization

The field of developmental victimology needs to consider gender as well as age in its efforts to map the patterns of victimization in childhood. In overall terms, many of the gender patterns seen for adults also apply to children. That is, boys overall suffer more victimizations than girls, but girls suffer more sexual assaults. On the basis of conventional crime statistics available from the NCVS and the Uniform Crime Report, the ratio of homicide involving boys to that involving girls is 2.3:1; for assault, it is 1.7:1, and for robbery it is 2:1. In contrast, girls suffer vastly more incidents of rape (8.1 female victims for every 1 male).[65,66] But these ratios pertain primarily to the experiences of adolescents, and they do not consider age, which adds a considerable wrinkle to the pattern.

Because gender differentiation increases as children get older, a plausible developmental hypothesis might be that victimizations are less gender specific for younger children than for older children because gender roles and attributes are less specific. That is, because younger boys and girls are more similar in their activities and physical characteristics, there is less difference between genders in the rate of victimization. And this pattern does indeed appear to be the case, at least for homicide, the type of victimization for which we have the best data. Rates of homicide are quite similar for younger boys and girls, even up to age 13, after which age the vulnerability of boys compared to girls increases dramatically.

The developmental pattern in gender differentiation may apply to some forms of victimization but not others. Some victimization types may have unique gender patterns reflecting their particular dynamics. Issues of reporting and disclosure also may influence gender patterns. More research on this issue is needed.

The Age-Crime Curve

The life-course patterns in crime and delinquency have been one of the most interesting threads for ongoing discussion and research in criminology. The empirical foundation for these discussions is the observation that criminal behavior accelerates dramatically during the adolescent years, reaches a peak in young adulthood, and then falls off in later years. This dramatic rise from preadolescence to adulthood has been ascribed to a variety of factors. One argument is that it reflects a biosocially based status competition for mates that gets its start in adolescence.[67] Others contend that crime rises in adolescence because at that stage young people begin to have adult aspirations but are excluded from the labor market.[68,69] Still others point to the lax social controls that operate during adolescence and young adulthood: singlehood, no family responsibilities, and little commitment to employers.

Does the risk of victimization demonstrate the same age pattern, accelerating during adolescence in the same dramatic fashion as delinquency? Official crime statistics say yes, but more comprehensive self-report surveys suggest otherwise. Police data, such as those from NIBRS jurisdictions, show that teens constitute three-fourths of juvenile crime victims, with risk escalating as the youth age.[70] Only a few crimes, such as kidnapping, forcible sodomy, and incest, appear more evenly distributed across developmental stages. But the police data have some serious limitations as true testimony to the age curve for victimization risk. Many of the victimizations of younger children—assaults at the hands of peers, abuse at the hands of parents, neglect, and other forms of child maltreatment—are forms of victimization considerably less likely to be defined as crimes or matters of police concern.

The age patterns in victimization rates are considerably different when the evidence comes from the victims themselves and their family members—for example, from the DVS, which assessed victimizations in children ages 2 through 17, using the same screening questions across all ages (see Fig. 2.5). Overall victimization rose slightly, not precipitously, for the adolescents.* The increase was largest for sexual victimizations and witnessing/indirect victimizations; there was no rise for assaults. Perhaps most surprisingly, child maltreatment also rose with age; this might be the form of victimization that we would most expect to decline with age. In fact, some studies of child maltreatment known to professionals show higher rates for older children. But it may be the case that the maltreatment of younger children is difficult to access or verify, both in surveys (which almost of necessity must get this information from the caregivers themselves) and among cases known to professionals, who are less likely to have contact with younger children.

The absence of a steep increase in victimization is also apparent in the NCVS data. Rates of violent crime measured in that study for 12- to 14-year-olds are as high as rates for 15- to 17-year-olds. Rape and aggravated assault are a bit higher for the older adolescents, but simple assault is actually more common among younger youth. The steep increases noted in self-reported delinquency studies[71] are not apparent in the self-reported victimization studies.

Why does the self-report information contrast so starkly with the official police data? Studies clearly show that the younger the victim, the less

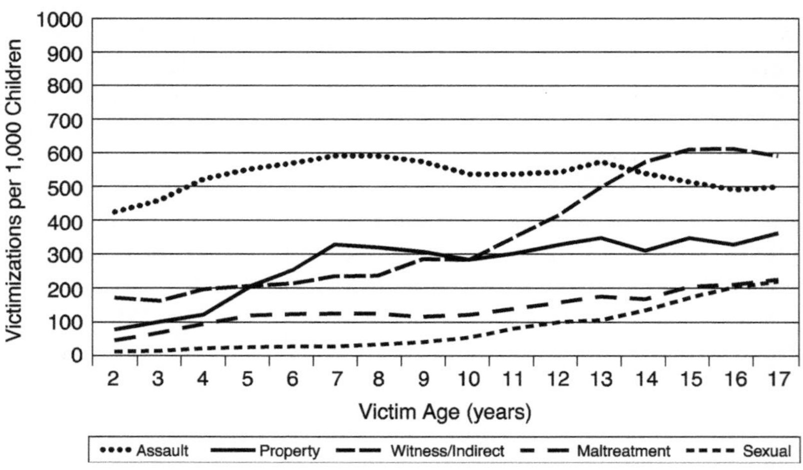

FIGURE 2.5. Major victimization types by victim age. Victimization rates given as 3-year running average.

likely it is that the victimization will be reported to law enforcement.[72] This may be because the public and police do not want younger victims caught up in the judicial system. Also, they are less apt to define juvenile victimizations as crimes. Families, schools, and child welfare officials lay claim to the arbitration of offenses against younger victims; younger victims themselves have a harder time independently accessing police. So, victimization does not accelerate in adolescence in the same way as delinquency.

Research Needs

The research needs in this new field of developmental victimology are vast and urgent, given the size of the problem and the seriousness of its impact. They range from studies of risk factors to studies of treatment efficacy to studies of criminal justice policy. But in the limited space of this review, we will mention only three important points.

First, if we are to take the subject seriously, we need much better statistics to document and analyze the scope, nature, and trends of child victimization. The National Crime Victimization Survey records crime victimizations only in children age 12 and older. In the past, the Uniform Crime Reports made no age information available about crimes, with the exception of homicide (something that is changing under the new NIBRS system, but the full national implementation of this system is still a long way off). The national data collection system about child abuse also has severe methodological drawbacks, limiting the way in which the information can be aggregated nationally or compared across states.[73] We need comprehensive yearly national and state figures on all officially reported crimes against children and all forms of child abuse. These statistics need to be supplemented with regular national studies to assess the vast quantity of unreported victimizations, including family violence, child-to-child violence, and indirect victimizations. While there are methodological challenges in such efforts, studies like the ones referenced in this chapter demonstrate that this is feasible.

Second, we need theory and research that cuts across and integrates the various forms of child victimization. A good example is the work on post-traumatic stress disorder in children, which has been applied to the effects of various victimizations such as sexual abuse, stranger abduction, and the witnessing of homicide.[74–77] Similar cross-cutting research could be conducted in other subjects, such as what makes children vulnerable to victimization or how responses by family members buffer or exacerbate the impact of victimization. To be truly synthesizing, this research needs to study the pandemic victimizations, not just the acute and extraordinary victimizations, which have been the main focus in the past.

Third, the field needs a more developmental perspective on child victimization. This would begin with an understanding of the mix of victimization threats that children of different ages face. It would include the kinds of factors that place children at risk and the strategies for victimization avoidance that are appropriate at different stages of development. It also would differentiate how children at different stages react and cope with the challenges posed by victimization.

Chapter 3

Children at Risk

Parents make considerable efforts, some more than others, to try to keep their children safe. They move them to the suburbs. They give them karate lessons. They drive them to school to keep them off the streets or the bus. They sometimes invest in wearable alarms, wristwatch Global Positioning System devices, and babysitter-surveillance cameras. There is no end to the ideas about how to protect children from harm. Sadly, social science has been little help. There is surprisingly little research about exactly which children are at risk and what works to reduce that risk. In this chapter, we summarize what is known about the risk of child victimization and organize the information conceptually in a comprehensive way that will help focus attention on what we can indeed do to help improve the situation.

As is often the case, the science that exists about child victimization is better for critiquing prevention strategies than proposing new ones.[88] Many common prevention ideas do seem to be based on mistaken perceptions about risk. For example, vast parental and public-policy efforts are targeted at stranger adults who might assault, molest, or kidnap children. But stranger molestations and abductions are quite rare—facts that have been fairly widely disseminated, but with only limited effect. In the most recent study on this topic, it was estimated that over the course of a year no more than a hundred children were victimized in a stereotypical kidnapping scenario, in which a child is taken a substantial distance, held for a substantial time, held for ransom, or murdered.[89] Stranger-molesters make up no more than 10% to 20% of the total of sexual abusers.[90] But for any offense against children—not just abduction and molestations—adult strangers are fairly uncommon perpetrators.[8] Children just do not have much contact with adult strangers; nonetheless, strong anxieties about strangers persist. In contrast, family members and good acquaintances commit a lot of the most serious crimes against children, yet it is considerably harder to get parents to warn and prepare children about these victimizations.

Many prevention advocates see this "stranger danger" preoccupation as simply a matter of providing better education. But the persistence of this preoccupation belies any simple solution. Unfortunately, there are probably bedrock features of human nature underlying such risk perceptions that will continue to make them difficult to counteract. In our tribal pasts, perhaps one of the most frequent dangers to children was a raid from an enemy tribe. But in our contemporary, more dense, more heterogeneous urban society, where hundreds of unfamiliar people and influences vie with one another to pull children away from their family sphere of influence, it is not surprising that these archetypal fears rest both symbolically and realistically on the dangers posed by strangers. Education may help parents to temper these fears, but they will probably always be a big factor in the emotions that motivate thinking about safety.

At the same time, our nature inevitably leads us to underestimate the dangers posed by family and friends. Family life and friendship networks cannot operate without trust and assumptions of reciprocity. It is hard to treat someone simultaneously with trust and suspicion, and the trust within networks of close kin mostly yields more benefit than harm. Unfortunately, family members and friends who exploit and hurt others take advantage of this general trust. Education can help people recognize the dangers close at hand, but people will never overcome the tendency to underestimate these risks or get people to instinctively put family members above strangers in their risk hierarchy.

Risk perceptions are also distorted by publicity. Newsworthy events are generally unusual in nature. Very unusual child kidnappings get a lot of publicity, in part because they are terrifying crimes that resonate with archetypal fears, and in part because the wide publicity is a legitimate aspect of the effort to locate and recover the child. This extensive publicity can make these kinds of kidnappings seem more frequent than they really are. By contrast, school bullying is widespread, but its commonness makes it less newsworthy.

Publicity also distorts the characteristics of child victim cases. The highly publicized kidnappings tend to involve younger children, for example; this is in part because police have an easier time diagnosing the disappearance of a young child as a true abduction. For older youth who go missing, it is harder to dismiss other possible scenarios, such as running away (a more common but less compelling story). So the public has not only a distorted perception of the frequency of kidnapping but also a tendency to think of younger children as the main targets. In fact, adolescent girls are the main targets for stranger kidnappings.[89] The main motive for kidnapping is to commit a sexual assault, and adolescent girls are the preferred target for most rapists. But teenagers do not elicit the same publicity or the same solicitude as do young children, and they are not recognized as the most common targets of stranger kidnappings.

Another mistaken idea about risk is that "small is bad." Parents with smaller children typically worry more about their children's risk of victimization, even to the point of stuffing them with growth hormones to "protect" them from bullies. Although it is true that bullies are more common among larger children, mere smallness of stature does not seem to confer risk.[91] Other personal characteristics stereotypically associated with smallness, such as passivity, weakness, and deference, may increase vulnerability more than size itself. There is obviously strong parental motivation to try to protect children; can those efforts be directed at remedies more likely to confer protection?

What Puts Kids at Risk?

Unfortunately the established risk factors for child victimization—the ones that are well identified—fall mostly under the category of "usual suspects." They include family disruptions, emotional difficulties, risk-taking, and neighborhood features—not factors easy to change with some sage parental advice or a cookbook-style education program. But it is important to understand not just that they are risks but why—something that is much more complicated.

Geography

For generations in America, parents have fled from the cities to the suburbs in search of protection for their children (and themselves). Hard as this may be on the tax base, school systems, and ethnic diversity, there is a rational basis to this perception of greater safety. Different geographic areas do confer considerably different levels of risk and safety for children. The idea that urban areas are more dangerous than suburban ones has a good statistical foundation, as does the judgment that high-crime neighborhoods entail higher levels of victimization for children. According to crime surveys, youth are safest in rural areas, and somewhat safer in suburbs than in inner cities.

But nonurban areas may not be as safe for children as parents might hope. According to the National Crime Victimization Survey (NCVS), children in rural areas actually experience *higher* crime-victimization rates than adults who live in urban areas (66 violent crimes per 1,000 for rural youth versus 42 per 1,000 for urban adults).[2] This is in part a function of the higher vulnerability of children to crime wherever they are; but in addition, nonurban living confers considerably less protection for children than it does for adults. The violent crime rate for children living in suburban areas is only 15% lower than the violent crime rate for children living in urban areas. In contrast, adults living in suburban areas benefit from a 32% reduction in the rate of violent crime compared to urban adults.[2] This may have to do with the fact that young people in nonurban areas end up congregating in schools with considerable exposure to potential offenders, so they don't benefit from the same population dispersion as do adults in nonurban areas.

The specific features of neighborhoods that are the most effective predictors of crime victimization, when everything is taken into account, are quite interesting and a bit surprising. According to Lauritsen's[92] thoughtful analysis in 2003, it is not racial composition, poverty, or central-city location that makes some neighborhoods more risky for youth; rather, the important features are a high concentration of youth in the neighborhood and the existence of a large number of youth from single-parent families. When these factors are taken into account, race and poverty are no longer important in explaining youth victimization. This suggests that when a neighborhood has a lot of young people who are not subject to effective or consistent parental supervision, conditions rapidly become far more dangerous. Interestingly, this danger is fairly specific for young people and does not explain adult victimization in these neighborhoods.

The importance of neighborhood and supervision is suggested by some other findings, as well. Youth who have lived for a while at their current residence are considerably safer than youth who have recently moved.[92] Being in a neighborhood for a considerable time may confer various protections for children. For instance, such children (and their parents) may know the neighborhood better and be aware of the risks and areas to avoid. Such children may also have better developed social networks in the neighborhood, meaning other adults who watch out for them and stable and friendly relationships with other children, who may be less likely to target them.

This finding raises an obvious dilemma for parents inclined to move from a longtime neighborhood that they perceive to be getting more dangerous. Will they be increasing their child's risk simply by moving? We do not know how much safer a new neighborhood has to be to offset the increased risk entailed with relocation. Moreover, we do not know for sure that moving itself raises the risk for children. But the obvious concern that parents feel about such dilemmas, and the suggestion that type of neighborhood and length of residency do make a difference, should make this a high-priority issue for researchers.

Family Disruptions

A variety of studies have clearly shown that children are at higher risk for certain kinds of victimizations when they are living in less conventional family situations: with a single parent, in a family including a stepparent, or with a parent's unmarried partner.[58,93] The increased risk applies to victimization both inside and outside the family. This is anxiety-provoking news for the increasing number of families with such characteristics. Unfortunately, the culprit behind this increased risk is not the family constellation itself but some features that accompany that constellation—though we do not know yet exactly what those features are. It is incumbent on those in the field to find out exactly what the pertinent features are so as not to stigmatize and alarm all such families. Here are some of the possibilities:

1. **Children in such families are exposed to more extraneous, unfamiliar, unrelated, and potentially predatory or aggressive people**. This could be because there are more frequent moves, there is a larger social network, or dating by the parent creates a transitional environment. Sociobiologists have pointed out that stepparents, stepsiblings, and new boyfriends see existing children as unwanted competitors for scarce parental resources, and therefore have an interest in abusing, neglecting, or minimizing the influence of these competitors.
2. **The supervision of children in some less conventional families may be compromised**. It may be obvious that one parent cannot supervise as well as two. It would then seem surprising that remarriage does not restore safety, but it doesn't. It may be that the remarriage process actually further distracts parents from their ability to supervise, or that stepparents or live-ins are not good substitutes when it comes to supervision.
3. **The children in these families may be more likely to experience loss, conflict, deprivation, adversity, and turmoil**. These are experiences that undermine their capacity to protect themselves. Some of the changes that yield these families—divorce, death, conflict, geographic transition—are challenging for children. If the children are depressed or emotionally needy, for example, it may make them easier targets for bullies or child molesters. If they are angry at their parents for divorcing or remarrying, the children may not avail themselves of parental help or may deliberately alienate stepparents and stepsiblings, thus inviting retaliation.
4. **Children who have experienced family disruptions may have been exposed to, and then themselves acquired, dysfunctional interpersonal patterns**. These children may have seen a lot of conflict, aggression, and even violence. They may not have learned conflict-reduction skills—in fact, they may have learned conflict-escalation skills. Thus they find themselves in more unresolved conflict situations, both inside the family with parents and siblings and outside the family with friends and acquaintances. These conflict situations lead to victimization.
5. **Family disruption may be a marker for groups of related people who are genetically predisposed to conflict and victimization.** Although some social scientists don't like to propose such explanations, the fact that the parents' marriage broke up may in some cases reflect the kinds of personalities predisposed to victimization, and children may have simply inherited these predispositions.

6. **Children in disrupted families may have less control over their environment and thus less ability to avoid danger and victimization**. Autonomy and positive choices may be constrained for these children on a wide variety of dimensions. They have more poverty. They may have less choice about where they live, so they end up in more dangerous neighborhoods. They may have less choice about who will come to live with them. They may have to share rooms and possessions. These situations can lead to more possibilities for conflict with others, as well as fewer alternatives that would allow the children to avoid risky situations.

Each of the above-listed risk mechanisms implies a different prevention approach, from financial support to child care to counseling. In the end, there are probably multiple mechanisms at work. Nonetheless, even if we do not know the exact mechanisms, we can start with the knowledge that children in less conventional family circumstances are at increased risk and thus should be priority targets for prevention strategies. The good news is that some of these circumstances are marked by public transitions, such as divorces and remarriages, around which prevention efforts can be organized. The bad news is that enormous numbers of children experience such transitions. It would be extremely useful to have more sensitive risk-prediction instruments for deciding which children really are most in need of prevention efforts. Still, this may be one of the most promising and currently underutilized domains for prevention studies.

Emotional Deficits and Difficulties

It is widely appreciated that victimized children suffer emotional difficulties after their experience, but it is less widely recognized that many children had these same or other emotional difficulties beforehand. In fact, the difficulties may have been part of the reason they were victimized, rather than just an effect of the victimization. Few studies have been able to evaluate victims prior to their victimization, but those that have show that youth who have suffered depression, anxiety, and other emotional distress have a higher likelihood of being victimized.[75] Mental health problems and emotional distress are, then, risk factors for victimization.

Once again, there is a fairly long list of specific mechanisms that could help explain why having emotional problems can increase a child's risk of victimization:

1. **Emotional problems may both reflect and exacerbate social isolation**. Children without friends or allies among peers or family may be easier targets. Without people to protect and support these children, bullies and aggressors can abuse them with more impunity and without suffering disapproval from others.

2. **Emotional problems may interfere with self-protective skills.** For example, an emotionally distressed child may lack the ability to sense when someone else is acting in a dangerous way, or the problem may interfere with the child's ability to stand up for himself or herself or ask for help from adults or peers to cope with or stave off a confusing or dangerous situation.
3. **Emotional problems may be a sign of vulnerability that serves to attract offenders.** The child who is depressed or has low self-esteem may seem to the bully, sibling, or parent to be someone who can easily be pushed around. The child who is needy or anxious may trigger the bully or offender's dislike. A sexual abuser looking for a compliant child may home in on the one who seems to be particularly deprived, lonely, and depressed.
4. **Emotional problems may lead children to provoke conflicts that lead to their victimization.** For depressed and anxious children, intentionally provoking conflict may distract them from their suffering. For angry and emotionally unregulated children, conflict may grow out of their biased perceptions that they are being treated unfairly.
5. **Certain emotional problems may lead to dependent, sexualized, or indiscriminately affiliative behavior that leaves a child open to victimization.** Such children may cling to whoever is available or anyone who expresses the slightest interest in them. This may lead them into the company of exploitative, poorly controlled, or abusive people.

Parents and professionals who are trying to help children with emotional problems often sense that the children are making dangerous choices regarding friendships or are acting in risky and possibly self-destructive ways. Changing these choices and behaviors seems challenging, but preventing these children's victimization is obviously a high priority.

Risk Taking

Children who engage in risky behavior are more likely to get victimized. Behaviors such as drinking and taking drugs appear to compromise safety. Stealing and harassing people cause offense to others that may invite retaliation. Joining gangs and hanging out with delinquent and risk-taking youth put children in proximity to other people who may take advantage of them. These risk-taking behaviors often put young people in situations of low supervision—for example, being out late at night or in places where adults are not present. The young people forfeit the protections that other youth enjoy from adults, authorities, and law enforcement. A considerable body of research shows that delinquents have high rates of victimization. In fact, some criminologists contend that victims and delinquents are a largely overlapping group of children.[94]

There are some important caveats that need to be voiced about the role of risk-taking in victimization, however. One caveat concerns the true causal relationship between the two. While much criminology work has emphasized the way delinquency creates victimization risk through risk taking, the reverse is also true: victimization can create delinquency. Children who have been victimized have a harder time controlling their behavior, have emotional effects that impel them to take risks, and may even end up in more risky environments, such as gangs, in a misguided effort to protect themselves from further victimization. So victimization may be the beginning of the sequence of risk taking and delinquency.

A second caveat concerns how easy it is to generalize the risk-taking–to– victimization sequence. Most of the professional observations about this pattern relate to adolescents. There may be parallel dynamics among younger children, but the model is not so self-evident. For example, children with uncontrolled behavior may be more annoying to other children or seen as appropriate targets for bullying, but many victims of bullying appear to be fairly passive. When young children fail to control their behavior and do dangerous things such as wander away or explore the medicine cabinet, it may provoke parental reactions that escalate into abuse. But much of the behavior that is known to trigger parental abuse (soiling diapers, crying, hitting parents and siblings) seems to involve developmentally normal failures of self-control. Are these problems of childhood self-control really parallel to the risky behaviors identified in adolescence? Probably not.

There has been enduring and acrimonious controversy in victimology about whether and how to use victims' own behaviors and characteristics to account for their victimizations. The mere mention of such characteristics often elicits complaints about "blaming the victim" and discourages further inquiry into such matters. There are several useful conclusions from this debate that are worth keeping in mind. First, there are victim behaviors and activities that have been clearly statistically associated with increased likelihood of victimization. Second, our psychological tendency is to overstress bad things that happen to people because of their own bad behavior ("he didn't get enough exercise," "she was dressed provocatively," "he was driving too fast"); this helps us reassure ourselves that we won't fall victim to the same fate. Finally, it is important to distinguish between seeing behavior as empirically contributing to victimization risk and blaming a victim or holding the person morally responsible for the victimization. So while risk taking almost certainly plays some role in victimization for some victims, we need to be cautious about how much and how often we associate the two.

Prior Victimization

One of the most reliable predictors of whether a child will be victimized is a child's previous victimization.[58, 95] This is not just the idea that the child who was bullied last year in school will be bullied again this year; this also means that a child who was bullied last year is at a substantially higher risk of being sexually assaulted this year, or vice versa. The child who had a stereo stolen is at higher risk of experiencing a gang assault, and so forth. There appears to be tremendous *transitivity* among victimization risks. The risk for a new victimization is typically three to six times higher for a child who has been victimized previously.[96] Moreover, it appears that any kind of victimization seems to apply, and no particular kind of victimization is far more predictive than others.

In addition, the kind of victimization that best predicts future victimization is multiple victimization. In Chapter 2, we introduced the concept of the poly-victim. This is a child who has an unusually high general level of victimization and of severity of victimization, and who also shows an unusually large number of stress symptoms. (We found it useful to categorize these children as those who experienced more than three victimizations in a given year.) Children who were poly-victims in the last year had seven to ten times the risk of victimization in the next year.[96] These are children whom we can think of as being locked into or trapped in a condition of victimization, rather than as experiencing victimization events. They also seem to be the children for whom victimization has the most serious adverse consequences.

Even more than to determine who is vulnerable to victimization, there is a need to figure out which children are vulnerable to *poly*-victimization. Although there has not been a great deal of research yet on this matter, available research and additional speculation suggest that there may be several pathways by which children arrive at this downward-spiraling condition that seems to attract additional victimization.

The Pathways to Poly-Victimization

The first pathway to a condition of poly-victimization leads through a dangerous and victimization-filled family environment. These would be families in which children are maltreated, sometimes in several ways, and in which there is also domestic violence that models violence and victimization. Obviously children in these circumstances have opportunities to experience multiple kinds of victimization within the family—violence, sexual assault, psychological maltreatment at the hands of parents and siblings—but these developmental experiences create both cognitive sets and emotional deficits that make subsequent victimization outside the family more likely as well.[41]

A second pathway to poly-victimization runs through family disruption and adversity, but not necessarily through direct family exposure to violence. We mentioned earlier some of the many mechanisms that possibly create risk in families experiencing disruption. Family illnesses, accidents, and homelessness can operate in similar ways. This pathway includes mechanisms such as poor supervision, emotional deprivation, and exposure to numerous potentially predatory persons. The deficits lead easily to peer victimization, sexual victimization, and other victimizations.

A third very probable pathway to poly-victimization traces its way through dangerous neighborhoods and risky community environments. Even children without dangerous, disrupted, or disorganized families may become poly-victims in such environments. These children live in neighborhoods where bullies and gangs abound, where there is a lot of vandalism and theft of property, where the schools are not safe, and where everyone's life is a gauntlet run past a line of criminal activities. The potential for multiple kinds of victimization, including the witnessing of violence, is obvious in these neighborhoods.

Finally, a fourth pathway to poly-victimization is paved through certain enduring personal characteristics of the children themselves. Some children, for perhaps a number of reasons, appear to act as magnets for victimization. What makes them magnets? Certain temperaments, for example, may be irritating or frustrating to peers and caregivers. Certain incapacities may be burdensome to parents or make children obvious targets. Children who are different in certain ways may mobilize dislike or resentment, especially in sociocultural environments that stigmatize such differences. Also, children who are disabled or inept may be easier targets. Children with certain kinds of traumas or mental health problems may actually seek out or trigger conflicts that they are unable to handle.

The "Lifestyles" and "Routine Activities" Theories of Crime Victimization

In the past, when academic scholars have tried to understand why people get victimized, one approach that has tended to dominate the discussion is to employ what have been called the *lifestyle exposure* and *routine activities* theories.[3,97–99] As expounded in the past, these theories highlight the lifestyles and routine activities of certain people that put them into environments or situations where they have more contact with potential offenders and risk of potential victimization.

Four central concepts have been used in these approaches to explain the connection between lifestyle and risk: proximity to crime, exposure to crime, target attractiveness, and guardianship.[100] *Proximity to crime* means living in a high-crime area. *Exposure to crime* includes behaviors like being out late at night. *Target attractiveness* applies to attributes that might entice offenders, such as owning desirable and portable possessions. *Guardianship* implies that spending considerable time alone or apart from the family or other protective individuals can create vulnerability. These concepts have proved useful in explaining important things about victimization—for example, why certain groups, such as men, blacks, and single people, have higher crime-victimization rates. For example, single people live in higher-crime areas. It has also been used to explain why rates of crime have increased over time in some places and during some periods—as when, for example, fewer people began living in families and more people began acquiring more conspicuously valuable items.

When these concepts are applied to the analysis of youth victimization, however, they do not yield a rich set of explanations. They have been used primarily to point out how increased exposure and decreased guardianship heighten youth vulnerability. Young people are viewed in this theory as engaging in risky behaviors, such as staying out late, going to parties, and drinking, which compromise the guardianship provided by parents and adults and expose them to more possibilities for victimization.[101] Much of the research on youth victimization has particularly stressed its connection to delinquent activities.[11,12] Delinquency is thought of as a lifestyle that puts a person in close proximity to other offenders—for example, aggressive or delinquent companions or rival gang members. Moreover, it greatly reduces guardianship because delinquents tend to avoid conventional social environments and, through their activities, largely forfeit their claims on protection by police and other authorities.[102] Empirical research has confirmed that delinquents are indeed more prone to victimization than other youth.[11,12]

A Critique of the Lifestyles and Routine Activities Theories

Ultimately, the lifestyles theory of youth victimization has been fairly limited in its ability to account for the diverse types of youth who get victimized. For one thing, many victimized youth are not involved in delinquency and do not follow a risky lifestyle—for example, young children molested by their fathers or relatives, or passive victims of bullies. Additionally, delinquent activities are primarily the domain of adolescents, particularly adolescent boys, but considerable numbers of quite young children are assaulted, kidnapped, sexually abused, or otherwise victimized,[8,103] again mostly without any connection to delinquent behavior.

In reality, the lifestyles and routine activities theories were designed for and have always been best at explaining street crime such as stranger assaults and robberies. They are not well suited to account for acquaintance and intrafamily offenses, which constitute a considerable portion of the victimizations children experience. For example, routine activities studies often measure *exposure to crime* as the amount of time routinely spent out at night or away from the family home. However, when used to try to explain why a child has been abused by parents, such explanations fall apart. It may explain a child's risk of stranger crime if the child is away from his or her parents or out at night, but it does not explain physical child abuse by members of the household. In fact, being out of the home may actually reduce the chance of such abuse.

Thus, it is not surprising that researchers trying to explain children's victimization by acquaintances and family members have virtually ignored the lifestyles theory and have relied on other concepts besides exposure and guardianship. For example, in trying to account for who becomes the target of bullying, observers have noted that these victims tend to be children with *avoidant-insecure attachment* relationships with primary caregivers, who lack trust, have low self-confidence, have physical impairments, are socially isolated, and are physically weaker.[104,105]

The literature on child maltreatment also takes a different tack from the lifestyles approach. This literature tends to equate victimization risk primarily with family and parental attributes such as family stress, isolation, alcoholic and violence-prone caretakers, and parents who have victimization histories and unrealistic expectations of their children.[58,106] Psychiatric disorders are another set of parental attributes cited as a risk factor.[107,108] When the literature cites youth characteristics that create risk, they include features such as oppositional behavior, difficult temperament, or impairments that are a burden or source of disappointment for caregivers.[109–112]

A still different victimization literature, that on child sexual assault, notes some other risk factors—being female, living in a stepparent family, having parents who fight or are distant and punitive, receiving too little parental supervision, and suffering emotional deprivation—that make children and youth vulnerable to the offers of attention and affection that predatory offenders sometimes use to draw children into sexual activities.[113,114] These also are more complicated than the usual factors offered by the routine activities theory.

Some concepts from these various literatures—as well as ones we highlighted earlier in the chapter—can, with some adaptation, be subsumed into the routine activities conceptual framework. Thus, for example, lacking parental supervision—as a factor that increases the risk for sexual abuse—does correspond to the guardianship concept of routine activities theory. Family social isolation (which can put a child at risk for physical abuse by parents) also has an element of the missing guardianship of the routine activities theory, but in this case the guardians are not family members themselves—the usual guardians in routine activities theory—since family members are the abusers. On the contrary, the guardians are members of a related social network whose supervision might inhibit the abuse.

Routine activities theory also has an important concept called *target attractiveness*, which can be adapted to incorporate some of these factors. Target attractiveness, in the routine activities literature, has primarily been utilized in a very narrow sense in reference to the value and portability of material objects that, as a result of lifestyle, a person may own or carry.[100,115] Thus, an attractive target is a man with a conspicuously fat wallet or an empty house known to contain a high-end TV.

Some features that make a child vulnerable to victimization might well be categorized under this notion of target attractiveness. For example, a child may be chosen (seen as attractive) by a bully or by an offender because the child has an impairment, is a girl, or is emotionally vulnerable. But target attractiveness takes on a different meaning when it comes to violent victimizations, a context in which the word "attractive" seems quite inappropriate. A child may be beaten by a parent because the child's disability disappoints and frustrates the parent, and in this sense some of the child's characteristics elicit parental anger. But this is an "attractive target" for parental anger only in an ironic and convoluted sense. Moreover, attractiveness as a factor implies that an offender has chosen one target from an array of available targets. But this is not always the case. In the example of parental assault, if the child victim were not disabled, it is not clear that some other child in the family would necessarily suffer the abuse instead. Maybe in this case no one would be abused. So while the routine activities theory does highlight the fact that victim characteristics sometimes play a role in determining who gets victimized, calling this "target attractiveness" is not an adequate characterization.

But perhaps the biggest objections to trying to subsume these child-victimization risk factors into routine activities theory are that none of these target attributes constitutes a "lifestyle," nor do they necessarily increase risk through routine activities. For example, femaleness, although it is a form of target attractiveness and does increase the risk for sexual abuse (in comparison to maleness), is not a routine activity. Moreover, while maleness may put men at differential risk for physical assault because men engage in more unsupervised and risk-taking behaviors (a lifestyle feature), femaleness does not put women at differential risk for sexual assault by virtue of anything they do: femaleness itself is the risk attribute. Similarly, while emotional deprivation may change a person's routine activities, if a molester preys on an emotionally deprived child because she is needy, it is not the routine activities of the child that necessarily elevate the risk. Thus, the routine activities idea of target attractiveness does not seem broad enough to be applied to child victimization.

A New Conceptual Framework for Thinking about Victimization

To explain the full range of victimizations that youth suffer, the lifestyles and routine activities frameworks need to be substantially modified. When it comes to victimization by intimates, concepts such as guardianship, exposure, and proximity need to be seen not as aspects of routine activities or lifestyles but as environmental factors that expose or protect children from victimization. Thus, when a child is placed at risk for sexual abuse because his or her parents are fighting and are inattentive, the lack of guardianship is an environmental condition conducive to victimization, not a problem of a lifestyle or routine activity for the child.

But in addition to the environmental conditions highlighted by the lifestyles theory to explain the risks for youth victimization, more attention needs to be paid to how individual attributes, such as female gender or emotional deprivation, increase risk. An individual's personal characteristics appear to increase vulnerability to victimization, not because they are inherently dangerous or entail any routine activity but rather because these attributes relate or appeal to something in dangerous individuals. The characteristics become risks when they have some congruence with the needs, motives, or psychological vulnerabilities of offenders. That is, because certain offenders are drawn to or react to certain types of victims or certain characteristics in victims, those potential victims are more vulnerable.

A good term for this process might be *target congruence*, with the term referring to the fact that some characteristics of potential victims are congruent with the needs or psychological vulnerabilities of potential offenders. This process might be broken down into three more specific subcategories, referred to here as *target gratifiability*, *target antagonism*, and *target vulnerability*. Each is described below.

1. **Target gratifiability**. Some characteristics of victims increase their risk because they are qualities, possessions, skills, or attributes that offenders want to obtain, use, have access to, or manipulate. For an offender interested in getting money or goods, a conspicuously wealthy person or well-appointed home is congruent with such a need. For a heterosexual sex offender, a female victim is a congruent target for the crime of sexual assault. Obviously, for other sexual offenders, gratifiability focuses on prepubescent children or, in some cases, boys. Clearly, the routine activities notion of target attractiveness falls into this category.
2. **Target antagonism**. Some characteristics of victims increase their risk by being qualities, possessions, skills, or attributes that arouse the anger, jealousy, or destructive impulses of offenders. Examples in this category are ethnic characteristics or being gay or effeminate (for hate crimes). For a bigot, or someone with anger toward a particular minority or segment of the population, a child's belonging to that ethnic group or sexual orientation creates congruence between their antagonism and that child's characteristic. Similarly, for a bully, whose need might be to prove his independence and toughness, a child who is anxiously attached—a "mama's boy"—might have the characteristics congruent with his antagonism. In the case of parental assaults, characteristics such as being a burden owing to a disability or being disobedient are common examples.
3. **Target vulnerability**. Some characteristics of victims increase risk because they compromise the potential victim's capacity to resist or deter victimization and thus make the victim an easier

> target for the offender. For child victimization, the prototypical risk factors in the vulnerability category are attributes such as physical weakness, emotional deprivation, or psychological problems.

Although these concepts of target congruence, particularly target gratifiabilty, have similarities to the notion of target attractiveness, the word "attractiveness" is obviously a poor choice. Its applications to the crime of sexual assault have victim-blaming connotations about physical appeal that reinforce a stereotype long contested by victimologists. The "attractions" implied in these concepts are not about beauty but rather refer to a range of predispositions, proclivities, and reactivities of the offender, hence the idea of congruence. Thus *gratifiability* works better, meaning that the target fits what the offender is looking for, whether that is conventionally desirable or merely satisfies the offender's idiosyncratic motive. Antagonism does not imply provocation in the conventional sense; for example, without some predisposition in the offender to resent or feel burdened by it, a crying baby does not provoke assault any more than a member of a minority group provokes a hate crime.

It is important to note, as the examples also illustrate, that target congruence changes considerably from crime to crime and from offender to offender. Thus, females may have considerable target gratifiability for a sexual assault, a crime that is mostly committed by heterosexual males. But a male may have more target antagonism for gay-bashing because male homosexuals are seen as more threatening to male assaulters. The characteristics that might increase target antagonism for parental assaults, such as disobedience, may have little if anything to do with risk for peer victimization. There may be some generalized target-congruence characteristics, such as weakness, but even this may be a relatively insignificant factor in many victimizations.

These elements of target congruence clearly play a greater role in some offenses than in others. In relatively impersonal street crimes or group victimizations (e.g., sniper attacks), and also in the case of family members who live with violent individuals, the offenders may not choose victims on the basis of personal characteristic at all, instead reacting only to proximity. The school sniper starts shooting at whoever is around when he pulls out a gun. The abusive parent lashes out at whichever child is in the room. Target congruence plays virtually no role.

In other victimizations, target congruence provides a virtually complete explanation of the crime. Take, for example, attempts to assassinate presidents or celebrities, such as John Lennon. Another example is the stalking of an ex-wife or a movie star. The congruence between the characteristics of the victim and the needs of the offender explains the crime, which would not have occurred with a different person. When a parent maltreats a colicky baby, there may be a similar, singular congruence: in the absence of the colicky baby, no crime would occur. In these cases, the congruence of the victim's personal characteristics with the motives or reactivities of the offender provides a virtually complete explanation of victim choice.

These three target-congruence concepts seem to encompass most of the characteristics cited in the literature on youth victimization, including characteristics such as low self-esteem and disobedience. But they also appear to be quite relevant to the prediction of forms of victimization, such as street crime, that have been the primary focus of routine activities research. They may be a useful elaboration on the most common conceptual framework used to talk about victimization, one that gives the model much greater general applicability.

A Comprehensive Dynamic Model

We can take these elements one step further and add a dynamic dimension. The routine activities concepts, and some of the concepts just introduced here, can be brought together in a model with some sequence and order, as illustrated in Figure 3.1. This model breaks down the offense–victimization experience into three sequential processes: *Instigation processes* are mechanisms that increase the likelihood or motivation for offending. *Selection processes* are mechanisms that govern the choice of particular victims out of a universe of all possible victims. *Protection processes* are mechanisms whose absence diminishes the ability of particular victims to ward off, deter, or escape victimization. These processes obviously occur in a temporal and logical sequence. The mechanisms in these processes can be further subdivided into two groups: first are mechanisms that pertain primarily to the environments in which victims live and interact, and second are mechanisms that pertain primarily to the victims themselves (in this case children) and their capacities.

Most of the risk and protection mechanisms discussed in this chapter can be classified within this grid. The grid illustrates, in its first stage, many of

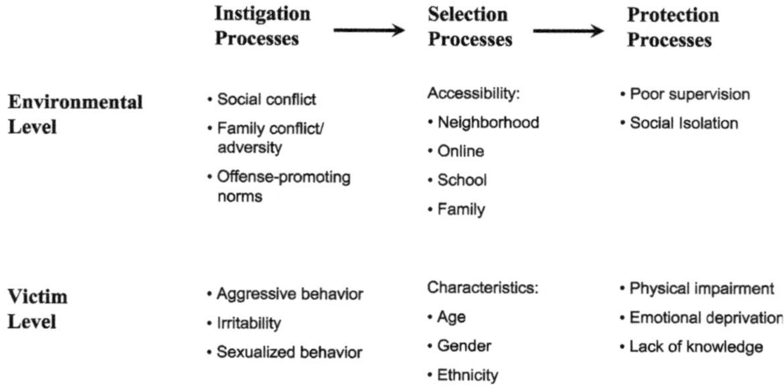

FIGURE 3.1. Victimization risk analysis model.

the conventional offense-instigation factors considered to promote criminal offending behavior, including conflicts, adversities, and offense-promoting norms (Environmental Instigation Processes). But the model also incorporates the fact that some victim behaviors may need to be considered instigatory as well (Victim-Level Instigation Processes)—for example, the processes we referred to earlier as target antagonisms. These might include the irritability of a small child who arouses the anger of parents, the aggressive behavior of a victim of bullying who provokes peers, or the sexualized behavior of a youth who makes overtures to adults online.

Next come the selection processes. When instigatory processes occur at the environmental level—that is, without the involvement of a specific child—then some kind of second stage ensues, during which offenders come to select particular children out of all possible targets. (This selection process does not really exist when a particular child is involved in the instigatory process, since the instigation and selection are simultaneous.) At the environmental level, the selection-process cell in the grid highlights some of the mechanisms emphasized by routine activities theory, such as exposure to crime and proximity to crime. Children are placed at risk by living in more dangerous neighborhoods, going to more dangerous schools, growing up in more dangerous families, and so forth.

There are also selection processes that might be seen as being more at the level of victim characteristics. These are the mechanisms discussed earlier, such as target gratifiability, and they include gender and age. In the case of sex offenses particularly, many offenders are looking for a victim of a specific gender and age. It would also include ethnicity for offenders who have racial and ethnic animosities that motivate offenses.

Finally, Figure 3.1 illustrates the final set of processes concerned with protection. At the environmental level, the main components of the protection web surrounding victims are the qualities of supervision and social connectedness. At the victim level, some of the main components of protection are physical capacities that allow resistance, deterrence, and flight. Other protection components at the victim level are emotional and cognitive capacities that allow individuals to assess danger, stand up for themselves, negotiate with potential offenders, and plan and execute escape and avoidance strategies.*

Conceptual frameworks like the one shown in Figure 3.1 can appear academic or abstract, but they can actually serve useful purposes. For example, they can help guide policymakers who might be trying to develop a comprehensive prevention program for an organization to serve abused youth or for prevention of bullying in schools. The conceptual framework orients planners to face the various components of the victimization process that a comprehensive prevention program ought to address. Thus, a bullying-prevention program in schools would have components that address the instigation processes at the environmental level, reducing sources of social conflict and counteracting offense-promoting norms. At the victim level, the prevention programs may want to educate children about how to avoid provocative behaviors. An analysis of selection processes can help planners identify individuals who may be at high risk for victimization, as well as provide the basis for educating victims about how to avoid being selected. Then, by analyzing protection processes, program planners may want to think about how to enhance protective capacities among potential victims and how to counteract vulnerabilities that put some young people at risk. Conceptual frameworks like this one can help ensure that a wide variety of processes are addressed.

Chapter 4

Developmental Impact

Victimization affects different children differently. Some of these differences have to do with how the child was victimized—a terrorizing gang attack versus having a CD stolen, for example. Some of these differences have to do with the particular capacities of the child—a depressed and anxious child will react differently than a successful and optimistic one. And some of those capacities pertain to the child's age and stage of development—for example, a knowledgeable teenager versus a naïve preschooler. These stages-of-childhood differences should be the focus of one branch of the field of developmental victimology. This chapter makes some suggestions about the developmental issues that should be taken into account by this field.

The Field of Childhood Trauma

If someone looks for information on how children react to victimization at different stages of development, they will find it in two places: research on the impact of specific kinds of victimization, such as child maltreatment,[116,117] and research on traumatic stress and posttraumatic stress disorder (PTSD), [76] a field that has become increasingly salient in conceptual and clinical thinking about child victimization.

In fact, the field of traumatic-stress research has grown enormously in the last 25 years, and increasingly this field has expressed an interest in children, including their maltreatment and exposure to interpersonal violence.[118] Those interested in child victimization have gravitated to this field, where research during the past decade has convincingly documented many trauma symptoms among victims of child abuse and victimization.[119]

Since the time when those interested in child maltreatment and child victimization joined forces with those interested in posttraumatic stress, there has been a fruitful period for the development of theory, research, and interventions. A large branch of the psychiatric profession became more interested in child victimization, bringing with it substantial funding, research capability, and institutional support. In part because traumatic stress is a diagnosable psychiatric condition with set criteria, research and epidemiology have also benefited. Links with the traumatic-stress field also helped overcome some of the fragmentation in the study of child victimization. In recent years, different forms of child victimization—such as physical abuse and sexual abuse—have been more universally recognized as resulting in similar subsequent problems,[117,120] and traumatic stress symptoms are one common denominator.[121,122]

Contributions from the literature on traumatic stress have also helped those concerned with child victimization to focus on specific processes that result in the most severe and conspicuous symptoms that various kinds of child victims manifest. Studies of child victims had always emphasized, and continue to find, that victimization has a considerable impact on indicators of child distress, cognitive functioning, interpersonal skills, academic performance, and emotional processes.[121,123–129] The literature on traumatic stress has additionally brought attention to another dimension, the physiology of trauma.[130,131] In the developing central nervous system, trauma can set off a chain reaction that influences levels of hormones and neurotransmitters and can impact the developing brain. Traumatized brains may have dysregulated systems, poorly equipped to handle subsequent psychosocial stressors. While adults primarily become sensitized to stimuli specific to the original trauma, traumatized children's entire neural systems may become organized around their traumas, sometimes to such a degree that the result is a generalized state of hyperarousal.[119,132]

The psychiatric contribution in this alliance also has highlighted the degree to which victimized children are more likely to develop not only PTSD but also other psychiatric disorders, including attention-deficit/hyperactivity disorder (ADHD), along with hyperactivity, impulsivity, irritability, restlessness and distractibility[133]; depression (Axis I); and borderline personality syndrome (Axis II). The literature on traumatic stress has offered the developmental observation that victimization in childhood "increases risk for rather than inoculates against later psychopathology."[134]

The links with the traumatic-stress field have also helped in the development of effective interventions for child victims. For example, PTSD therapists had found various ways to help relieve some of the most disruptive and disturbing symptoms of traumatic exposure, such as flashbacks and intrusive thoughts, and these techniques were quickly adapted for victimized children. In recent years, a variety of clinical interventions with concrete behavioral strategies aimed at relieving traumatic symptoms and cognitions have proved effective in work with victimized children.[134–137] So, the marriage of child victimization theory and treatment with the traumatic-stress field has had many undeniable benefits.

At the same time, increasing identification of child victimization with the traumatic-stress literature has deemphasized or obscured some issues related to the impact of child victimization that might merit renewed interest. Moreover, it is useful to keep in mind that, conceptually, child victimization and traumatic stress are somewhat distinct phenomena. As the collaboration between these fields seems likely to continue, some points of distinction are worth discussion.

The central issue in the PTSD field has been trauma, which originally meant an acute, overwhelming, frightening, and frequently life-threatening experience. In the original PTSD literature, these experiences were thought of as traumatic *events*, which also meant they were largely time-limited or at least episodic. The prototypical traumatic events on which most of the clinical experience and research activity originally focused were rapes, terrorist attacks, and wartime battles. Many child victimizations, such as encounters with a physically violent parent, an intimidating school bully, or a teenage rapist, do indeed fit these criteria, but not all child victimizations do. A neglectful parent may not attend to a child's need for a clean environment or medical care or may not protect a child from developmentally inappropriate exposures. An abducting parent may not be intimidating or brutal but may simply deprive a child of access to the other parent or the child's familiar environment. These experiences are not time-limited, and they may also not be intense in the manner of a violent attack. They may be degrading, humiliating, and stigmatizing, but not necessarily frightening or threatening to bodily integrity. Their bad influence may be due not to the emotional overload but to the long-term distortions of development and self-perception. They may be characterized as *mis*-socialization. The children may be locked into a harmful victimization *condition*, which may be as or more damaging compare to a traumatic event.

The confrontation between these kinds of victimizations and PTSD conceptualization has led to reformulations in the field of traumatic stress. One concept is that of *complex PTSD* or *complex trauma*, which recognizes trauma-inducing conditions (in contrast to events) that may, like neglect, continue over a lengthy period and which may entail different cumulating victimizations and stressors.[121,138] In the complex-trauma formulation, for example, an effort is being made to incorporate the disruption of attachment as a traumatic process.[121]

This new direction in trauma conceptualization is promoting useful discussions that should motivate more investigation into the varieties and differences among responses to victimization. But one possibility that also needs to be considered is that not all reactions to child victimization, even serious ones, should be considered traumas or some subcategory of traumatic responses.

Indeed, victimizations can have harmful effects, including developmental effects, that some might not want to categorize as *trauma* in the clinical sense. For example, what if being the victim of a crime tended to lead someone to form racist or reactionary political attitudes?[139] The person might come to hate everybody of the same race or ethnicity as the victimizer. These are important effects, and they have been the subject of some developmental analyses in the study of political and social attitude formation,[140,141] but they might be better considered as falling outside the realm of mental health or PTSD.

This discussion highlights another limiting feature of the traumatic stress conceptualization—that it has tended to emphasize victimization's impact on emotions and emotional regulation. Trauma itself is generally conceptualized as a result of emotionally overwhelming, frightening events or processes. The major diagnostic criteria for PTSD emphasize emotion-based symptoms and their underlying physiological processes: hyperarousal; the unbidden intrusion of frightening thoughts, feelings, and images; and the numbing of emotional responses.[142] The main thrust of inquiry in the PTSD field has been on documenting and explaining these emotional injuries.

But this focus does not exhaust the variety of ways in which victimization can be harmful. Many of the serious harms that come from victimization are not strictly emotional but also cognitive and attitudinal. Victimized children acquire distorted views of the trustworthiness of others. They learn about the efficacy of violence and bullying to accomplish one's goals. They internalize a view of themselves as weak and unloved. They adopt a paranoid and defensive view of other people's actions—what has been called a *hostile attribution bias*.[143] They come to see the world as unfair and morality as relative. A question to ask is whether the traumatic stress field, with its emphasis on emotions, has given secondary status to these other impacts. Perhaps the emotional impacts are the most serious ones, but based on the literature it would seem that cognitive impacts are also widely noted and should be seriously studied.

Yet another distinction is worthy of consideration. While the connection with the field of traumatic stress may have overcome some of the fragmentation of the field of child victimization, it may have also discouraged efforts to find and explain victimization-specific effects. Perhaps the most conspicuous of these is the sexualization of children who have been sexually abused. This is one of the most frequently identified symptoms of sexual abuse.[144–147] It is not a dimension well explained by the PTSD orientation, which is primarily concerned with the effects of intense fear and powerlessness. It may be a form of emotional dysregulation, in which case it roughly fits into the trauma paradigm. It may have a physiological basis, in that premature sexual stimulation or exposure may potentiate certain hormonal or neurological changes. Or it may represent learning or conditioning of certain behaviors as a result of socialization experiences that other children have not been exposed to. This may be better thought of as deviant socialization than as trauma; in any case, it does suggest that there are impacts specific to certain kinds of victimization that are not part of a generic traumatic-stress model. Efforts to understand and treat such specific effects should be part of the overall agenda for developmental victimology.

Another possible biasing result of the connection between child victimization and the PTSD field is the tendency to focus on the most extreme forms of victimization; in early stages, this meant violent sexual assaults, kidnappings, or playground shootings,[148–150] and more recently it has included multiple and cumulative child maltreatment.[121] On the other hand, the vast majority of childhood victimizations—experiences such as being bullied or being assaulted by peers—are of a much less serious nature than those that are most frequently studied in this literature.[56,151]

A good case in point is the growing literature on the negative effects of corporal punishment.[152] Is corporal punishment damaging (e.g., associated with more aggression, depression, and lower academic performance) only because it is a traumatic stressor? Or do the corrosive effects of corporal punishment operate more typically by undermining the parent–child bond and internalizing the punitive and physically aggressive responses to conflict situations? It may take very different concepts to understand the full effects of these less extreme kinds of victimizations. There may be useful ways in which study of less serious forms of victimization can complement and elaborate the study of more serious victimization.

Because traumatic stress has been thought of as a psychiatric category, its study has been concerned almost exclusively with individuals, and relatively little attention has been paid to the effects of victimization on *groups*. But even individual victimizations have group effects when the victimization becomes known to a larger group. For example, when a child is kidnapped or murdered, whole communities are affected. Groups need to assimilate and make sense of any serious norm violation, and their reactions can include alienation, the breakdown of social ties, religious responses, and political and social mobilizations.

Child victimizations seem to have particularly strong group effects, as evidenced by public, media, and community responses to events like the murder of Megan Kanka (after whom the offender notification laws were named) or Polly Klaas.[153–157] Children themselves may respond collectively to victimizations in ways that are distinctive. The formation of protective cliques or gangs is one response to threats of childhood victimization.[158] Other group-level responses among children can include exclusion of the victimized individual, collective elaboration of fantasy to cope with fears, or adoption of collective superstitions.

There may also be group or generational effects to collective victimizations such as the bombing of Pearl Harbor or the destruction of the Twin Towers. These primarily relate to the impact of such events on children as a cohort. While the impact of these events has been studied on children at the individual psychological level, it may be useful to posit group-level effects as well. The study of these processes is an appropriate domain for developmental victimology.

Toward a More General Model of Victimization Impact

The study of developmental victimology needs to be expanded substantially from the approach taken in the PTSD literature. First, it should encompass a broad range of victimizations. In Chapter 2, we grouped child victimizations into three categories based on their relatively frequency: the extraordinary, such as homicides and stranger abductions; the acute, occurring to a minority of all children, such as child physical abuse and sexual abuse; and the pandemic, occurring to a majority of children at some time, including peer assault, sibling assault, and theft. We think pandemic victimizations in particular need to be included in the purview of the field.

Second, any study of the impact of victimization should encompass a broad range of effects, including effects that do not necessarily fall within the realm of psychopathology, such as effects on personality (e.g., shyness), social skills, and political and social attitudes. It might even include effects that would be regarded as normative, such as acquiring personal safety skills—for example, learning to lock up one's possessions or to handle firearms.[159] It should include effects that have a group or social, as well as individual, dimension—for example, the observation that, starting in the preschool years, girls begin to express fear of and distaste for boys, perhaps in part as a result of their being hurt and threatened by boys' aggressive play.[160,161]

Third, developmental victimology should focus most particularly on effects in their developmental context—that is, on how effects differ at different developmental stages. This has not generally been done in the existing literature. For example, among the most widely cited effects of sexual abuse is what has been termed "sexualized behavior," which is often mentioned without any developmental context. The term is sometimes made slightly more precise with references to frequent masturbation, play that is focused on sexual themes, and play that draws attention to the sexual organs of oneself or others. It was not until much more recent studies conducted by Friedrich, using the Childhood Sexual Behavior Inventory, that this issue was given clearer developmental dimensions. Friedrich et al.[162] found that *overt* sexualized behavior among abused girls was primarily confined to girls between the ages of 2 and 6, and that among somewhat older girls a more common response pattern to sexual abuse took the form of *inhibition* of sexual behavior. In adolescence, there is again an association of sexual abuse with sexual risk taking. This illustrates well how the impacts of victimization may differ at different developmental stages.

In addition to the issue of developmental differences, there is the matter of *developmental trajectory*. The developmental trajectory perspective looks at the reactions to victimization as they transform over the course of an individual's development. The consequences of victimization are not static or fixed; they have ramifications that may be quite different in different stages of development.

In fact, much of the literature on victimization impact does have a static and nondevelopmental quality. Associations are found, for example, between childhood sexual abuse and adult PTSD or depression. Although rarely articulated in these terms, the predominant notion behind these findings is that victimization engenders a stress disorder or depression at the initial time of the offense that then persists or recurs on a continuous basis in response to that initial insult. But more recent research and writing conceptualizes the connection between childhood trauma and adult outcome differently as more of a chain of cascading developmental effects, with each effect influencing the next one.[163]

Thus, victimization in early childhood may inhibit a child from forming close ties with peers. This in turn may lead to associations with other marginalized youngsters. Continued association with these youngsters may expose the child to delinquent influences or acts such as stealing and drug use. This may then result in experiences with the criminal justice system that negatively affect employment prospects. Poor earning potential may lead to restricted choices in romantic and marital partners. The mental health problems of the young adult may be due to a bad marriage and financial problems, proximal problems that cascaded from the victimization but are not the direct and lingering mental health effects of the abuse or victimization.

A developmental perspective also should encompass interest in the existence of critical periods, phases of development when reactions to victimization may have some special potential for impact. For instance, victimization at certain critical periods may have a heightened effect on peer relationships, sexual development, or the development of aggression.

Finally, a developmental approach should ultimately be part of a full life-course approach that includes tracking the effects of victimization into the adult and later life stages. As part of the goals for this field, developmental victimology needs to integrate the developmental observations that have been made in the separate literatures on victimization. For example, in the literature on sexual abuse, there has been debate and speculation about whether earlier or later sexual abuse has a more serious impact.[164] This issue has often been framed as a discussion of whether younger children are protected by their lack of understanding of the implications of the sexual activities in which they were involved or made more vulnerable by their lack of alternative sources of information or experience. The empirical findings have not produced a clear endorsement for either view, suggesting that real developmental effects are more complicated and contingent on other things.

Other developmental hypotheses about victimization have posited specific developmental periods of vulnerability. Thus those who have studied dissociative disorders have noted that a common factor seems to be serious sexual and physical victimization that occurred prior to age 8.[165,166] The idea is that abuse that occurs when children are developing capacities for normal dissociation may lead to the formation of chronic dissociation as a way of coping with stress.

Still another common point of developmental attention in the literature is the different family and social responses that are encountered by victims of different ages. Thus teenagers seem to be much more likely to be doubted or disbelieved by mothers or criminal justice officials when they make allegations about sexual abuse than are elementary-school-age children.[167] These are developmental differences based less on intrinsic developmental capacities and more on the ways in which children of different ages are viewed socially.

A Developmental Dimensions Model

The kinds of observations just discussed have led us to formulate a general conceptual framework for thinking about the differential impact of victimization, which we call the Developmental Dimensions Model of Victimization Impact (see Fig. 4.1). We suggest that developmental differences can affect four relatively distinct dimensions with bearing on how victimizations impact children. These four dimensions are as follows:

1. **Appraisals of the victimization and its implications.** Children at different stages appraise victimizations differently and tend to form different expectations based on those appraisals.
2. **Task application.** Children at different stages face different developmental tasks, upon which these appraisals will be applied.

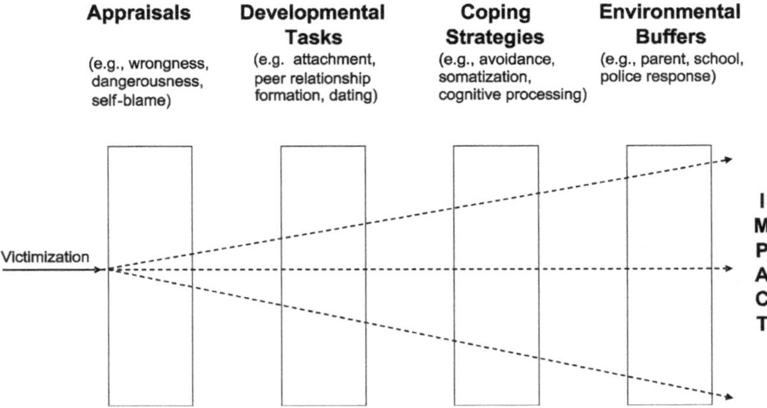

FIGURE 4.1. Four-developmental-dimensions model of victimization impact.

3. **Coping strategies.** Children at different stages of development have available to them different repertoires of coping strategies with which to respond to the stress and conflict produced by victimization.
4. **Environmental buffers.** Children at different stages of development operate in different social and family contexts, which can alter how the victimization affects them.

This conceptual framework presupposes a certain sequence in a child's response to victimization. When a victimization occurs, children must appraise what is happening to them during the course of the victimization and then in its aftermath. These appraisals apply to a wide range of aspects: the nature of the event ("I am being robbed"), the cause of the event ("I led him on"), the motives of the perpetrator, the nature of the harm ("I could have been killed"), or the nature of their own response ("I can't handle this"). These appraisals get applied to the developmental tasks facing the child. For a child trying to learn cooperative play with peers, it's "I can't trust them"; for a child adjusting to dating, it's "It's dangerous to look attractive"; for a child trying out independence from a parent, it's "I can't survive without Mother's presence."

Children also express the conflict in a vocabulary of behaviors or coping strategies available to them in that developmental context. If the child is at the stage of fantasy play, then the conflict gets expressed through fantasy play; if the child is at the stage of testing independence from parents, then the conflict can get expressed through radical break (for example, running away) or through regression (for example, a retreat back into family dependence). Other people in the child's environment respond to the victimization and the child's coping strategies in ways that also depend on the child's developmental stage—for example, whether they blame the child, whether they believe the child, whether they are alarmed, whether they take steps to protect the child, whether they involve social authorities, and whether they seek help. All these will be influenced by their view of the child's developmental capacities.

Thus we can analyze victimization developmentally for any child by asking (1) how does this child's stage of development affect his or her appraisal, (2) what developmental tasks are at the forefront that may be most prominently impacted, (3) what developmental vocabulary is the stress most likely to be expressed in, and (4) what environmental reactions are likely for this developmental context. This framework posits the existence of some general differences according to age in the answers to these questions, but it also answers them in relation to a particular child and that child's specific developmental history.

To illustrate how this conceptual framework can be generalized across a variety of victimizations and developmental contexts, let us use some highly schematic examples that illustrate developmental observations made in the literature.

Cicchetti and a variety of others[168–170] have found that early child abuse appears to be associated with patterns of insecure attachment to caregivers. We might represent one instance of this as follows:

- **Victimization:** Mother hits, shakes, and roughly handles a young child in response to crying.
- **Appraisal:** "Mother hurts me when I cry or have needs."
- **Task application:** Attachment formation; "I do not feel safe with my caregiver."
- **Coping strategy:** "I avoid my caregiver or am reluctant to express needs."
- **Environmental buffer:** No other significant relationships are available in the child's environment to buffer the insecure adaptation.

Another example is the observation from the literature on sexual abuse that sexually abused young children manifest sexualized behavior.[162]

- **Victimization:** A father repeatedly puts his 6-year-old girl on his lap and bounces her against his naked penis until he ejaculates.
- **Appraisal:** "I make Daddy happy and he treats me like I'm special when I touch his penis."
- **Task application:** Getting affectional needs met from adults.
- **Coping strategy:** "I offer to touch Daddy's penis and the sexual parts of others when I want them to be nice to me."
- **Environmental context:** Variable; others may either reinforce or be alarmed by this behavior.

What follows are two other examples.

- **Victimization:** A 4-year-old watches his mother being killed by his father.
- **Appraisal:** "It was my fault for making my father angry."
- **Task application:** Apportioning causality to bad events.
- **Coping strategy:** "I use extreme passivity to avoid the possibility of angering anyone else."
- **Environmental buffer:** Passivity in a 5-year-old may not be noted as a problem, and minimal rehabilitative efforts may be directed toward the child.

- **Victimization:** A 16-year-old boy suffers repeated attacks and threats from peers.
- **Appraisal:** "I must look like a pushover"; to threaten others creates authority and safety.
- **Task application:** Formation of a consistent personal identity.
- **Coping strategy:** "I must use toughness"; preemptory aggression toward others.

- **Environmental buffer:** Gangs of other aggressive youth may reinforce toughness and help bolster an ideology to support it.

This four-dimensional framework is not the only way in which the impact of victimization can be analyzed, nor does it encompass all the components of the process that determines how a victimization will be processed. For example, the nature and severity of the victimization itself play a big role. But the framework highlights the elements of the victimization-response process that are most affected by developmental changes. These four dimensions—appraisal, developmental task, coping strategy, and environmental buffers—are those domains that best encompass the developmental differences noted in the literature on victimization. We will use them as a framework for talking about some of the findings from this literature.

Developmental Factors in Victimization Appraisal

Appraisals concern the cognitions, however primitive, about what is happening in a victimization and why. They can be as simple as the appraisal that a certain person or event causes pain. Clearly these appraisals are affected by developmental considerations, even in regard to such a basic issue as the perception that victimization is occurring. While many forms of victimization, such as violent assault, can be appraised as unpleasant and painful even by a very young child with an almost entirely undeveloped cognitive system, there are other forms of victimization that cannot be recognized as such without some knowledge of social norms and interpersonal expectations.[171].

The notion of theft, for example, requires the concept of ownership, which is not yet present in a very young child. This suggests a useful developmental distinction between what might be called *pain-mediated victimization* and *meaning-mediated victimization*. Pain-mediated victimization (such as assault) can presumably be appraised as noxious at an earlier developmental stage than meaning-mediated victimization (such as theft). But it is also important to note that pain-mediated victimizations generally are not pure; they acquire negative meanings that children come to appreciate quite quickly as they develop, which can change the impact of the victimization. Thus, even very young children experience the physical pain of being spanked by a parent, but the intense humiliation a teenager experiences at being spanked comes into play only after the child acquires some awareness of social norms. So pure pain-mediated victimizations hardly exist, but there are victimizations, such as theft, that are purely meaning-mediated and have no element of physical pain.

Smetana [172] has drawn a related distinction between moral and social-conventional rules: moral rules ("don't hit others") have some intrinsic basis for our acceptance, whereas social-conventional rules ("boys don't wear pink") are arbitrary and culturally specific. Most victimizations—whether pain- or meaning-mediated—involve violations of moral rules, but meaning-mediated victimizations may have more normative or social-conventional rule components. Thus the wrongness of theft has a strong intrinsic component—the pain of being deprived of a valued possession—but there are also social conventions that, to some extent, control the distinction between theft and socially tolerated use of others' property: for example, norms about borrowing, sharing, and the transitivity of property among members of a family or a classroom. Little work has been done on how the acquisition of such norms affects appraisals of victimization.

The research shows that children as young as 3 years of age can distinguish between familiar moral and conventional transgressions, but that appreciating moral violations is to some degree affected by a child's familiarity with the class of events.[172] In regard to victimizations, this might be extrapolated to mean that children would be better able to identify the theft of an object as a victimization, an event with which they had familiarity, than they would the theft of money. The research also shows a transformation with age in the ability to judge transgressions as wrong because they are unfair, rather than simply because they cause harm.[172] Presumably, this would relate to the ability of children to identify as victimizations classes of events in which the harms are less immediately evident—for example, thefts of money or sexual violations—in contrast to obviously wounding events such as being hit.

The issue of how development can alter the appraisal of victimizations has not been widely explored, but it has perhaps received more attention in regard to sexual abuse than elsewhere in the literature. The sexual implication of behaviors, including forms of bodily contact, is acquired in later stages of development, so questions have from time to time been raised in the sexual abuse literature about whether children can be harmed by behaviors they do not understand.[173] One would expect vastly different subjective reactions from a 10-year-old who was touched on the genitals by an older sibling than from a 2-year-old, based on each child's ability to understand the inappropriateness of the contact.

Yet, in spite of this theoretical idea that children cannot be harmed by what they do not understand, there are thousands of clinical reports of sexually abused preschool children who manifest marked disturbances in behavior,[174] and the many studies comparing the impact of early and later sexual abuse have failed to conclude that very young children are protected from psychological harm by their age.[116,144,175]

Unfortunately, there has been relatively little careful analysis of the traumatic components of early sexual abuse. However, it is important to bear in mind that such abuse, at least the cases that come to professional attention, frequently entail some components of pain-mediated victimization—for example, the forced penetration of a penis into an anus or vagina—that may explain some of the impact. Moreover, the conduct of the perpetrators in these cases frequently includes other readily appraised noxious activities, such as threatening or restraining the child. There is also some suggestion in the literature that the sexual stimulation itself, even when the young child does not understand its full adult meaning, has a negative effect. This may be because powerful physical sensations are being evoked in a context (e.g., the mother–child relationship) or with associations (e.g., as a condition to meeting the child's other needs) that distort development. This is obviously a complex area worthy of much more attention than it has received, not just in regard to sexual abuse but also for other meaning-mediated victimizations such as thefts and abductions. In spite of the complexity, especially in the case of sexual abuse, it is probably safe to say that some victimizations have little or no impact, or at least a different impact, because of the child's inability to recognize the occurrence of the victimization. But as the examples show, we must be careful not to assume that the child is ignorant of all elements of the victimization.

There are many cognitive capacities that need to be investigated in terms of how they affect the appraisal of victimization in general or certain kinds of victimization in particular. For example, the development of concern for one's social reputation in middle childhood[176] can have a substantial influence on a child's susceptibility to peer aggression and how it relates to his or her image in a group. Knowledge of social rules governing the use of property could affect reactions to theft. The level of understanding of the finality of death affects how a child appraises a potentially lethal assault on another family member.[177,178] Acquiring conceptions about how to attribute causality in complex social interactions may determine how much a child blames himself or herself for a crime committed against that child or a relative.

Issues related to perceptions of justice, fairness, and morality also presumably affect a child's appraisal of victimization, and these perceptions have a developmental trajectory. For example, Kohlberg,[179] in his model of moral development, posits that very young children assess wrongness primarily by the magnitude of the negative consequences of an act and that only later does an assessment of the actor's intent come into play. Empirical research shows that there are indeed developmental changes in children's ability not just to assess the intention of a harmful act (was the perpetrator trying to produce the harm?) but also to judge an act's causality (was the perpetrator the true cause of the harm?), avoidability (could the perpetrator have avoided the harm?), and motive acceptability (were the perpetrator's motives benign or malicious?).[172,180–182] These studies suggest that older children, because they are more discriminating, make fewer categorically negative moral judgments based just on harm. They appreciate that sometimes the harm was unintentional or justified and thus a real victimization did not occur. Does this mean that there are many conflict situations in which older children are less likely to feel victimized because they are better able to interpret information about the causality and intentionality of the harm done? Unfortunately, because most of the studies in this literature use vignettes involving thefts and aggressions against third persons, it is unclear exactly how they might apply to perceptions about personal victimizations.

Interestingly, this literature on moral development has not intersected extensively with the literature on victimization and trauma, where issues of blame, particularly self-blame, have been discussed widely but in different terms. In the latter literature, victims are believed to cope better if they do not engage in what has been called *characterological self-blame*—seeing uncontrollable aspects of oneself ("I'm too trusting") as the cause of the victimization.[183]

But there has been substantial debate about whether some forms of self-blame may actually be salutary. An article of faith among therapists who treat sexual abuse, for example, is that in order for children to recover they need to be taught categorically that they were not to blame in any respect for the abuse.[184] But some have argued that attributing all responsibility to the perpetrator diminishes a child's sense of efficacy,[185,186] and that some self-blame (what has been termed *behavioral self blame*—"I should have yelled") may be adaptive because it gives a child a sense that he or she may be able to do something different to avoid victimization in the future.

Although some child victimization research has found that younger children blame themselves more, perhaps because of their developmental egocentricity,[187] little in the way of a developmental perspective has been offered in this discussion about how attributional capacities or tendencies may change the reactions to victimization among children. Celano [188] does point out that some children do not have the cognitive capacity to distinguish between characterological and behavioral self-blame. For these young children, the most important issue may not be whether they think they have the power to prevent future victimization (the result of behavioral self-blame) but rather whether they think their parents do. Also, more crucial than whether they blame themselves or others for the victimization (internal or external attribution) may be whether they think the cause of the victimization is constantly present across time and across situations (termed *stable* and *global* attributions, respectively). Celano also identifies specific attributional issues that may come into play selectively for children of different ages; for example, a latency-age child might feel a responsibility for failure to protect a sibling that a preschool-age child would not. Clearly a developmental analysis of blame attributions may help greatly in understanding children's reactions to victimizations.

Another appraisal issue that has been actively discussed in the victimization and trauma literature is that of dangerousness. Studies from the PTSD field have suggested that certain kinds of appraisals about a negative event—for example, the belief that one could have been seriously injured or killed—are associated with more harm and more symptoms.[189] One of the developmental principles suggested by the PTSD research is that the danger appraisals of young children are more socially referenced.[190] Thus a young child who has been party to a kidnapping may take many of his or her cues about how dangerous the situation is (or was) by appraising fear or distress in his or her parents, rather than from facts about the actual event. Research on the Buffalo Creek Dam disaster, in West Virginia, found that young children were one group whose symptomatology was not predicted by their direct proximity to the devastation but rather by the proximity of their parents to the devastation.[191]

Children's ability to discriminate among classes of events obviously has relevance to victimization appraisals as well. One of the prominent theories of trauma impact suggests that in the wake of traumatic events, "fear structures" get elaborated that link together cues, associations, and information related to the experience.[192–194] Fear structures are easily triggered and hard to extinguish.[192,195] So if a child is victimized in a playground, at night, with a red T-shirt on, and just prior to the victimization the child was having fun, all these stimuli—the playground, the night, the shirt, the feeling of having fun—can be tied together in a fear structure. Research has found that people victimized in familiar and previously safe environments tend to have more symptoms and greater difficulty recovering.[195] One reason may be that their fear structures encompass more cues from their normal and ordinarily safe environments, so that previously safe cues come to trigger the fear structures and signal danger. For children, an important factor in the generation of fear structures is how well they can discriminate among different classes of events and individuals. If a child cannot readily distinguish the perpetrator from other classes of people (e.g., a stranger from an acquaintance) or the crime context from other contexts (e.g., the particular park from all other parks), then his or her fear structures may be larger, more general, and more impervious to extinction. This process may be part of what is so globally disabling about early parental maltreatment: its highly generalized aspects—insecure attachment or lack of basic trust—get so readily transposed onto all other or future relationships.

A good example from research illustrating the operation of such discrimination in a developmental context is Pynoos and Nader's [196] finding concerning children who witnessed their mother's rape. Among school-age witnesses to these rapes, there were no gender differences in resulting symptoms, but adolescent girls were found to be more affected than adolescent boys. The authors theorize that by the time of adolescence, the children had learned that rapes primarily happen to women and girls, so the older boys were protected from much of the impact and did not see themselves as vulnerable to rape, whereas the younger boys had no such defenses in place. The ability to make discriminations about classes of events resulted in a different appraisal that, in turn, resulted in a different impact.

Another study, related not to victimization but to children's reactions to parental divorce, showed that 10- to 12-year-olds could distinguish among different kinds of threats in the divorce situation (threats to themselves, threats to others, and loss of desired objects and activities) that 8- and

9-year-olds could not.[197] Here again, the ability to make distinctions could possibly mitigate impact.

An important theme in the literature on victimization is not only how the appraisal process affects the impact of victimization but also how the impact of the victimization can affect appraisal. Thus, once a child has been victimized in a certain way, his or her appraisal process may be altered.[198] Dodge and colleagues[199,200] point out that harshly punished children develop a bias to attribute hostile intentions to others or a tendency to interpret accidents and normal social conflicts as motivated personal attacks,[201] which in turn contributes to the development of aggressive social interactions. This suggests that experiencing certain victimizations can create a proclivity to appraise many other events as additionally victimizing. But victimization may also potentially desensitize a child to the potential for future victimization by inculcating a sense of helplessness or making victimization appear normative. Thus, some previously sexually victimized girls seem less able to discriminate future sexually dangerous situations, explaining in part why they appear to be at greater risk for subsequent sexual victimization and rape.[202] All these findings and speculations suggest the kinds of questions investigators with a developmental orientation might systematically ask about the victimization-appraisal process.

Developmental Tasks and Victimization

While the appraisal process concerns how victims "interpret" the victimization experience, an important additional dimension is the developmental task that a child may confront at the time of (or after) victimization, and to which the appraisal gets applied. Thus the appraisal process involves, for example, whether a child "understands" the sexual implications of a sexual abuse experience; but there is a separate dimension that concerns how this understanding will affect the child who is approaching the developmental task of starting to date versus one who is not yet facing this task. Clearly, the sexual abuse may be much more disruptive for the child who is actively testing his or her sexual desirability in the dating world.

Developmental tasks come in a wide variety of forms, and we use the term *task* here in a broad sense. They can be the slow and steady accretion of competencies in a certain area, such as independent decision making. They can include tasks that children face in a more confined developmental period, such as adjusting to school. While no task is ever fully completed, there appear to be stages when a particular task is at the forefront.

Obviously, appraisals and developmental tasks are related. Certain cognitive capacities and appraisals are the products of having entered into or progressed through a developmental task. But a developmental task is a valuable organizing concept, and some of the most developmentally oriented literature on victimization has used such tasks to formulate differential hypotheses about the impact of victimization and trauma.

For example, we have mentioned the literature on early maltreatment and the attachment to a primary caretaker, considered one of the early developmental tasks of childhood. Thus young children victimized at an early age by their primary caretakers seem to suffer a significant developmental impact in the form of insecure attachment to these figures, according to child-abuse research.[169,170] This mode of relating seems to be carried into subsequent phases of development and other relationships.[203] Another developmental task that has been discussed in the literature in relation to victimization is the process of emotional regulation. An early developmental task of childhood is to learn to modulate emotional arousal using cognitive skills, shifting with some voluntary control among various emotional states and maintaining a certain equilibrium.[204,205] In normal development, disturbances to this equilibrium are met with internal working models of the world and other internal resources that allow a child to reorganize existing frameworks at a higher level that includes new information or a resolution to the challenge.[171] Among children traumatized at an early stage by victimization, however, the ability to modulate emotional arousal and maintain equilibrium may be overwhelmed by intense fear or other physiological reactions and compromised by immature cognitive skills.[206] Such children may operate at permanent levels of high emotional arousal and have a relatively difficult time managing disturbances to their system that require self-regulation.

A question raised by these analyses is whether there are sensitive periods in regard to various developmental tasks, and whether victimization during these periods has a unique capacity to cause permanent developmental distortions. There are suggestions about sensitive periods, for example, in the literature on dissociative disorders. Research has found that of those suffering from multiple personality disorder and other extreme forms of dissociation, almost all suffered victimization prior to age 8 or 9.[165,166] Even less severe forms of early victimization may leave dissociative scars, as indicated by the observation that children who have been physically punished are easier to hypnotize (a benign form of dissociation).[207] There may be a sensitive period when children have the opportunity to learn to use dissociation as a coping method to deal with pain and stress.

Another of the basic developmental tasks affected by victimization is the formation of peer relationships. This process goes on over an extended period and in fact includes a variety of developmental tasks. Parker and associates,[208] in their general review on peer relationships, mention some of the milestones. Although these have not been systematically studied in connection to victimization, there are many suggestions in the victimization literature about how they can be distorted. For example, in the preschool period, children begin to form stable friendships for the first time and also learn to engage in cooperative play. Victimization can delay the formation of friendships or make it even more difficult for naturally shy children to initiate this process. It can also aggravate and extend the early patterns of antagonistic play. Pynoos and colleagues[190] have pointed out that in this preschool period, when fantasy play predominates, the victimization experiences can lead to play dominated by posttraumatic fantasy and trauma processing—for example, reenactments of the victimization or rescue fantasies preoccupied with mastering the victimization-related fears. This can sometimes make it hard for victimized children to play cooperatively or be readily accepted by peers. On the other hand, sometimes the traumatic themes of victims get incorporated into the play of nonvictimized peers.

In middle childhood, there are other peer relationship tasks that can be disrupted by victimization. For example, in middle childhood, children normally learn to take the role of others into account and accommodate others' desires and feelings.[208] Victimization can delay or block this process. Friendship groups during this period tend to develop more around common interests. Victimized children, who may be preoccupied with self-protection, may find themselves bonding primarily with other victimized children or having a hard time relating to the interests of nonvictimized peers.

While some research has pointed out how parental maltreatment can lead to peer–relationship difficulties, mediated especially by attachment problems,[209] it is important to note that other forms of victimization can presumably have this disruptive effect as well. Thus, witnessing parental violence, being the victim of a kidnapping, or being subjected to serious sibling violence or harassment by older children all may have ramifications in the domain of peer adjustment.

The literature concerning developmental tasks suggests that victimization may impact these tasks in three conceptually distinct ways. First, the victimization can interrupt or substantially delay the accomplishment of the task; thus, as a result of bullying, a child can be intimidated about trying to form peer relationships. Second, the victimization can distort or condition the way in which the developmental task is resolved; thus an abused child, instead of forming a secure attachment, will form an anxious attachment. Third, the victimization can result in regression, so that the achievements of a previously resolved developmental task are disrupted. Newly acquired achievements are those most vulnerable to disruption.[210] In this case, a victimized child who has recently been able to tolerate separations from his or her parents is thrown back into close dependency on them. An important implication of this discussion is that victimization can result in departures from normal development in both directions—for example, hypersexualization or inhibited sexuality—so that simply looking at the average characteristics of a victimized group can sometimes obscure the effect.

With a better understanding of how victimization can affect developmental tasks, researchers in developmental victimology should strive to look at their progression. One of the few general attempts to do this is that by McCann and associates,[211] who organize the developmental tasks on which victimization has its impact into five categories: the formation of a sense of safety, a sense of trust, a sense of power, a sense of self-esteem, and a capacity for intimacy. They argue that there is a developmental sequence to these tasks, but they do not associate them with particular ages. Although this seems a somewhat limited inventory of developmental tasks (for example, where does emotional regulation fit in?) and may be at too high a level of generality (for example, peer relationships may be a subcategory of intimacy, but it is an important independent domain), it does suggest how a framework of developmental tasks may help researchers and clinicians orient themselves to the potential impacts of a victimization experience.

Coping Strategies and Victimization

While some of the developmental impact of victimization is governed by how it is appraised and what developmental tasks are at hand, another relevant factor is the repertoire of coping strategies available to the child. A child who is capable of talking introspectively about how an experience felt may be able to process it and recover better than one who is not. Similarly, children who are able to control their environment enough that they can avoid contact with the perpetrator will react differently from those who have little control. Coping strategies might be thought of as generalized modes of responding to stress or challenge. Thus the reliance of preschool children on fantasy and the reliance of older children on rationalization and intellectualization are responses specific to certain stages of development. The literature on victimization suggests that some coping strategies are relatively confined to certain developmental stages, and others cut across stages. Actions such as running away, attempting suicide, abusing substances, causing deliberate self-harm, and engaging in promiscuous sexual activity are noted as behavioral responses to victimization that tend to be limited to adolescents[144,212] Generalized anxiety and nightmares are more apparent among younger children; other coping strategies such as depression, withdrawal, and belligerence seem to appear at many stages of development.

On the whole, children's repertoires of coping strategies become more diverse, complex, and situationally specific as children get older,[171] presumably allowing for a more adaptive response to victimization. For instance, an older child might respond to parental violence by talking about it with another trusted adult, an option that might not be available to a younger child. Other advantageous developmental changes may help older children to cope; for example, older children may have more effective cognitive techniques for dealing with anxiety, fear, and anger.[190] They may also have more experience managing stressful situations.

At the same time, older children, for a variety of developmental reasons, may forfeit certain effective coping strategies and thus be at a disadvantage compared to younger children. For example, older children have typically learned to inhibit or restrain their emotions, [213] and so, for example, may not allow themselves to benefit from the positive effects of crying and abreaction, which may be helpful in the wake of an upsetting victimization. Older children, particularly adolescents, are more likely to mistrust or feel alienated from parents, and thus to forfeit the comfort and empathy that younger children can receive from parents. Older children may also have more entrenched world assumptions that are harder to modify or exchange in the wake of an assumption-shattering victimization, while younger children may be better able to cope by changing their world views.[190] All this suggests that easy developmental generalities may not hold and that there is a complex interplay between coping resources and victimization.

One plausible if complex hypothesis about coping is that development interacts in some ways with gender, class, and other personal characteristics. So, for example, since gender (and other) differences become more pronounced as children develop, one might see more gender differences in coping among older children than among younger children. Thus while all children seek less help from adults as they get older, boys, in reaction to cultural norms about self-reliance, appear to cut back on seeking help even more than girls. As they get older, boys also manifest fewer fear-related and other "internalizing" symptoms than do girls in response to victimization.[191,214–216] This may be due to cultural prohibitions that inhibit older boys from expressing fear, but it may also be due to cultural training in overcoming feelings of fear.

Because coping strategies and resources change with development, some observers have posited that child victims' responses may differ from stage to stage not in reaction to external events but as a result of what might be called *symptom substitution*.[217] Thus the victimization-related depression that may manifest as withdrawal in middle childhood may metamorphose into drug usage in the teenage years, as drugs become available as a resource and coping strategy during that period of development.

Environmental Buffers and Victimization

Those studying the impact of victimization have come to recognize the importance of the child's social environment.[218,219] One of the most consistent empirical findings in the sexual abuse literature, for example, is that the response of the child's social support system, and particularly the child's mother, is the most important factor in determining outcome—more important than objective elements of the victimization itself.[220–223] Children have more strongly negative outcomes when mothers do not believe them, blame them, are allied with perpetrators, do not listen to them, or have strong personal reactions of their own that override those of the child. Studies show that positive support is more forthcoming for younger than for older children.[222,224] While these findings pertain primarily to sexual abuse, other research has found that the family environment mediates child response to community violence in general,[218,225] and it is easy to extrapolate this conclusion to other victimizations such as experiences with bullies, assaults by siblings, thefts, and gang victimizations. The dynamics are more complicated when the victimizations involve parents as perpetrators or as co-victims, as in parental abductions or the witnessing of spousal assault, because these events may compromise the ability of parents to be supportive, but these principles would still generally hold true.

Although parental response is obviously crucial, the notion of *environmental buffers*, as defined here, includes a much broader set of reactions. For example, peers have an important and potentially damaging response to victimization. Research with 6- and 8-year-old children suggests that when these school-age children suffer from peer victimization, it lowers their popularity in the eyes of other children [226] in ways that may be hard to reverse. Our notion of environmental buffers also includes the reactions of social institutions such as schools, police and courts, and the media, and the generalized reactions of society as a whole within the cultural context. It is clear that people respond differently to child victims of different ages. But, curiously, there has been little specific developmental analysis of these environmental responses to victimization and their impact on children. Nonetheless, some obvious principles can be discerned.

For example, it appears that parental responses have a more direct impact on younger than on older children. This is illustrated by previously cited findings about the degree to which younger children's symptoms are associated with their parents' appraisals of danger and seriousness.[191] Parents constitute a larger portion of the overall social environment of young children; they are more influential in younger children's lives. By contrast, older children are additionally affected by peer reactions, community reactions, and their awareness of general social norms. A possible hypothesis is that social factors, such as discrimination, and cultural factors, such as norms regarding honor and shame, have more impact on the victimization experiences of older children.

Another general principle relates to the degree to which parents and others hold children responsible for victimization episodes. Older children, teenagers in particular, are more likely to be blamed for their own victimizations than are younger children.[167,227]This may stem from a variety of factors: (1) a belief that teens have more skills to avoid and resist victimization, (2) the perception that teens voluntarily engage in risky behavior, and (3) the fact that adults actually are expected to take less responsibility for teens. Interestingly, this principle of holding teens responsible even characterizes the scholarly analysis of adolescent victimization: the predominant theoretical explanation is the greatly oversimplified notion that teens' victimization is primarily the result of their own delinquent behavior.[11,42] Being held responsible by others for one's own victimization certainly affects the degree to which one blames oneself.

Another related developmental principle concerns not just the blameworthiness but also the credibility of victimized children. Here the relationship appears to be more complex. In the case of sexual abuse, at least, there is evidence that adults are more likely to disbelieve reports made by older children, especially teens.[227,228] Teens are seen as having the motivation and capacity to willfully deceive (for example, in order to cover up voluntary sexual activity, to get someone into trouble, or to gain feelings of power). Younger children are seen as naïve and as having less reason to fabricate. When young children display knowledge about sexual behavior, it is presumed that they couldn't have gotten it from any source other than the abuse experience.[229] But skepticism about abuse allegations also sometimes applies to very young children.[167,227] These children are seen as prone to exaggeration, misinterpretation, and suggestion.[230] In one mock juror study, 9-year-olds (in contrast to 6- or 12-year-olds) were judged to be ideal witnesses.[227] It is not clear that this credibility pattern necessarily pertains to other kinds of victimization besides sexual abuse, but it suggests the possibility that there are major developmental questions as to how much child victims are believed by those whom they tell about their experiences.

Because these social responses to victimization are, to a great extent, governed by common attitudes and stereotypes, we can examine the attitudes and stereotypes toward victimizations of children at different ages to infer something about the environmental buffers. For instance, the fact that some victimizations are seen as normative, particularly for younger children, is an important developmental difference in the environmental context for these victims. That is, a 3-year-old who describes being spanked by a parent will not elicit much sympathetic attention from other adults, but a 14-year-old might. Similarly, young children who complain about sibling assaults often receive little more than frustrated and perfunctory responses because these assaults are seen as a normal part of family life and growing up. The view that these incidents are not true victimizations certainly carries over into how the victims feel about the episode and the extent to which they are likely to blame themselves.

There are also some clear developmental patterns about the degree to which social authorities are invoked in response to child victimizations. Parents tend to be the prime social arbiters of much child victimization in the preschool years, but once children get to be school aged, school authorities, with their more formal sanctions, become involved. For school-age children, police and the criminal justice system tend to respond only to child victimizations that involve adult perpetrators or, in rare cases, to child perpetrations that exceed a certain threshold of severity, such as a child-on-child rape or homicide. As children become teenagers, police do respond even to peer violence; thus, for example, a brawl between two teens might precipitate police intervention, whereas one between two elementary school children would likely not.

The literature on court involvement suggests that district attorneys are also less likely to prosecute in the victimizations of preschool children, even holding constant other features of the victimization.[231] This may reflect some concern about the credibility of such children before juries, as well as the possible impact of prosecution on their well-being. Interestingly, the same study shows that testifying in court is actually less stressful for preschool children than for those of other ages, perhaps because they are less aware of and less self-conscious about the importance of the procedure.[232]

The involvement of social authorities certainly has the potential to affect the impact of victimization. It tends to increase the degree to which knowledge of the victimization is disseminated in a larger community. It can increase the number of reminders about the victimization as children are interviewed about the episode and as investigations, court cases, or disciplinary actions drag out. It can also affect the sense child victims have that justice is being carried out. In spite of some of these obvious concerns, it is interesting that a number of studies looking for adverse impact on children from criminal prosecutions of sexual abuse incidents have been unable to find many systematic effects. In general, more extreme forms of court involvement, such as drawn-out cases or the child's having to testify on multiple occasions, seem to delay recovery,[233,234] but children do not seem to be worse off overall simply from the case's proceeding to a criminal prosecution.[235]

Types of Victimization Impact

Thus far in this chapter we have outlined four dimensions that we think should be probed for generalized developmental principles relating to the impact of victimization. However, in undertaking this generalized approach, we must review some important conceptual issues concerning how to classify the various types of victimization impact.

One problem here is that relatively little comparative analysis has been done among different kinds of victimization. Since much of the literature on the impact of victimization has focused on specific types of victimization, there are uneven patterns in victimization types that have and have not been compared and contrasted. Thus, within the field of sexual abuse, it has been common to compare the impact of intrafamilial with extrafamilial victimization, but there has been little comparable analysis of intrafamilial versus extrafamilial physical assault, since studies of physical abuse involve samples made up almost entirely of children assaulted by their parents.

Another problem is that the typical research paradigm used in impact research is not necessarily conducive to highlighting important differences.

Typical research studies choose one or two linear psychological scales, such as PTSD or depression, on which to evaluate victims. While such studies have sometimes found that intrafamily abuse is more serious than extrafamily victimization, that chronic victimizations are more serious than single events, and that experiences involving injury are more serious than ones without injury, these findings have been less consistent than one might expect.[144,175] One problem is that not enough effort has gone into trying to ascertain how different aspects of victimization are related to different kinds of problems or symptoms. For example, violent sexual abuse may be related to specific PTSD symptoms such as hyperarousal because of the fear and life-threat perceptions. Repetitive sexual abuse may be related to sexualized behavior as a result of conditioned sexual responses; elsewhere we have suggested some of these correspondences in the response to sexual abuse.[147]

Generic Versus Specific Effects

The above discussion suggests that several analytic distinctions might be useful in discussing the impact of victimization. One such distinction is between generic and specific victimization effects. There are probably certain kinds of effects that are common to a great many kinds of victimizations. These may include generalized stress-response symptoms such as depression; they may also include reactions to the inherent properties of a victimization—the sense of trust having been betrayed, or of powerlessness, or the violation of expectations of justice or fairness. So reactions such as anger, reevaluation of reciprocity, increased wariness or willingness to trust, and fear of the recurrence of an event might all be considered generic victimization effects.

In addition to these generic effects, certain effects seem specific to certain kinds of victimizations and might be unlikely to occur in other victimizations. For example, the sexualization seen in sexually abused children appears to be an effect related to the specific conditions of that abuse. (Interestingly, however, sexualization has been reported in some other, not sexually, maltreated children,[236] although the mechanism or motivation for this effect has not been well analyzed.) Insecure attachment is an effect that seems specific to parental maltreatment; it is not thought to occur as a result of other victimizations, unless these victimizations affect the nature of the parent–child relationship.

Localized Versus Developmental Effects

Another distinction that should be particularly important for those interested in a developmental analysis is that between effects that are truly developmental in character and others that might be termed *localized*. Localized effects are common reactions that tend to be rather readily dissipated. These can include fear, disorientation, re-experiencing the event, feeling numb, and feeling guilty. These symptoms can be called "localized" both because they are usually short term and also in the sense that they primarily affect behavior associated specifically with the victimization and similar experiences. Among children, these localized effects include the fear of returning to the place where the victimization occurred, anxiety around adults who resemble the offender, nightmares, being upset by television depictions of violence, and so forth.

By contrast, developmental effects are deeper and more generalized. They are impacts more specific to children than to adults and result when an experience and its related trauma interfere with developmental tasks, as discussed earlier in this chapter. They include, for example, impairment of self-esteem, development of very aggressive or very withdrawn general styles of behavior, inhibition of a whole realm of activity such as sexual functioning or academic achievement, and use of drugs or other dysfunctional ways of dealing with anxiety. These broad changes can result from victimization, too, but they are of a different nature and course than localized effects. In a way, these are the kinds of effects that distinguish childhood victimization from adult victimization.

Most victimization results in some localized effects—at the very least, an increased level of fear and increased vigilance. Localized effects can actually be pervasive and persistent without interfering to a great extent with development. For example, as a result of victimization by a person of a different race or ethnicity, a child may be afraid of people of that ethnicity for the rest of his or her life but have relatively normal functioning otherwise. By contrast, developmental effects have broad ramifications.

Direct Versus Indirect Effects

A conceptually important distinction related to the localized versus developmental consideration is that made between direct and indirect effects. Most of the immediate or proximal impact of a victimization can be classified as *direct effects* of the victimization and the context surrounding it. Once a victimization has developmental effects, however, the delayed or distorted resolution to a developmental task may result in other negative outcomes that can be called *indirect effects* of the victimization. Thus, if victimization trauma results in an inability to form peer relationships, and the lack of peer relationships leads to isolation and depression, then the depression is, conceptually speaking, an indirect effect of the victimization.

There are plenty of difficulties in distinguishing indirect from direct effects. They cannot be recognized necessarily by the nature of the symptoms, which can be similar across direct and indirect effects. When, as is often the case with sexual abuse, disclosures of the victimization come years after the event, the victimized children will by then likely be suffering both direct and indirect effects. Moreover, when chronic victimization occurs, it may be hard to disentangle the two effects—the indirect effects of the early victimization and the direct effects of what is happening currently. Also, since revictimization can be one of the effects of victimization,[95] it may be very difficult to discern which victimization is resulting in which effect. The ideal approach, of course, is to be able to follow victims longitudinally, but relatively few studies have had the luxury of this trajectory model design.

Browning and Laumann [163] illustrated empirically the process of indirect effects with a cross-sectional survey that gathered detailed life-events data. They found that the common association between childhood sexual abuse and adult relationship dissatisfaction is actually mediated by other intervening negative events, such as teenage pregnancy and childbirth or the acquisition of sexually transmitted infections. In other words, the association disappears statistically when these other events are accounted for. Thus sexually victimized girls are more likely to get pregnant as teens, and this event disorders their subsequent lives and relationships more than the sexual abuse itself, so the distal effects may be indirect rather than direct.

Future Directions

The current social and political concern about crime and violence has resulted in a large mobilization within the social scientific community to understand the childhood roots of the crime.[237,238] However, this mobilization has focused exclusively on why children become offenders and has too often neglected why they become victims and with what results. Not only are children the most frequent victims of violence, but the problems of victimization and offending are clearly intertwined. Moreover, it is a mistake to focus, as has often been done, on victimization primarily as an attempt to understand the sources of delinquency. Violence, crime, and abuse cause suffering, too, that is worthy of study and remedy, whatever their additional consequences. There are aspects of this suffering, besides its contribution to delinquency, that need additional attention by those with a developmental orientation.

Policy makers and researchers have recognized that fear of crime, in addition to crime itself, has major social and psychological consequences. Studies have illustrated the operation of this fear on certain vulnerable populations, such as the elderly.[239,240] But fear of victimization can certainly have major consequences in the lives of children as well. The extent of these fears and their consequences for child development have hardly been charted.

The problem of child victimization has spawned a wide variety of preventive educational programs.[241] The main, overt aim of these programs is to reduce the number of victimization episodes.[159] Less attention has been paid to another goal, however: the possibility of preventing psychological morbidity in the aftermath of victimization.[223] There are suggestions that preventive educational programs can alter some of the factors thought to be associated with victim impact, such as self-blame.[54] Victimization first-aid—rapid responses to children who have experienced victimization—may be a way of reducing other impacts as well. Developmental studies of the effectiveness of preventive education and victimization first-aid could provide a useful basis for program development that could make widespread improvements in public health.

Psychotherapy for the effects of victimization on children is a relatively recent development. Many programs and models have proliferated in the last decade, many with the aim of treating the effects of sexual abuse[242,243] and others focused on physical abuse[223] and the witnessing of violence.[47,244,245] While the evaluation studies of these treatments show promising results,[246,247] the research has done little to delineate what works most effectively with which kinds of victims. Little consideration has been given to the extent to which the widespread sexual abuse treatment models are applicable to other kinds of victimization. There is much room for developmentally oriented research to improve the effectiveness of treatment for child victims, including more theoretical guidance in the selection and design of treatments.[223]

The longitudinal study of child development is one of the most potent tools in social science. While such longitudinal studies have been or are underway on related topics of child abuse[248] and delinquency,[71,249] gathering information about some forms of victimization, longitudinal studies whose central focus is the full range of child victimizations and their impact are rare. The goal of such studies should be to see how proneness to victimization develops, how different kinds of victimizations might be interrelated, what effects victimization has, how and whether such effects persist, how they interact with development, and whether there are such things as "sleeper effects" that appear at a remote developmental distance from the victimization to which they are related. All of these undertakings would greatly assist the advancement of the study of child victimization and provide an increasing foundation for knowledge in assisting child victims.

Chapter 5

Just Kids' Stuff? Peer and Sibling Violence

Joyce, busy at her desk, didn't see it coming. The assailant ran through the door, clobbered her on the head, and ran off. Joyce fell to the floor screaming.

a. (Joyce is 25) Her co-worker reached for the phone and dialed 911.

b. (Joyce is 5) The kindergarten teacher, Mrs. Coyle, looked up and asked, "What's going on here?"

Children experience a lot of violence from other children. Surveys suggest that more than half of all children experience violence from a sibling in the course of a year,[7,250–252] and a quarter to one-third from a nonsibling peer.[151,253–256] However, we tend to regard this violence between children, especially young children, differently than we do violence in general. The same violent act—a punch to the head or a whack with an object—that would readily be labeled an assault and treated as a crime if done to an adult is rarely so labeled when committed by one young child against another. Child-on-child violence is more often described as scuffles, fights, or altercations. This chapter looks at the question of whether there is scientific support for regarding this violence as different from adult violence.

How Scholarship Discounts Peer Violence among Children

Despite the widespread presumption that they are dissimilar, there have been few studies of exactly how child-on-child violence is different from adult violence. Research has rarely considered such basic questions as whether child violence is fundamentally less overwhelming, less injurious, less psychologically harmful, differently motivated, or characterized by different sequences of interaction. Rather, there are difficult-to-avoid, widely shared stereotypes about this type of violence that color even scholarly thinking on the topic.

Examples of the difficulty of escaping the stereotypes can be found in a paper by Garofalo, Siegel, and Laub,[3] one of the studies most frequently cited as demonstrating the less serious nature of juvenile peer victimization. The authors analyzed narratives of school-related victimizations from the National Crime Survey, the predecessor to the National Crime Victimization Survey (NCVS), the federal government's large, annual epidemiological survey on crime. They concluded, "Generally, victimizations of juveniles tend to be less serious than victimizations of adults" (p. 336). In support of their conclusion, the authors cited episodes provided by teenage interviewees in response to questions intended to elicit crime victimization scenarios.

> The emerging picture is not one of the offender stalking an innocent prey, but of teasing, bullying and horseplay that gets out of hand. The following excerpts are not unusual: "While walking down stairs in school, two boys threatened to throw respondent down stairs unless she walked faster." "Boy had been bullying respondent for several months. One day respondent knocked him down when he called respondent names. The next day offender knocked respondent down, causing injury to the jaw" (p. 331)

In another section of the article, the authors add that "72% of the narratives contained additional information about injury and most served to confirm its minor nature. For example, 'while on school grounds respondent accidentally spilled milk on another student who turned on the respondent with great anger and hit her on the head with clenched fist. Offender's ring caused pain and a lump to form' " (p. 332).

These are good examples of how easy it is to impute "minor nature" to episodes involving children when in truth a range of seriousness could be inferred from the available descriptions. Being thrown down stairs could be life threatening in some stairwell constructions, and the true seriousness of the threat is unclear from the narrative. An adult knocked down, injured in the jaw, and verbally abused by a co-worker two days in a row might well be described as being terrorized, and the victim could end up with a large damage award. If a man hits his wife in the head with a clenched fist "with great anger," causing a lump to form, police and prosecutors have no difficulty construing this as an arrestable and prosecutable spousal assault, with a presumption of serious emotional harm done to the victim. When the authors of this article contrast their cited juvenile episodes to the crime-thriller stereotype of "offenders stalking innocent prey," they ignore the fact that this stereotype does not characterize most adult crime in general or most adult-victim NCVS episodes, which frequently grow out of arguments, disagreements, and bullying.[257]

In fact, more quantitative analyses of NCVS data do not confirm a lower level of seriousness for violence occurring against juveniles. Overall, the rate of serious violent crime—that is, rape, robbery, and aggravated assault—has been twice as high for 12- to 17- year-olds as for those 18 or older.[2] In addition, the proportion of all NCVS assaults that involved injury is around 28% for both 12- to 17-year-olds and adults.[258] This is despite the fact that the vast majority of the assailants who attack juveniles are other juveniles, while most of the adult assailants attacked other adults.[2] So the NCVS does not support claims that peer victimization of juveniles is less serious than the violent crime that adults experience.

Common Presumptions about Child-on-Child Violence

If child-on-child violence is regarded as different from other kinds of violence, the main reason for this belief derives not from empirical evidence but from moral and philosophical presumptions about young offenders. Children, according to long traditions in law, religion, and psychology, are deemed to be more impulsive; less aware of society's norms, standards, and consequences; and less capable of harboring so-called criminal intent, or *mens rea*.[259] Some of the aversion to using crime-oriented labels like *assault* is the belief that children should not be judged by the same moral or legal standards as adults and should be spared the stigma inherent in such labels. This principle forms the basis for having a separate and less punitive system to handle juvenile offenses.

But along with presumptions about child offenders, perceptions of child-on-child violence appear also to contain parallel presumptions about child victims. These presumptions consider the victims of peer violence to be less violated, less injured, and less affected than similarly victimized adults might be. This presumption of lesser impact can be seen by again substituting adult victims in the examples from the previously cited article by Garofalo, Siegel, and Laub.[3] Would it be considered unreasonable for a man who is knocked down, injured in the jaw, and verbally abused by a co-worker to pursue a grievance about such treatment a year after the episode? Would it be considered unreasonable for a woman hit on the head in great anger with a clenched fist to seek a restraining order against her offender? In recent instances, when children have filed such grievances or sought restraining orders, typically in the face of more serious abuse, questions have been raised about whether the children or their families were "going to extremes."[260–262]

Presumptions that people hold about child victimization at the hands of peers apply to both the severity of the event's objective features (level of violence involved) and the severity of its impact or harmfulness. One element is the idea that child-on-child violence is objectively less threatening and injurious in its physical and interpersonal dynamics. Child assailants, at least in the case of younger children, are thought of as not as strong, not as calculating, and not as callous as older individuals. It is assumed that they could not create as much fear or cause as much physical damage as an older offender might.

A second element in the presumption is that child-on-child violence is less harmful because the normative violation is not so severe. Presumably, child-on-child violence is more common, expected, developmentally normal, and less associated with malevolence or criminal intent.[263] Children are less impacted by such violence because they, presumably, appreciate its normality and do not feel so violated or stigmatized by it.

A third element in the presumption of lesser impact is the idea that children are simply developmentally more resilient when child perpetrators are involved. There is so much novelty in the world of children; things are continually changing, and children can be miserable at one moment and elated the next. The anguish and suffering of being a victim of violence is therefore short-lived.

There may be other elements in the presumption of diminished impact as well. Terms like *scuffle*, *fight*, *squabble*, and *altercation*,[263] often used to describe child-on-child violence, imply that responsibility for the violence is mutually shared, that everyone may have been using violence in the episode, or that the self-described victim may have done something to provoke or prolong the assault. If a victim is culpable or even an aggressor, then that child is likely less harmed by the violence of the episode.

Yet another element in this presumption about child-on-child violence is that such experiences are character building.[264] There is a tradition of thought among parents, and even developmental authorities, that it is important for children to learn to defend themselves from assaulters and bullies.[261] Even if being the victim of violence causes pain and suffering, these are thought of as salutary and educational experiences, and this benefit mitigates whatever harm someone might otherwise impute to the experience.

A Critique of These Presumptions

Though rooted in popular thinking, these presumptions do not have a strong grounding in empirical evidence or developmental theory. In fact, in some cases, there is basis for an opposing premise. For example, far from being less threatening and injurious, the impulsive, unrestrained nature of child aggressors—combined with large differences in size and physique, youthful strength, and lack of socialization to the concept of chivalry—makes young child assailants generally more threatening and injurious than slightly older assailants. In addition, while the developmental immaturity of children may make it easy to move beyond a victimization episode, this same immaturity may allow an episode to inflict a more pervasive and catastrophic effect on developmental trajectories. Notice, for example, how, according to popular presumption and some of the research evidence,[144] sex crimes are believed to be more injurious the earlier they are experienced precisely because of this developmental immaturity.

Also, the apparent normality of peer violence in childhood could be an exacerbating rather than a buffering factor. When violence is more common, children have more difficulty achieving a sense of security. The presence of frequent violence may be a traumatic reminder of children's own victimizations, which according to traumatic stress theory could make it more difficult to recover from the episodes.[265] In general, children may have much more intensive and ongoing contact with their assailants—classmates and siblings—than would most adult victims (with the exception of spousal victims). This may also make it more difficult for a child to recover from the trauma of a victimization episode. Obviously, the comparative seriousness of child-on-child violence needs to be settled through empirical comparisons and evidence, not by presumption and selective application of popular thinking about child development.

Although in this chapter we have been discussing the seriousness of peer and sibling violence with regard to children in general, the presumption of lesser seriousness applies more strongly to certain types of child-on-child victimization than to other types. A relatively more "discounted" type is the victimization of younger children. The perceived seriousness of victimization could be said to decrease with declining age, such that the peer-on-peer violence among 16-year-olds is regarded as more serious and crime-like than peer-on-peer violence among 10-year-olds, which in turn is more serious and crime-like than that among 4-year-olds.[266]

Another relatively more discounted type of peer-on-peer violence is sibling victimization. Sibling victimization is almost certainly regarded as more benign than other peer victimizations, and the basis for this belief might once again be the idea that it is among the most normal, frequent, and expected forms of violence. However, one might also argue that the pervasive and inescapable nature of contacts with siblings makes it a form of violence with great capacity to harm.[267]

Our Study of Peer and Sibling Violence

In a study of some of these issues, we were able to compare the peer and sibling violence experienced by children ages 2 to 9 years with the violence experienced by older youth ages 10 to 17.[43] The children in this study were selected from a nationally representative sample of 2,030 children ages 2 to 17, conducted in 2002 and 2003. The families were recruited and interviews were conducted by telephone. The experiences of the youth 10 to 17 years old were obtained directly from the youth themselves, while those of the younger children were collected from interviews with the parent who knew most about the child. Violent episodes were signified by a yes response to one or more of five screeners concerning an assault with an object, an assault without an object, an attempted assault, a generalized peer or sibling assault, and a nonsexual genital assault.

To ensure that information on equivalent kinds of experiences was solicited, the same questions were used for episodes occurring to the younger and older children. Episodes of peer or sibling violence were distinguished from each other and from those committed by other types of perpetrators. Considerable other information was gathered about the dynamics of the episodes and about possible abuse-related mental health symptoms.

There was little evidence, we found, to support the conventional presumption that peer violence was less serious or less consequential for younger victims. Compared to peer assaults on older youth, very young children (ages 2 to 5) were actually more likely to be injured and more likely to be hit with an object that could cause injury. Younger children (ages 2 to 9) were somewhat less likely to be victimized by multiple perpetrators. But in terms of impact, when we asked about symptomatic behaviors that tend to be the result of violent victimization, such as anxiety and depression, even low-frequency peer violence against younger children was significantly associated with elevated trauma symptoms. For young children, the association between peer violence and trauma symptoms was just as strong as the association for older children. Thus, there was little suggestion that young children were more resilient to or less affected by peer violence.

We found that sibling violence, by contrast, did have some different patterns. Sibling violence appeared on some dimensions to fulfill its stereotype as a less serious form of aggression. Compared to peer violence, it entailed fewer injuries, the use of fewer objects that could cause injuries, and fewer multiple assailants. But sibling violence was much more likely than peer violence to be a chronic condition. Over half of the children under 10 years old hit by a sibling in the previous year had experienced five or more such episodes during that year. Living together with the assailant could easily explain this high frequency. Younger children were even more likely than older children to experience this chronic sibling violence. Thus, this risk of *chronicity* may offset sibling victimization's lower level of physical injuriousness. Indeed, we found that being a victim of sibling violence independently elevates a child's trauma symptoms, for both younger children and older youth.

One potentially important difference in our findings was apparent in sibling victimization compared to peer violence. For younger children, increased trauma symptoms appeared only for victims of chronic sibling violence (five or more episodes a year), not for children suffering infrequent episodes. These young chronic victims were the juveniles most affected by sibling violence. The older youth showed some weakly increased symptoms at low levels of sibling victimization and none at chronic levels. This suggests that younger children in particular may be more resilient to a modest amount of sibling aggression. But bear in mind that one-fifth (19%) of the sample of younger children (half of all children with a sibling episode) experienced chronic sibling victimization—the level at which symptoms increased. These findings do not paint a picture of sibling hitting as a benign condition or of young children as a broadly impact-free group.

The findings also suggested that older youth show fewer effects of sibling victimization, especially at higher levels. It may be that the sibling violence against older youth is more frequently at the hands of their younger siblings, who have a harder time exercising behavioral control. Aggression by younger siblings against older siblings may be associated with fewer consequences because the older siblings feel less threatened. Unfortunately, the study does not provide information on the age differentials between perpetrators and victims in the peer and sibling victimization episodes.

Overall, the findings of our study can be interpreted as evidence against popular inclinations to discount the seriousness and potential impact of peer and sibling hitting, as well as other violence against younger children. Its implications are bolstered by the use of a nationally representative sample that includes a broad spectrum of children and youth and a broad spectrum of victimization episodes.

So the empirical data do not confirm what many people take for granted: that peer and sibling violence among younger children is less serious than among older youth. One implication is that such violence *needs* to be taken more seriously by schools and parents, and not dismissed as just normal, minor, and inconsequential. Schools and parents need to set clearer standards against such violence and intervene earlier to prevent recurrences and to protect victims. Parent and teacher education programs need to provide more tools to prevent the initiation and recurrence of such violence. Child protection workers need to assess such violence in considering child safety in the home and in institutional environments. Mental health providers need to adapt treatments to prevent the long-term consequences that result from exposure to such violence. There are signs that such reevaluation of attitudes and approaches has been taking place—for example, in the increased efforts to prevent bullying among school-age children.

A particularly recent and relevant reevaluation of another type of so-called normative violence is the case of spousal hitting, which was once seen as squabbles or altercations, normal in occurrence, different from real crimes, and with minor impact—much as peer hitting among young children is sometimes currently viewed. Views of spousal hitting, however, underwent reevaluation in the light of victim testimony, a new ideology emanating from the women's movement, and considerable empirical research. One of the main differences regarding children in comparison to spouses is that testimony from child victims is not nearly as available to the public or as credible, which makes the role of research even more important.

However, spousal assault may not be an adequate model for the development of interventions and responses to peer and sibling violence. Even if a peer hitting a young child were to prove more harmful and offensive than an adult hitting an adult, it would not make sense to treat these actions in the same way; few would propose police, courts, or even juvenile criminal proceedings in regard to the violence of young children. The main rationale for different treatment of young offenders lies in their likely different motives, capacities, cognitive abilities, and so forth. Insofar as child victims are concerned, it makes more sense to think about applying interventions that would be comparable to what is done for older youth and adults. This might include testing for posttraumatic symptoms and applying cognitive-behavioral techniques that have proved effective in alleviating those symptoms.[246]

The implications of taking peer and sibling violence more seriously are more straightforward with regard to victimization assessment and instrumentation. Some have questioned whether it makes sense to include peer and sibling hitting in an inventory of victimizations or potentially traumatic events, and whether it should be counted when calculating cumulative event scores such as with the Juvenile Victimization Questionnaire.[57] Analyses here suggest that such experiences should be considered victimizations and should be included. These victimizations appear to make independent, incremental contributions. It may be that for younger children, only chronic sibling violence should be counted.

A related question concerns the advisability of using the same screening questions to inquire about victimization across the developmental spectrum. Our study showed that peer victimizations of younger children were disclosed in response to a somewhat different set of screeners from those that elicited victimizations of older youth. It remains to be seen whether this finding reveals true differences in the dynamics of the episodes reported or whether it reflects differences in how they are categorized by the participants and observers. Our experience is that the similarities are more salient than the differences, in terms of both the victimization characteristics and their ability to predict trauma. While we urge more investigation of this issue, we think that the advantages of studying and assessing youth of different ages using the same kinds of questions strongly advocate for keeping the assessment instruments as comparable as possible. Among the main advantages of this approach is the ability to plot developmental trajectories and make developmental comparisons.

Another concern is how systematically victimization researchers should inquire about and include sibling victimization in their analyses. Sibling violence is among the most common kind of violence that children experience. Counting it in inventories will certainly inflate the victimization rates, and for this reason sibling victimization might be segregated out for analytical purposes. Sibling violence also seems to have characteristics that differentiate it from peer violence. On the other hand, our study provides evidence that sibling victimization, and especially chronic sibling victimization, contributes to trauma symptoms. It strikes us as a mistake to choose not to assess it. This form of violence may turn out to be an important precursor to other kinds of victimization and may possibly be confounded with the effect of other victimizations. Something that is clear from the study, however, is that respondents will not disclose sibling victimization unless it is mentioned specifically as an event of interest to the researcher.

We believe that these kinds of findings[43] have implications for the future of crime victimization epidemiology. We cannot find, based on the results of this analysis and the study in general, much justification for limiting crime victimization surveys to teenagers or excluding the experiences of younger children. The rates of victimization are not substantially higher for teens.[8] We did not find caretakers to be an obviously inferior source of information when it comes to the victimizations of children under 10.[55] Moreover, the episodes that occurred to younger children appear to be as serious as those that occurred to older children.

Should the NCVS continue its policy of excluding younger children from one of the nation's most important and widely cited sources of crime information? On the one hand, peer assaults against younger children are not regarded as crimes, even if they may qualify according to statute, and our research is unlikely to change that view, nor should it. Policy makers might reasonably object if the NCVS started counting peer assaults against young children in aggregates of "Crime in the U.S." On the other hand, the current policy of excluding all persons under 12 also excludes many episodes of what everyone would agree is serious crime and of great public-policy interest, including child molestations and serious physical abuse. Exclusion of these crimes also contributes to a mistaken belief that crime does not occur frequently to younger children. In reality, most studies now confirm that children face frequencies of assaultive violence far above the levels that most adults encounter, although this reality is not widely recognized. There may be good reasons for not calling or counting much of this as criminal violence. But our above-mentioned study undercuts at least one of the earlier rationalizations for ignoring or discounting violence against younger children: the idea that such violence tends not to be that serious or consequential.

A solution for a major national crime survey such as the NCVS might be to include the experiences of younger children in the data gathering but to report the experience of all juveniles, both younger and older, in separate reports about juvenile victimization. At the same time, the NCVS could count only the victimizations of older children in the official crime statistics or add in some narrowly defined subgroup of victimizations (for example, sexual assaults) from the younger children.

Conclusion

Professional and public attitudes about violence in the lives of children have been undergoing a shift. Concern about parental child maltreatment represented an early indication of this shift.[268] In recent years, the shift has advanced to include concerns about even more normatively accepted forms of violence, such as school bullying and corporal punishment.[46,269] Even the United Nations has placed the matter of violence in the lives of children on its agenda as an important human rights issue.[270] As moral, legal, psychological, parental, and public-health views on these topics come under scrutiny and discussion, it will be important to have dispassionate scientific evidence to inform the debate. Many questions remain to be answered, and the need is urgent.

Chapter 6

Getting Help: What Are the Barriers?

Most crimes involving child victims are not reported to the police. Most child victims also do not receive any other kind of professional help. Does this mean that society is failing to provide adequate justice and support for its youngest crime victims? For the most part, yes: underreporting and lack of professional help are indicators that we do not yet have a system that is fully responsive to child victims. But that's not always the case, and some victimizations may be better dealt with outside of formal systems.

This chapter reviews what is known about both of these processes—police reporting and seeking professional help—among child crime victims, once again generalizing across a variety of domains of child victimization. Although reporting to the police and seeking help are very different processes that involve different organizations and different outcomes, they are linked. That is, many of the factors that predict one also predict the other. So this chapter discusses both processes. First, it reviews what is known about police reporting in regard to adult as well as child victims. Then, it looks at how child crime victims get treatment for psychological problems that result from victimization, including which victims are most likely to be treated and what factors commonly facilitate or stand in the way of treatment. Finally, it proposes a simple conceptual model to help analyze and research the factors that promote or hinder police reporting and the seeking of help among child victims.

Most Crime Is Not Reported

Children are not alone in their failure to report crimes. Among the general population, over half of all violent crimes—including rape, sexual and physical assault, and robbery—are never reported to the police. The National Crime Victimization Survey (NCVS) is the main source of data about reports of violent crime for persons age 12 and older, excluding homicide. Across all age groups covered by NCVS, only 41% of violent crimes are reported to the police. Completed robberies involving injury are the most reported of violent crimes (66%), and attempted rapes are the least reported (19%).

Several factors are known to influence whether a crime is reported to the police. The most obvious determinant is the seriousness of the crime. Violent crimes are more likely to be reported than crimes against property, and violent crimes are more likely to be reported when they are completed, as opposed to attempted, and when they involve an injury, particularly a serious injury.[271] Rapes are more likely to be reported when the victim sustains an injury in addition to the rape or when a weapon is used.[272]

In addition to the severity of the crime, victims' attitudes toward the police and the influence of the victim's family and friends are important factors in whether a violent crime is reported to the police. Victims who have previously had positive experiences with the police after reporting a crime[273] and rape victims who were advised by friends and family to report[274] are more likely to report. Demographic characteristics, however, have only slight predictive value in terms of whether or not violent crimes are reported. Analyses of the NCVS suggest that crimes are somewhat more likely to be reported when victims are women or African American.[271,272,275]

Underreporting of Juvenile Victims

While all crime, then, is likely underreported, crimes against children are even more underreported. Only 28% of the violent crimes suffered by youth are reported to the police, compared to 48% of those suffered by adults.[72] This is emphatically *not* a matter of juvenile victimizations being systematically less serious. The underreporting of violent victimizations of juveniles compared to those of adults holds across most categories of crime victimization, including crimes committed with weapons (40% of juveniles reported versus 62% of adults), crimes resulting in injury (42% of juveniles reported versus 62% of adults), and crimes committed by all categories of perpetrators including strangers (32% of juveniles reported versus 49% of adults). Violent crimes committed by juveniles against juveniles are particularly underreported (2% of juvenile victims reported versus 41% of adult victims). The one crime domain where juvenile victims in the NCVS do not systematically report less to the police compared to adults is the crime of sexual assault. However, this is not because of high levels of reporting by juveniles but rather because of particularly low levels of adult reporting—about 30% in each case.[72,275] Other general population surveys confirm the generally low levels of police reporting for youth victims.[26,276–278] In addition, there is evidence that many professionals employed by mental health and social services agencies, as well as medical and educational institutions, fail to comply with laws mandating the reporting of child victimization.[279]

Factors in the Underreporting of Juvenile Victimization

The reasons that crimes involving child victims are underreported to the police can be usefully grouped into five general categories: definitional, jurisdictional, developmental, emotional/attitudinal, and material (Table 6.1). These are not mutually exclusive categories, but they do convey the range of factors that may be relevant. The first three factors apply differentially to the situation of juveniles, while the last two apply to the underreporting of adults as well, although some of the specifics relating to children may differ.

Definitional Factors

Definitional factors concern the way in which child victimizations are viewed—whether the acts are seen as crimes, serious normative violations, or anything else that would be of potential interest to police. For example, many juvenile victimizations are not defined by victims, parents, or police

TABLE 6.1. A Taxonomy of Factors in Juvenile Underreporting to Police

Factors	Description
Definitional	Episodes are seen as less criminal because of: • Normative expectations that victimization is part of childhood • Image of shared culpability, fighting • Juvenile offenders are not seen as criminals • High proportion of child victimizations involve acquaintance offenders
Jurisdictional	Nonpolice resolutions: parents, schools, child protection agencies
Developmental	For younger children, parents are gatekeepers to police For adolescents, youth subculture discourages police reporting
Emotional	Embarrassment and shame Avoiding blame or mistreatment by system Powerlessness, cynicism Avoiding negative reminders Loyalty to or protection of offender Fear of retaliation from offender
Material	Time Financial costs

as crimes that fall within police jurisdiction. Assaults, robberies, and thefts involving young people are sometimes viewed as a "normal" part of youth, or as "learning experiences" rather than crimes. Reporting of offenses committed against children by other juveniles is substantially lower than reporting of offenses committed by adults.[278] Juvenile-on-juvenile victimizations, especially, are apt to be defined as fights in which responsibility is shared, rather than perpetrator–victim crimes.

In addition, when juveniles are victimized by other juveniles, the cases are handled by a different branch of the justice system (juvenile and family courts), one that emphasizes rehabilitation rather than punishment. This situation may foster a perception that police and courts are less concerned about youthful criminal behavior or are likely to take it less seriously. Likewise, juveniles are victimized disproportionately by family and acquaintances, and acquaintance victimizations, even between adults, have been more difficult to define as crimes.

To some extent, this definitional problem is revealed in NCVS data. In the NCVS reports for 12- through 17-year-olds, 31% of juvenile victimizations, compared to 21% of adult victimizations, were not reported to police because of reasons coded by interviewers under the heading "not important enough to report."[53] Almost half of the Boston parents who did not report incidents of sexual abuse involving their children said they thought the incidents were not serious.[26]

Another definitional factor that influences reporting is how victims and families define their needs. Police and the justice system are agencies with certain potential resources to dispense, such as justice and protection. If families and children feel in imminent danger, for example, they are more likely to report, according to one study.[278] But to the extent that victims and families define their salient needs in the wake of victimization as something other than what police can provide, they may direct their attention in other ways. For instance, a victim's salient need may be to get a vandalized bike repaired or a CD player replaced, and in such cases the police are deemed irrelevant. Other research on adult crime victims has pointed to the extent that a victim's needs may be beyond the scope of services that law enforcement is thought to provide.[280]

Jurisdictional Factors

Jurisdictional factors have to do with what authority—such as parents, the school, police, or a child protection agency—may initially take charge of the handling of an episode. A major factor in underreporting of juvenile victimization to the police may be that children have many authorities in their lives, including parents and schools, who routinely deal with such victimizations. The most common childhood victimizations—assaults by siblings and peers—are ordinarily investigated by parents, who then dispense justice to the offending parties. Even in the case of sexual assaults, parents often want to handle matters on their own. For instance, in a Boston sample, 90% of the parents of sexually abused children whose abuse went unreported cited a desire to handle the situation themselves.[26]

Similarly, crimes against children may be handled directly by teachers or other school authorities or referred to a child protection agency instead of being passed on to the police. School officials, an especially common authority in the lives of children, can mete out justice for physical assaults, thefts, and robberies more swiftly than can any law enforcement agency, usually by punishing, suspending, or expelling the offending students (although they do not always do so). Their informal operation may also be seen as more victim-friendly; this may make schools a more popular avenue of redress for victims than the police. Schools, for a variety of reasons including concerns about reputation, are often reluctant to pass along knowledge of crimes to the police.

The child welfare system is another authority that receives reports of child victimizations and often handles them outside of police jurisdiction. Child protection agencies are akin to police in that they are formal governmental agencies that investigate and present cases to a court system that then provides due process to accused abusers. However, most instances of physical assault by family members, except when extremely serious, are handled by providing services rather than labeling and processing the assaults as crimes. Parents, schools, and child protection agencies all refer some victimizations to the police, but they handle others independently.

The NCVS and other data confirm the existence of important alternative jurisdictions for crimes against children. According to the NCVS, about 39% of the violent crimes against children that are not reported to police are dealt with another way—that is, reported to another authority or handled informally between families. According to another study, when offenses occur in school, they are less likely to be reported to the police.[278] That study found that violent victimizations of 10- to 16-year-olds were over three times more likely to be reported to schools as to police (21% versus 6%), the disproportion being greatest for nonfamily physical assault (33% versus 7%) and least for sexual assault (5% versus 3%) or family assault (5% versus 4%).[276]

Developmental Factors

The different relationships that children of different ages have to social institutions, and the cultural and legal structures that govern those relationships, are considered developmental factors. These developmental factors can be barriers to reporting. First, young children in particular cannot access police directly and must contact them through the intercession of adults. Adult victims generally, although not always, determine on their own whether their victimization will be revealed to the police. For a child victimization to be reported, generally the child has to disclose the offense to an adult, and an adult has to make a report. Parents in turn have their own possible reasons for nonreporting, including personal interests that may be antithetical to those of the child victim—for example, fear that a police investigation might lead to complaints of neglect against the parents. So there are two opportunities for the report to be squelched.

Developmental issues for adolescents also create barriers to police reporting. The developmental tasks of adolescence put emphasis on developing autonomy and weaning oneself from reliance on adults, and this independence from adult norms and adult institutions gets exaggerated in many youth subcultures. Youth who report violations may be subject to teasing, stigmatization, or social ostracism by peers, which for adolescents may be a greater price to pay than being victimized. So victims may not want adults and adult authorities such as police involved, even when they have been victimized.

Emotional and Attitudinal Factors

Emotional and attitudinal factors are individual reactions that inhibit or motivate victims and their families when it comes to reporting child victimization to authorities. In adult studies, victims' concerns about reporting have ranged from fear of embarrassment to fear of retaliation by the perpetrator,[274,281] and may include concerns about being revictimized by the system. Rape victims are often concerned about not being believed or being blamed,[282,283] and battered women may fear retaliation or loss of financial support or have mixed feelings about the offender.[284,285] Finally, the adult crime victim's sense of powerlessness and related perception of the police as unable to intervene effectively may contribute to the decision not to file a police report.[282] Some adult crime victims who reject police involvement instead seek help from social service agencies or turn to family and friends.[275]

Many of the same factors apply when parents decide not to involve police after their children have been victimized. Parents may fear that involvement in the criminal justice system will make a bad situation worse by upsetting and embarrassing the child and family. For example, among the previously mentioned nonreporting Boston parents, 45% did not want friends or neighbors to find out.[26] Moreover, while parents, or children themselves, may wish for the satisfaction of seeing justice done, many may regard justice as an uncertain outcome and fear the children will be doubly traumatized if they are not believed by a judge or jury. They may distrust the police or believe the children will be treated insensitively, will not be believed, or may even be blamed. When parents do not believe that the police will take an incident seriously, they are much less likely to report.[278] They may also just want to put the episode in the past to avoid reminders of the negative event.

Parents may have their own emotional reasons for not wanting to involve legal authorities. The offender may be a spouse, child, relative, or family friend. This may create divided loyalties or fear of the loss of valued relationships, and victims or families may not want the offender to suffer criminal sanctions. For instance, half the nonreporting Boston parents of sexually abused children said they felt sorry for the abuser and did not want to get him in trouble.[26]

The emotional and attitudinal barriers to police reporting are well illustrated by the large percentage of child victims who do not disclose to anyone at all, let alone the police. In self-report studies, as many as one-third of all victimized children do not disclose to anyone.[276] Even among studies of clinical samples of children already known to authorities, it is interesting how much of the victimization—45% in the case of one group of sexually abused subjects—was revealed not through self-disclosure but through other avenues such as direct adult observation or medical evidence.[286]

Another emotional barrier is the fear of retaliation from offenders, an especially important consideration among children who may not be confident that the police or other authorities can protect them from their offenders. Underreporting of juvenile victimization is particularly high for weapons crimes, possibly for this reason.[72] Fear also seems to be a prominent reason for nondisclosure among those sexually abused children who have suffered the most serious kinds of abuse.[279,286] In addition, children are also particularly sensitive to stigma among peers. Reporting may be seen as an acknowledgment of weakness or an act that will only encourage the dissemination of shameful or embarrassing information to a wider audience. Children, who are disproportionately victimized by friends, neighbors, or family, may also avoid or be encouraged to avoid reporting in order to protect the offender.

Material Factors

In studies of adult crime victims, some of the victims cited time and financial losses that might be incurred in reporting the incidents as deterrents to reporting.[282,287] There has been little examination of this factor in regard to juvenile victims. Because children are less likely to be employed, loss of income from time taken up with the justice system may be a minor consideration for children, but to the extent that parents need to chaperone children during their encounters with the justice system, this may be a motivating factor for parents not to report.

Does Reporting Serve Justice and Victims?

When citizens fail to report crimes, it is fair to presume that in many cases they are making a judgment that reporting does not promote their own interests or even those of the larger community. This judgment should not be rejected summarily as irrational. In addition to creating personal inconvenience and distress, reporting to police may burden law enforcement with investigations and paperwork concerning minor crimes that might be better handled privately or by some other authority. It is not clear that, even in an ideal world, 100% reporting of crimes would be a desirable outcome for all involved.

But it is likely that some increased level of reporting would both serve the community and benefit victims. The community is clearly appalled when serious offenders fail to come to justice. While there have been charges of overreaction, most observers agree that the historically recent revelations of child abuse, domestic violence, and acquaintance rape—crimes that previously were rarely disclosed—have been, on the whole, major advances for justice in our society. Data from the NCVS and other methodologies[80] show that large numbers of serious child victimizations are still not being disclosed. Even people concerned about overreporting acknowledge that efforts should be expanded to identify the large number of serious child victimizations still hidden.[288,289]

On the crucial question of whether there is a benefit to victims themselves, unfortunately there has been far too little research to determine whether victims who do report ultimately feel well served by the justice system. Many in the past have not. In an early study,[286] prior to most of the justice system reforms in the handling of sexual abuse, for example, almost half of families with a sexually abused child felt the criminal justice experience had been harmful. They cited police insensitivity and the stress of testifying as key concerns. But, by contrast, in more recent studies of sexually abused children,[290] children's views of the justice process were generally positive, with all but one child saying that reporting had been beneficial and 100% recommending reporting to other children. Similarly, three-fourths of a sample of 126 Canadian child victims[291] said that after their experience they would call the police again if they needed to. The weight of the current evidence does not confirm the jaundiced view that reporting is a mostly negative experience for victims and families. Rather, it supports a policy of encouraging more police reporting among juvenile crime victims.

What about the issue of the potential impact of increased reporting on perpetrators? Some commentators have the perception that the criminal justice system is often unfair and inept in handling many types of perpetrators and that it has limited options to offer them. In this view, increased reporting, particularly of crimes committed by young offenders or family members, will increase injustice and disrupt informal and perhaps more effective means of handling certain offenses.[292]

Discomfort with the tools of the criminal justice system is in part what prompted the creation and sustains the existence of a separate intervention system—child protection agencies—to deal with certain offenses against children. Debate about what belongs in the purview of the justice system is a central policy issue of our era, as evidenced by discussions about arrest policies in domestic violence cases[293] and whether to turn child welfare investigations over to the police.[294]

Nonetheless, encouragement of greater police reporting for offenses against children appears warranted, based on several factors. First, considerable research indicates that some serious and patently criminal forms of child victimization are still not being reported fully. Second, recent historical experience with increased police reporting of child abuse and domestic violence has led to outcomes that have, on the whole, been favorably viewed by child welfare professionals and the public. Third, as indicated earlier, almost all the research to date has contradicted the impression that police involvement in child victimization cases typically results in negative experiences for the children.[295] In fact, there are indications of better outcomes, including more services provided when police are involved. This may be particularly true now that police departments have better trained and more specialized personnel working with juvenile victims. Fourth, there are reasons to believe that police involvement may bring general benefits to society, if not the victims directly, in the form of greater deterrence and stronger reinforcement of general norms against these forms of victimization.

The obvious question that looms from the generally positive results of greater police involvement is how far their involvement should extend. There are still forms of child victimization in which society is reluctant to involve the police. Offenses that occur in elementary and middle schools, for example, are typically handled by school authorities rather than police, although increasingly youth crime specialists, sometimes called School Resource Officers, have been given a role in handling these offenses. Forms of child maltreatment, including physical abuse and most neglect, have been deemed unsuitable for law enforcement to handle.

Based on past trends and evidence of the successful adaptation of law enforcement to social problems involving families and children, we think that experiments should be undertaken to encourage more reporting to police and more police involvement in other forms of violence and victimization that have so far not had it. As with sexual abuse and domestic violence, this may require the development of specialized law enforcement practitioners to handle these problems and new hybrid, multiprofessional institutions and interventions. But the notion that the police should not be involved in family conflicts or in the resolution of cases involving younger children may now be outdated.

Help-Seeking by Child Crime Victims

If most crime victims fail to report their incidents to the police, still fewer seek or receive help from other victim-assistance organizations. Victim service groups are a relatively recent innovation, dating only from the early 1980s. Although these programs have been substantially expanded since they were first started, evidence from across the country shows that only 2% to 15% of victims access these services,[296–298] and less than 4% of victims receive any financial compensation, even though many states have crime-victim compensation funds.[299]

Nonetheless, it is clear that a need exists. One study found that over half of the victims of violent crimes had experienced symptoms of posttraumatic stress disorder, but only one-third of the symptomatic victims had received any mental health services.[287] Almost a third of youth victims in the National Youth Victimization Prevention Study (NYVS) were depressed during the year subsequent to their victimization,[300] but few sought help.

In general, the studies suggest that only a minority of child victims get the mental health services that are recognized as one of their major needs. A general population survey of juvenile crime victims found that only 20% received any kind of counseling.[301] A National Institute of Justice review suggested that 25% to 50% of reported child-abuse victims receive some mental health treatment.[302] Two recent studies of child protective caseloads found that 20% were referred for mental health treatment in Pennsylvania,[303] and 58% in Massachusetts.[304] Sexual abuse victims tend to be referred more—estimates range from 35% to 77%.[286,305–307] The receipt of mental health services by victims of offenses besides sexual abuse has not been common.

Even among those receiving mental health treatment, the average duration and number of sessions may be relatively modest. Many come for just a few sessions and drop out. Managed-care programs in the United States may not support extended treatment for child victims.[308,309]

Factors Associated with Seeking Mental Health Help

While there has been little study of which juvenile victims receive mental health services, the predictors of which juveniles in general get services are much better understood. According to mental health surveys, in any given year about 20% of young people suffer from diagnosable mental disorders, with only a small percentage receiving specific mental health treatment for their problems.[310–313] Given that disorders put youth at risk for victimization,[75] and vice versa, there is a large overlap in the populations of youth with mental health problems and those who are victims, so examination of this literature is highly relevant. For the remainder of this section, we discuss access to mental health services, rather than victim services in general, recognizing that mental health services are one of the most important forms of help that victims can receive and that they are the only form of help that has been extensively studied.

We have identified a number of factors from the literature that have been found or hypothesized to influence whether children with mental health problems seek help. Many of these factors are similar to those that impact crime reporting for juvenile victims, so we have sorted them into parallel categories: definitional, jurisdictional, developmental, emotional/attitudinal, and material (Table 6.2).

TABLE 6.2. A Taxonomy of Factors in Juvenile Access to Mental Health Services

Factors	Description
Definitional	Symptoms seen as normal to childhood Problems seen as transient Defined as school problems Internalizing problems not motivating to family
Jurisdictional	Doctors, teachers, more accessible sources of assistance
Developmental	For younger children, parental concerns inhibit help-seeking For adolescents, issues of autonomy and self-image inhibit help-seeking
Emotional	Embarrassment and shame Powerlessness, cynicism Avoiding of negative reminders
Material	Time Financial costs

Definitional Factors

Whether a child obtains services or assistance depends on whether a child is perceived as having a problem and, if so, whether that problem is viewed as a mental health problem or some other issue, such as a behavioral or academic problem. Most children with psychological problems, even children who are functionally impaired by diagnosable mental disorders, are not perceived by their parents as having mental health problems.[314,315] Parents often view symptomatic behaviors, such as aggressiveness in boys, as normal. They tend to view school-conduct problems as school related and not related to mental health. And even when they recognize behaviors as problematic, they often treat them as transient concerns that will ease as the child gains maturity.

Naturally, more serious symptoms are more likely to lead a child to mental health services,[310,314] a finding confirmed even among the few studies of juvenile crime victims.[286,306,307] More serious victimization episodes (e.g., sexual assault involving penetration or a family perpetrator), independent of symptoms, are also more likely to result in treatment.

But seriousness is not the entire story. Problems that cause difficulty for parents are more likely to be defined as requiring treatment than are problems that do not.[314,316–318] Thus, children with externalizing disorders characterized by defiance and aggression are more likely to be treated than children with internalizing disorders such as depression and anxiety because these children, although very distressed, tend to be quiet and withdrawn and to not cause trouble at home or school.[314,319] One study of juvenile crime victims did find that aggressive symptoms were more associated with the receipt of counseling[301]; however, another study found higher rates of service among those suffering from PTSD than among those with other symptoms.[309]

Interestingly, parents who have their own mental health problems or have used professional mental health care are more likely to arrange treatment for their children.[311,316–318] Parents with their own psychological problems may feel more burdened by their children's problems or, because of their experiences, these parents may be more likely to attribute behavioral or other difficulties to psychological distress. In addition, children's own perceptions of their problems play a role. For example, child and adolescent victims of bullying and peer assaults are more likely to disclose and seek help when they suffer high levels of negative emotion.[320]

Jurisdictional Factors

Jurisdictional factors have to do with what person or group defines the child's problem and makes decisions about how it will be treated. Children, obviously, face jurisdictional complexities that adults do not. For instance, children's access to services is mediated not just by parents but also by schools, child protection agencies, and criminal justice authorities. These jurisdictional factors can facilitate as well as impede access.

For example, research has found that child sexual abuse victims who are involved in the justice system when their offenders are prosecuted are more likely to receive mental health services.[321] This may be in part because these children get referred to the services by their criminal justice contacts, but it also may be because the justice system sees it as being in the interests of the cases for the children to get support or have ongoing contact with professionals. It may also be that these children are more likely to be eligible for victim's compensation funds.

Another jurisdictional issue flagged in the research on children is that parents are more inclined to turn to physicians and teachers for help with their children's problems than to mental health care providers such as therapists, psychologists, and psychiatrists.[310,312,317,322,323] It makes sense that parents who have established relationships with physicians, teachers, or other professionals who know their children would turn to them first for help. But researchers have found that while pediatricians are responsive when parents raise concerns about their children's psychological problems, they often fail to diagnose such problems in young patients unless the parents bring them up.[317] This may be particularly true when physicians treat adolescents.[315,324] On the other hand, physicians report that they often manage the psychological problems of young patients within their practices, referring only the most severe problems to specialists.[323] There is little information about what physicians do with reports of victimization.

While physicians can be seen as responding to parents' concerns, teachers and schools have a more complicated relationship with parents whose children exhibit problems. Schools are the major providers of mental health care to children and adolescents in the United States. In some areas of the country, as many as 80% of the children receiving mental health services are seen by providers affiliated with the schools—mostly guidance counselors and school psychologists.[310,322,325] Parents probably consult with teachers about their children's behavioral and emotional problems more often than with any other source of assistance.[319,326] At the same time, teachers and other school personnel are major players in identifying and referring children for mental health problems.[312,325,326] Children victimized at school appear to be more likely to receive counseling than other children.[301] But it is also likely that school referrals are governed primarily by issues of academic performance or disruptive school behavior. When victims do not have one of these symptoms, it is doubtful that school personnel will take much initiative in referring them for treatment.

In summary, jurisdictional issues overall have a complex relationship with victims' seeking help with mental health, and contacts with other institutional spheres are perhaps as likely to facilitate as inhibit access to services for child crime victims.

Developmental Factors

Age does not appear to have a strong influence on the absolute likelihood of receiving services. Teenagers may be somewhat more likely to obtain services,[327,328] possibly because the kinds of problems that older children have are seen as more serious, disruptive, or threatening. But once the level of symptoms is controlled, age does not appear to make much of a difference.[313] While that may mean that barriers to service are not substantially greater at any particular age, the nature of the barriers probably does change with age. For younger children, the reticence of the parents to define a problem as meriting mental health consultation may be a major factor. For older children, their own resistance, concerns about stigma, or threats to their personal autonomy may be more salient. Research has found that many teens find it intrusive to have to get parental permission and may forgo medical or mental health care for problems relating to sexuality, substance abuse, or emotional upset if they are required to tell their parents about it.[329] Adolescents who have access to age-appropriate, confidential services through school-based clinics are more likely to get help for psychological problems than are other teens.[330,331]

Emotional and Attitudinal Factors

Emotional and attitudinal factors are individual reactions that inhibit or motivate victims and their families with regard to seeking services for children. Among these may be attitudes toward service providers, the desire to avoid embarrassment or blame, feelings of powerlessness or cynicism, and not wanting to acknowledge weakness or compromise personal autonomy. The role of autonomy is highlighted in one study of adolescents that found the central barriers to seeking help were their beliefs that they, their families, and their friends were sufficient support for dealing with their problems.[332,333] Many adolescents believe that friends alone are sufficient.[334] A study of preschool-age children found that the most common perceived barriers to seeking help were (in this order) the belief that the problems would resolve on their own, the belief that parents should be strong enough to handle children's problems on their own, and a lack of knowledge as to where to go for help.[335]

Material Factors

Material factors are practical resources like money, medical insurance, time and transportation, and knowledge that can inhibit or promote access to mental health services. Interestingly, general research on access to mental health services does *not* show lower utilization by the poor. In fact, poverty, in some research, is associated with the receipt of more mental health care for juveniles.[310] Part of this is certainly the higher incidence of juvenile mental health problems among the poor, but part is the availability of subsidized payment systems such as Medicaid[310,311,322] and the targeting of community mental health services at vulnerable groups. In one study,[301] child victims in families with health insurance were found to be more likely to get counseling. But many mental health services are provided in public schools and clinics, and private health insurance is associated with higher income and thus lower incidence of mental health disorders, so there may be a curvilinear relationship between socioeconomic status and mental health services.[311,322,336]

This seemingly rosy picture of access for lower-income children is undercut by findings from the sexual-abuse-victim research that show, for example, that victims without phones or those referred to public (versus private) mental health services were less likely to follow up on referrals to treatment or to actually obtain services.[337] So, low income may still be a barrier to child victims' receiving services.

The Utility of Mental Health Services

As was the case in our discussion of police reporting, it is not clear that failure to seek or obtain mental health or other victim services is necessarily a problem. Often the choice may be quite appropriate. Studies have found, for example, that as many as 40% of child sexual abuse victims are not suffering from symptoms and perhaps do not need treatment.[144,338] For most children, levels of distress drop over time, regardless of whether treatment is given.[144] Many victims get adequate help from family and friends and other informal sources.

Nonetheless, there is evidence that treatment is effective for children in reducing symptoms resulting from victimization. In randomized, controlled trials, children receiving abuse-specific treatment have shown significantly greater reductions in behavior problems, anxiety, and posttraumatic stress symptoms.[246] These trials reinforce other emerging evidence for the effectiveness of treatment of childhood PTSD.[339] Thus, given interventions with demonstrated efficacy, it seems that the promotion of mental health assistance among the population of juvenile crime victims has some clear empirical justification.

The dilemma remains concerning what to do with victimized children who do not have symptoms. It cannot be assumed that symptoms will appear at some later time. These children's natural and environmental coping strategies may, in fact, be adequate. Nonetheless, we do know that there are possible "sleeper effects," and victimized children are at higher risk of future victimization. Prophylactic intervention or simple education may help forestall these outcomes. The downside of providing prophylactic intervention for children without symptoms is that it may reinforce the stigma of being a victim or lead children to have anxiety about effects they may never experience. Given that substantial numbers of victimized children do not have symptoms, we need to study what kinds of interventions, if any, make sense with this group.

A Summary of Empirical Findings

So far, we have identified a variety of factors that might be seen as barriers to or facilitators of reporting victimizations to the police and seeking help for mental health problems. Police reporting is more likely when crimes are more serious (e.g., entail injuries or weapons), but reporting is less likely when crimes involve family members, juvenile perpetrators, and sexual assaults. There is evidence that juvenile victimizations are particularly underreported because the offenses are not seen as criminal in nature, the offenders are often other juveniles, and reporting to other authorities, school officials in particular, is seen as a sufficient and appropriate response. Issues of privacy and autonomy are particular salient when victims and families cite reasons for nonreporting.

A variety of parallel factors can be conceptualized as barriers to and facilitators of juvenile crime victims' seeking professional help. For instance, the seeking of professional help is more likely when children's symptoms are more severe, particularly when they involve aggressive, disruptive, and acting-out behaviors. It is also more likely when parents are distressed themselves and have experience with or current involvement in the mental health system. Reliance on alternative, nonprofessional help sources can be associated with the choice to not seek additional help, and some professional help sources fail to refer. Also, schools play an important role in this process, with juveniles getting more mental health services when these are provided through schools. Concerns about autonomy and a desire to handle things on their own stand out among the reasons people give for bypassing services.

In contrast to these barriers, a small body of research points to the potential advantages for victims of reporting and seeking mental health help. Victims and families report relatively high levels of satisfaction after having reported, and randomized studies show that victims can benefit from treatment.

Implications of the Review

Several implications can be drawn from these findings for efforts to stimulate reporting and help-seeking. First, since perceptions of seriousness play a role in both police reporting and help-seeking, a program to educate the public and promote public awareness about the seriousness of these victimizations and their potential impacts are likely important priorities. Recent examples of such successful efforts include education and media efforts leading to greater awareness of juvenile and adolescent sex offenses, for which police reports have increased greatly in recent years.[340–342] Information needs to be conveyed not only to victims but also to parents and others who work with children, since they have a great deal of influence over how situations are defined and what gets referred.

The research also makes clear the important role that schools play in access to both justice and mental health services. In the case of mental health services, schools play a facilitative role. In the case of justice, it is not clear whether schools are a barrier to the more formal justice system or the dispenser of alternative justice that may be better suited to the parties involved. But obviously those concerned with the response to juvenile crime victims need to work with schools to make sure that the justice and mental health needs of victims are satisfied. Educators may need more training about youth victimization and more formal protocols for making referrals. The move toward assigning mental health and law enforcement officials (called School Resource Officers) to schools and giving them office space in school facilities seems a warranted step in facilitating communication and referrals. But other steps short of full co-location would make police and mental health professionals more accessible to schoolchildren and could promote more police reporting and seeking of helping services by crime victims.

The literature also suggests that there are prejudices about and stigmas attached to both police reporting and the seeking of mental health help that could potentially be broken down. In one study, families were much more likely to report to the police when they had prior experience with the police or when they were advised by other trusted persons to report.[278] This suggests that some barriers can be overcome relatively easily through familiarity and encouragement. Police might take advantage of this in a variety of ways. Procedures for accessing both resources could be made more "user friendly," as the Community Policing Initiative has proved. For example, specially trained juvenile victimization officers may make reporting to the police a more pleasant experience for families and children. Mental health services might improve child victim receptivity by providing more immediate and emergency consultations, reducing waiting times, and providing home visits (something that police are often willing to do). Both sources could also produce educational materials that give a more accurate and positive image of the kind of reception and attention that victims might expect to receive.

Special efforts need to be made in particular to undercut the prejudices among teenagers about police and mental health institutions. Both institutions are seen as compromising teenagers' claims to self-sufficiency, autonomy, and independence, and as antagonistic to youth values and aspirations. But there are ways both institutions could align themselves with youth aspirations as well, particularly around victim services, for example, by helping young people achieve justice, respect, and independence. To the extent that both police and mental health services can redefine what they offer, not as help to those who cannot help themselves but in terms of enhancing options and achieving justice or power, they may circumvent one of the bigger attitudinal obstacles.

The research is less clear about the degree to which financial factors are barriers to police reporting and help-seeking. However, there are steps that could be taken to enhance the material incentives that might improve the situation. For instance, victim compensation systems in many areas are not well publicized and are slow. Police are not active in publicizing such benefits. Beyond money, there are other incentives that youth might respond to. For example, they might respond positively (in both reporting to police and consulting mental health services) if they knew they could receive valuable help and information that would protect them and their friends. It does seem as though there are many avenues that could be explored to enhance reporting if a concerted campaign were inaugurated toward this goal.

A Conceptual Framework for Analyzing Barriers

Another use for the foregoing review is to suggest a conceptual framework to help analyze and improve the police reporting and help-seeking processes. Here again there are parallels to the two processes that suggest a common conceptual framework might be applied. In this framework, the barriers to both reporting and help-seeking might be usefully broken into two types: (1) those that inhibit the recognition of a problem for which a service would be relevant and (2) those that inhibit or discourage the accessing of the services, even after some possible need or relevance is recognized. This has led us to propose the following two-stage conceptual

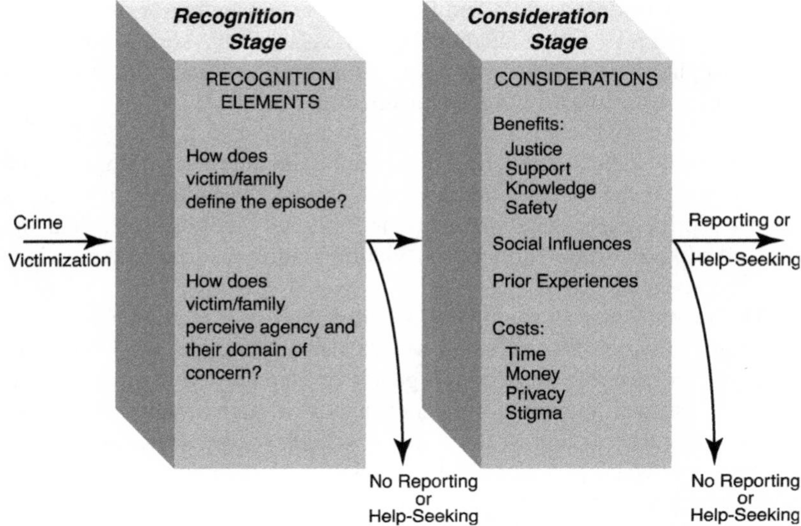

FIGURE 6.1. Two-stage model of police reporting and victim help-seeking.

model about the problems of police reporting and seeking victim services; the model is illustrated in Figure 6.1.

The first stage of this model is called the Recognition Stage. It posits that before police reporting or help-seeking can occur in the wake of an episode of violence or victimization, the victim or victim's family needs to recognize the relevance of the events to some external social agency. In the case of the police, this means recognizing that the police would probably be concerned about the event. In the case of a mental health agency, this means recognizing that a mental health agency has a service to offer someone who has had such an experience. The barriers to recognition of this relevance can occur at a number of levels:

1. The victim or victim's family may not know about the existence of a particular class of agency or service. This is more likely to be true in the case of mental health assistance than of police.
2. The victim or victim's family may know of the agency but not the range of events that falls within its purview (e.g., they may know mental health agencies exist but think they are only for psychiatrically disturbed people, or they may think that police are strictly concerned with crimes committed against adults).
3. The victim or victim's family may know of the service but believe that the episode in question does not qualify for the agency's level of concern. That is, they may think that the crime is too minor or that the harm to the victim does not qualify as serious trauma.

4. The victim or victim's family may fail to conceptualize the event as a crime or a victimization. If a person sees a physical assault as a fight, then the idea that police or mental health services might be relevant would never enter his or her mind.

Obviously factors that affect recognition include such things as the seriousness of the offense, the degree of injury, the victim's or victim's family's prior experience with similar kinds of victimizations, and the amount of knowledge the victim or victim's family has about the various relevant agencies.

The second stage of the model is called the Consideration Stage. It is the stage in which the victim or victim's family weighs the benefits of accessing or invoking the service, agency, or help they have recognized as relevant; assesses any costs or risks connected to such access; and is open to the influence of their social network or prior experience. Barriers to access occur when costs are thought to outweigh the potential benefits or when members of a social network discourage such reporting. Temporally, the Consideration Stage occurs subsequent to the Recognition Stage, once the relevance of an agency has been considered, but in practice these considerations may occur simultaneously, and some of the factors that affect Recognition also affect Consideration.

Some of the generic benefits that victims and families consider are justice, support, knowledge, and safety. So in the case of police, the victim or victim's family may consider it a benefit of reporting that (a) the police will catch and punish the offender or return stolen property, (b) the police will help them understand what happened or gather information about the crime, or (c) the police will help protect them or other people from similar events in the future. In the case of mental health service, the victim or victim's family may consider benefits to include sympathy, protection against negative effects of the crime, or improved understanding about what happened.

On the other hand, some of the generic costs that victims and families will consider in getting involved with an agency are time, money, privacy, stigma, and the risk of revictimization. In the case of police reporting, specific concerns that fall into the cost category are things such as retaliation by the offender or getting caught up in the machinery of the legal system and the time and energy that it will require. In the case of victims' service agencies, the costs that the victim or victim's family may consider include the stigma of being seen as mentally ill, the expense involved in paying for services, and time taken away from other activities.

While this two-stage process helps to organize some of the factors that go into reporting and seeking help, there are other sequences that occur somewhat apart from the model. Police, for example, can find out about the crime independently—from an observer, from the offender, or by just being at the scene—in which case victim and family decision making does not play a role. Similarly, counseling can be undertaken or even imposed on victims for problems that may not be viewed as related to the victimization, even if they are. One study found that schools may connect child victims to counseling even when parents have not recognized the need because the schools see the victims' possibly aggressive or disruptive behavior as needing management in the school environment.[301] Thus there are some limitations to the universality of this proposed conceptual framework.

There are also other conceptual frameworks used to understand help-seeking behavior, particularly in the health-care field, such as the Health Belief Model,[343] the health-care access model of Anderson and Aday,[344,345] the Trans-Theoretical Model of Change,[346] and the Social Organization Strategy Model.[347] All of these models have elements potentially useful for understanding the process of police reporting and crime-victim help-seeking and in the identification of important potential variables. But for the most part, their level of generality, as with the Trans-Theoretical Model, or their specificity to health care, as with the health-care access model, make them less useful than the model proposed here, which captures some of the unique concerns operating in the context of crime victimization decision making.

Conclusion

In the public-health arena, the topic of health-care utilization has become a major area of research and conceptualization. There is an obvious parallel field of justice-system-resource utilization, but it has been much less well developed. If there is any population that warrants analysis from this perspective, it is child victims of crimes. As society struggles to provide some measure of justice and healing to this group, it is hard to think of any other topic where new research and analysis would have more immediate policy and practice applications.

Chapter 7

Good News: Child Victimization Has Been Declining—But Why?

There have been some fascinating and important recent developments about child victimization that have not received much attention. Various types of child abuse and crimes against children have been declining since the early 1990s, and in some cases declining dramatically (for information on sources for the following trends, see Table 7.1):

- Sexual abuse started to decline in the early 1990s, after at least 15 years of steady increases. From 1990 to 2005, sexual abuse substantiations went down 51% (Fig. 7.1).
- Physical abuse substantiations joined the downward trend starting in the mid-1990s, in a decline that was most dramatic between 1997 and 2000. From 1992 through 2005, physical abuse substantiations declined 46% (Fig. 7.1).
- Sexual assaults of teenagers have dropped, according to the National Crime Victimization Survey (NCVS). From 1993 to 2005, overall sexual assaults decreased 52% (Fig. 7.2). The subgroup of sexual assaults by known persons decreased even more.
- Other crimes against juveniles 12 to 17 years old have also gone down dramatically, as measured by the NCVS (Fig. 7.2). Aggravated assault went down 69%, simple assault down 59%, robbery down 62%, and larceny down 54%. This has been in the context of a crime decline for victims of all ages.

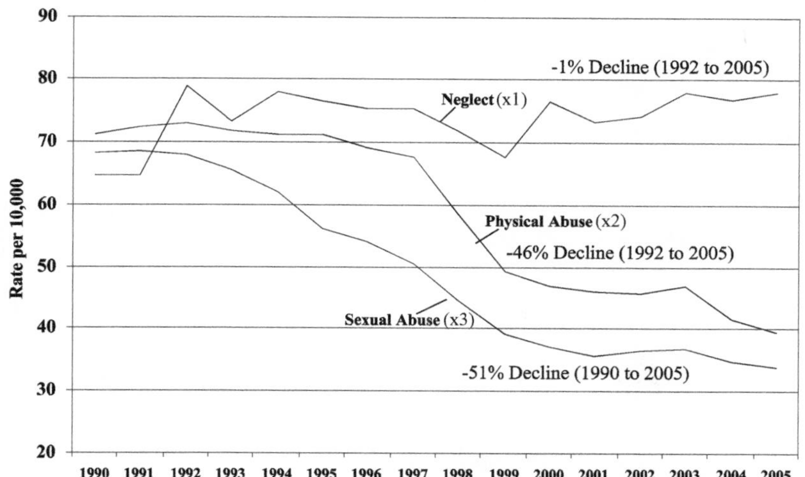

FIGURE 7.1. U.S. trends in child maltreatment, 1990 to 2005. Declines calculated from peak year by rate to 2005: neglect calculated 1992 to 2005, physical abuse 1992 to 2005, sexual abuse 1990 to 2005. *Source*: U.S. Department of Health and Human Services, Administration on Children, Youth and Families. (2007). *Child Maltreatment 1990–2005: Reports from the states to the National Child Abuse & Neglect Data System*. Washington, DC: U.S. Government Printing Office.

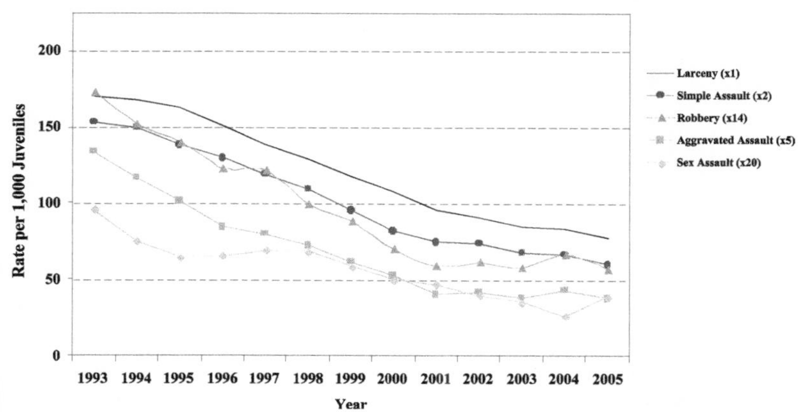

FIGURE 7.2. Juvenile victimization trends, 1993 to 2005 (NCVS). Ages 12 to 17 years; 3-year averages. Percentage declines are as follows: larceny—54%; simple assault—59%; robbery—62%; aggravated assault—69%; sex assault—52%. *Source*: U.S. Department of Justice, Bureau of Justice Statistics. (2006). *National Crime Victimization Survey, 1993–2004*. Survey conducted by U.S. Department of Commerce Bureau of the Census. 8th ICPSR ed. Ann Arbor, MI: Inter-University Consortium for Political and Social Research.

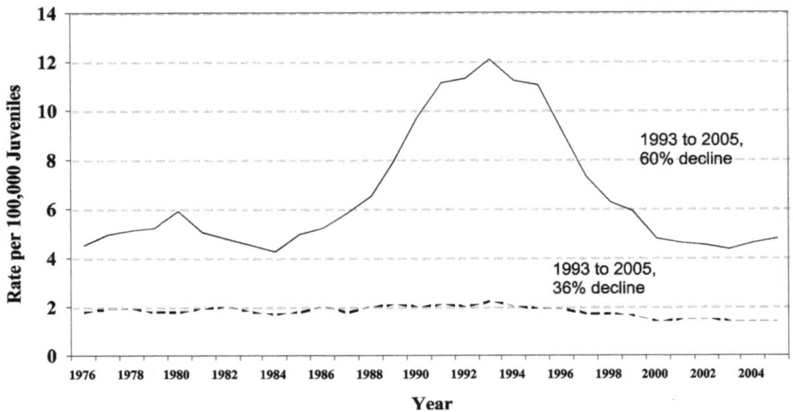

FIGURE 7.3. Juvenile homicide trends, 1976 to 2005. Solid line: juveniles 14 to 17 years old; dotted line: juveniles under 14 years old. *Source*: Fox, J. A., & Zawitz, M. W. (2007). *Homicide trends in the United States*. Retrieved September 19, 2007, from http://www.ojp.usdoj.gov/bjs/homicide/teens.htm.

- Juvenile-victim homicides declined 48% from 1993 to 2005, a drop that was larger than the 40% drop in homicide for victims 18 years and older. The drop has been more dramatic for youth 14 through 17 years old (down 60%) than for younger children (down 36%) (Fig. 7.3).
- Intimate partner violence has also been declining; according to the NCVS[348] rates went down 55% between 1993 and 2004, meaning that children were probably being exposed to fewer violent parents.

This chapter provides some speculation on why these declines have been occurring. First we consider the question of whether these are real trends or only statistical or administrative artifacts. Then we try to characterize the declines in terms of their dimensions and commonalities, and we designate some core features that need to be explained. We illustrate the benefit of looking at these trends in a comprehensive, holistic way. Then we review explanations that have been forwarded for the declines, many of them from the field of criminology, evaluating the extent to which they account for some of the core features. Finally, we suggest some implications of the declines for public policy, practice, and research.

Is the Improvement Real?

Some of the statistics showing declines have provoked skepticism,[349] particularly the drop in sexual abuse. Because the sexual abuse (and other child maltreatment) figures are based on reported cases known to and substantiated by state child protection agencies, observers have speculated that the decline might not be real. The drop might simply reflect changed standards for investigation; decreased reporting to agencies; reduced funding, staff, and interest; or statistical or other artifacts.[349,350]

But after considerable efforts to study the Child Protective Services (CPS) data in context, we have concluded that they probably reflect at least in part a real decline in sexual abuse. The following are among the most important findings that suggest that the sexual abuse declines are real:[350]

1. The decline in agency statistics is paralleled by declines in victim self-reports from at least two other sources, the NCVS (data on sexual assault to teens by known persons) and a statewide survey of students in Minnesota.[351]
2. The patterns in the CPS data do not bear the hallmarks of declines owing to decreased reporting, changed standards, or other artifactual explanations. For example, declines are strong for all categories of reporting source and for all types of sexual abuse. Cases with more equivocal or problematic evidence have not declined more than other cases.[350,351]
3. There have been declines in the most clear-cut, unambiguous, and uncontroversial cases of sexual abuse, such as those involving offender confessions and sexually transmitted diseases.[350]
4. Other closely related child welfare indicators have also declined over the same period. For example, in addition to other forms of juvenile and adult crime victimization, there have also been declines in teen suicide, running away, juvenile delinquency, and teen pregnancy.[353,354] These other problems are generally thought to be outcomes of or connected to sexual abuse. The related declines, from independent data sources, give plausibility to the decline in sexual abuse.

Much of the same argument applies to the decline in physical child abuse. The agency data probably reflect a real decline because there are confirmatory victim surveys, broad declines across categories, and few indications of data artifacts.

The downward trend shown for juvenile victims (and adult victims) in the NCVS data has prompted less skepticism. The NCVS is a large national survey conducted for many years under rigorous conditions by the Census Bureau for the U.S. Department of Justice. Questions have been posed about whether some methodological factors might have lowered NCVS incidence,[355] but the dramatic drops uncovered by the NCVS have been backed up by parallel changes noted in police statistics from the Uniform Crime Reporting system.[355,356] Almost all criminologists accept the NCVS's evidence for a major crime decline,[17,357,358] and there is little reason to believe the juvenile victim trend is any less valid than the overall pattern.

The Breadth and Variety of Declines

The evidence for major declines is fairly strong and well accepted among criminologists. Some of the details of the declines, however, are more complex and less widely acknowledged. These details, if they show variable patterns in what declined and among whom, could provide clues about what was behind the trend. However, most of the declines have not occurred in patterns that would give strong clues. For example, the declines have been pervasive in regional and demographic terms. The sexual abuse declines have occurred in 41 states and the physical abuse declines in 38 states, with no apparent regional pattern.[352] The NCVS declines have also shown little regional variation. There is little evidence that the declines were confined to certain races or ethnic groups.[2]

The declines have also occurred across a broad range of victimization types. They include victimizations that are rare, serious, regionally variable, and indicative of more pathological circumstances like homicide, but they also include victimizations that are fairly common, such as simple assaults. This is important because some of the factors that affect homicide trends, such as gun availability and the quality of medical care, are not likely to be factors in explaining trends for simple assaults among youth.

The declines have also occurred across victimizations that involve different motives and contributory factors. For example, victimizations that occur primarily at the hands of adult caregivers, such as physical abuse, have declined, but so have victimizations that occur primarily at the hands of other youth, such as peer assaults against teenagers. Offenses that have their etiology in frustrated and incompetent parenting have declined, but so have those that have their etiology in sexual deviation. Some of these offenses are probably sensitive to short-term and situational stresses (for example, child abuse may increase when child care is no longer available or affordable). But other child victimizations may involve more long-developing etiological factors (like sexual deviations).

Our analysis of the sexual abuse decline, for example, found that both extrafamilial and intrafamilial offenses were down.[349] This may mean that pedophiles—persons with an enduring disturbance of sexual orientation and who are much more numerous in the extrafamilial-offender population—have been as affected as incestuous abusers, who are typically considered situational offenders.[359]

One large exception to the overall decline pattern, however, concerns child neglect. Whereas declines occurred first in sexual and then a few years later in physical abuse, child neglect, one of the other major categories of child maltreatment, has *not* declined. By 2005, substantiated neglect cases were down just 1% from a peak in 1992 (see Fig. 7.1), making neglect one of the few forms of child victimization that did not show a marked decline for the decade. The trend for neglect may be misleading, however. One analysis suggests that a true, underlying decline in neglect has been masked in recent years by an expansion of definitions and identification efforts.[352] There have been recent child welfare mobilizations regarding the children of drug abusers or the children of domestic abusers, whose situations are often categorized as cases of neglect after investigation. Canadian researchers have explained a dramatic rise in neglect in that country as the result of such sensitization factors.[360] An analysis of state data in the United States found at least some evidence consistent with this hypothesis.[352] But if, contrary to these findings, neglect did have a different trend than other forms of child victimization, then this is an important exception that theories of the decline need to explain.

Another exception to the pattern has been the data on child maltreatment fatalities. While homicide in general and child homicide in particular have declined overall, child maltreatment fatalities have not shown such a trend. The rates calculated from state reports by the National Child Abuse and Neglect Data System (NCANDS) went from 1.68 per hundred thousand in 1995 to 2.03 per hundred thousand in 2004,[9] but the rise is probably due to data system changes. (The system began augmenting fatalities known only to child protection agencies with fatalities from other sources.[361]) Child maltreatment fatalities differ from homicide in that they are heavily concentrated among very young children and include many cases, particularly those involving neglect, that would not be viewed by law enforcement officials as homicides. It is likely in our view that the development, implementation and growing use of Child Fatality Review Boards[362] and other intensive forensic efforts have masked a decline in child maltreatment fatalities by identifying child maltreatment as a feature of a considerable number of child deaths that might not have been previously so identified.

The Context for the Declines

As already suggested, juvenile victimization has been declining in parallel trends with a number of other closely related social improvements. On the one hand, crime victimization for adults has been declining in almost equal measure with the decline for juveniles. Looking in another direction, other child welfare indicators have also registered improvements during the period that juvenile victimization was declining. Teen suicide fell 41% from 1994 to 2003, although it has risen a bit since then.[363] Births to teens fell 45% from 1991 to 2003.[364,365] The number of children living in poverty declined 24% from 1994 until 1999, when it leveled off.[366–368] Running away declined, both in police statistics and in reports from children and families.[354] The 1990s also saw an improvement in child behavior problems and competence scores on the Child Behavior Checklist, reversing an earlier period of significant deterioration in this widely used child assessment measure.[369]

One other indicator not synchronized with the general trend was juvenile drug use. The use of illegal drugs continued to rise in the 1990s (after a drop in the previous decades), and it only started to decline in the late 1990s. For example, illegal drug use among eighth graders declined 27% from 1998 to 2004.[370]

Taken together, a large number of child welfare indicators were showing improvement, mostly starting in 1993 or 1994. These improvements may be independent or connected, but their conjunction is thought provoking when it comes to formulating explanations.

The Timing of the Declines

The data suggest that the child victimization declines of the 1990s were something new, and not simply the extension of trend lines from the past. For example, available data on child abuse show strong increases in all forms of maltreatment from the mid-1970s into the 1990s.[64,80,371] After a short plateau, the sexual abuse decline seemed to start in 1992, and the physical abuse decline gained momentum after 1996. Many analysts did not interpret the earlier rise as necessarily indicative of a real increase in child maltreatment but rather as the result of a new public and professional mobilization to identify and report cases. But some data suggested real increases in the 1980s.[80] Nonetheless, the decreases of the 1990s meant that something had changed, and that needs to be explained.

Similarly, the declines in the 1990s in the NCVS crime victimization rates are not simple extensions. NCVS trends show fluctuations prior to the 1990s, with violent crime up from 1973 to 1981, then down during the mid-1980s, and then up again from the mid-1980s until 1993. Homicide data also show a big rise in youth victim homicide in the late 1980s prior to the drop in the 1990s. So youth crime victimization also went up in the 1980s before declining more recently.

In another similar pattern, Land and his colleagues[372] analyzed some three dozen indicators of child well-being and concluded that there had indeed been a deterioration of the overall social environment for children from the mid-1970s until the 1990s, but then a variety of indicators appeared to turn positive after 1993. So a number of independent sources suggest that the improvements of the 1990s were a departure from what had been happening just before.

Explanations for the Declines

In the social science discussions of social trends in the 1990s, most of the attention has been given to the general decline in crime.[17,357,358,373] In fact, much of that discussion has been confined to homicide or other serious crimes such as robbery. But homicides are relatively rare events subject to effects from relatively local conditions (e.g., gang outbreaks). Factors relevant to homicide may have little to do with trends for something much more general, such as simple assaults against juveniles. In addition, none of the discussion about the crime decline has factored in the information about child maltreatment or some of the other improving child well-being indicators, which may well be related and direct the attention to a broader range of factors than do discussions of homicide and other serious crime.

So the following discussion starts by reviewing some of the major factors that have been mentioned in regard to the crime decline, but it brings in considerations that have not been widely discussed in that literature. In general, little empirical evidence is currently available to evaluate any of these factors and their explanatory power, so the discussion will of necessity be speculative. The main goal is to see which of these factors have the power to account broadly for or at least be consistent with the features of the declines that we have outlined. Among the key features are the simultaneous declines in multiple victimization and child problem indicators, the breadth of the declines across demographics and crime characteristics, and the convergent onset in the mid-1990s. Some of the factors seem to have more explanatory breadth than others.

Factors to Explain Declines in Crime Rates

Several factors come up frequently when sociologists and criminologists discuss the declines in crime that occurred during the 1990s, and these are an obvious place to start when considering explanations for the declines in child victimization. We first discuss two factors that do *not* seem relevant to the juvenile victimization picture: demographic changes and capital punishment policies. We then discuss two other factors that are probably relevant only to juvenile homicide trends and possibly robbery, but not to broader changes: gun control policies and the crack-cocaine epidemic. Finally, we discuss other factors whose contribution to a broader variety of juvenile victimizations is plausible. They include four hypotheses from the crime decline debate that have been frequently discussed: the impact of legalized abortion, improvements in the economy, expansion of imprisonment and other serious legal sanctions, and the hiring of more police and agents of social intervention.

Demography

Demography is a powerful factor in social change, and criminologists have often invoked it to try to explain changes in crime—but they have also often been wrong, as they were when they anticipated a crime boom for the 1990s.[374,375] Some of the obvious demographic suspects were simply not present to predict a drop in juvenile victimization, which is why almost no one anticipated it. There had not been dramatic drops in the size of the youth population during or leading up to the decline.[376] The number of children in the prime juvenile victim pool over age 6 has actually been increasing modestly while the decline in victimization has been occurring.

Many of the changes in family structure during this period have been on the negative side—for example, increasing numbers of children living in single-parent families.[377] Risk models have generally shown that children who are not living with both biological parents are at greater risk for victimization,[93] so changed family structure cannot account for the decline.

There was a modest reversal of the divorce trend, or at least a leveling off of the rate of increase, during the 1990s. It is possible that this has had some ameliorative effect, although it has not been dramatic or long-term enough to be responsible for the large changes of the 1990s.[358] The other strong and obvious demographic development in the United States has been the growth in the percentage of the youth population from minority backgrounds, particularly Hispanic and to some degree Asian backgrounds, and the decline in the percentage from white European backgrounds.[378] Here again, for the most part the growth in the proportion of minority children would have led observers to predict an increase, not a decline, in child-welfare-related problems and child victimization. Victimization rates have generally been found to be higher among minority children, for reasons that are thought to pertain primarily to economic conditions and social stresses.[8] So demographic changes do not provide much leverage in understanding why child victimization may have declined.

Capital Punishment

The 1990s witnessed a dramatic increase in the number of prisoners put to death in the United States, up from 117 executions in the decade of the 1980s to almost 500 in the 1990s. Some researchers have presented arguments in favor of the deterrent effects of capital punishment, while others have disputed such effects.[379–383] While it is possible to hypothesize that capital punishment could deter capital crimes such as homicide, it is hard to construct plausible explanations for how capital punishment would curb the huge volume of relatively less serious offenses committed against youth, especially by other youth, most of which is not reported to police or prosecuted, let alone subject to capital punishment.

Drug Epidemic Trends

In the crime-decline discussion, a great deal of attention has been paid to the role that the crack-cocaine epidemic played. Crack cocaine became a very popular drug in the late 1980s because it produced an intense high and could be purchased at relatively low cost. It was marketed by youth gangs who competed intensely with weapons and violence for shares in this lucrative market, and it appears to have been responsible for a steep increase in homicides of young people in the late 1980s.[357] The crack-cocaine epidemic then subsided in the 1990s, and markets became more stable and the related violence abated. Although this factor could well have been responsible for the rise and fall of homicide, gang violence, and drug-related robberies, particularly in certain localities, it seems less well suited to explain the broader declines in child victimization and improvement in child welfare that occurred in the 1990s. The fact that child victimizations declined over such broad demographic areas, including in rural areas and rural states and for both whites and minorities, and that it included declines in simple assault for younger youth and sexual abuse, all suggest something beyond the crack-cocaine-epidemic abatement.

In recent years alarms have been sounded about a new drug epidemic—this one involving methamphetamine—and its possible impact on child maltreatment and crime.[384] With the exception of homicide in some selected urban areas, few of the indicators of crime and child maltreatment showed any sign of an increase in the most recent years available up to 2004.

Gun Policy

A variety of gun control laws have been enacted in attempts to reduce crime, such as the Brady Handgun Violence Prevention Act of 1993 and other laws increasing penalties. A crackdown on guns in the hands of juveniles was widely touted as the cause of a dramatic decline in youth homicides in Boston in the 1990s.[385] While some criminologists have contemplated the impact of these laws on the most serious of violent crimes, such as homicide, it seems unlikely that they had much impact on the broader spectrum of juvenile victimizations we have been describing, including child abuse. The vast majority of offenses against juveniles do not involve guns. This is especially true of physical and sexual abuse. Such laws would also be very unlikely to explain the improvement in other child welfare indicators.

The previous four factors probably had little to do with the broad decline in general child victimizations or in the other improving child welfare indicators, with the exception of homicide, which may have been affected by changes in the drug market and gun availability. The next four factors to be considered, however, could have had much broader effects, especially if considered in somewhat broader terms than has been the case in some of the criminology discussions.

Wanted Children, Fertility Factors, and the Legalization of Abortion

In their popular book *Freakonomics*, economist Steven Levitt and a colleague have given great visibility to the hypothesis that crime declined in the 1990s as a result of ripple effects from the legalization of abortion in the 1970s.[386–388] Five states legalized abortion in 1970, and *Roe v. Wade* legalized abortion for the rest of the country in 1973. According to this theory, the ensuing decline in fertility affected crime because it reduced the number of what would have been otherwise unwanted children who would ultimately have been at greater risk of commiting crimes. As one might expect from a theory touching on the abortion controversy, this has been a hotly debated idea.[389–391]

The argument might have generated considerably less controversy if it had centered less on abortion and rather highlighted the idea of women and families making various fertility and contraception decisions that have allowed the birth of fewer unwanted children and have enabled more children to grow up in environments in which there are adequate financial, supervisory, and emotional resources. This trend has been facilitated not only by the availability of abortion but, perhaps even more considerably, by the availability of contraception. The changing role of women and changes in the desired number of children have also contributed to declining birth rates, decreased family size, and increased spacing between child births.[392] Unfortunately, the focus on abortion alone likely stems from two factors: continuing controversy about abortion and the fact that the effect of abortion legalization on fertility was a dramatic statistical event occurring in a short time frame, which makes its effects easier to analyze than other effects on fertility.

Reduction in unwanted children is a fertility change that could indeed have some of the broad impacts we might be looking for in the way of an explanation. It could have had a positive impact on many different kinds of child victimization, and it could also help explain other child welfare indicators. Presumably, wanted children would experience less child maltreatment. They would grow up with better supervision and parental instruction, perhaps leading to less victimization. They might encounter fewer adversities and disadvantages that would lead to risk taking and aggressive behavior.

Is there any evidence for such effects outside the general crime trend data? Indeed, an analysis by Sorenson, Wiebe, and Berke [393] finds that the legalization of abortion may have been associated with a subsequent decrease in the homicides of children ages 1 to 4. The researchers did not find a significant effect, however, on the homicide of children under 1 year of age—an important omission, since many homicides of young children seem to be motivated specifically by a desire to dispose of an unwanted child.[394] Nonetheless, the failure to find effects for the very young children may have been due to the fact that not long after *Roe*, dramatic efforts were undertaken across the country by child welfare and law enforcement to investigate and identify homicides of young children and distinguish them from accidental fatalities, a movement epitomized by the development of child fatality review teams all across the country.[362] This effort may have been most successful in identifying homicides of infants, whose deaths have always been among the most difficult to investigate. Such differential increases in the rate may have masked the effects that were strictly a result of abortion legalization. Other researchers have concluded that increased abortion availability reduced the likelihood by 40% to 60%

of children's dying in infancy, being born into a single-parent family, or living in poverty or as a welfare recipient.[395]

Although an increase in the proportion of wanted children in the cohort, boosted by abortion legalization, might be an important piece of the puzzle, several results that one might expect from such a scenario are not immediately apparent, and their absence at least calls for further investigation. If abortion legalization resulted in a marked increase in the percentage of wanted children in a new cohort of children, then the effect of this change should be visible as a ripple of improvement moving forward as the cohort gets older. Thus, long before one saw a reduction in the amount of homicide committed by that cohort's young men, presumably one would have seen a reduction in the amount of child maltreatment committed against that cohort as young children. What is curious about the improved indicators in crime, child maltreatment, and other child welfare factors is that they seem to have had a simultaneous onset in the mid-1990s. Why weren't the homicide declines of the 1990s preceded by dramatic declines in child maltreatment in the 1970s and 1980s, during the formative years of the *Roe v. Wade* cohort?

As indicated earlier, the data generally show big increases in reports of child physical and sexual abuse throughout the 1970s and 1980s and no drop until the mid-1990s. Of course, it may be that increased reporting efforts in the earlier period masked underlying reductions that actually had been occurring. But the NCVS-based crime victimization increases of the 1980s are harder to dismiss. Moreover, Land's trend data for child well-being indicators mostly show a deterioration in the 1970s and 1980s.[372] In other words, there are limited indications of what demographers call a "cohort effect"—a change limited to the experience only of people born at or after a specific time. The declines, with their changes to groups both young and old around the early 1990s, have more the signature of a "period effect" than a cohort effect.

Another puzzle not easily explained by the *Roe* explanation is why sexual abuse might have been at the leading edge of the decline in child maltreatment. Sexual abusers have an age profile considerably older than other violent criminals, as well as than other child abusers.[5] They tend to be men in their 30s and older who victimize preadolescent or adolescent children. This contrasts with physical abusers and neglecters, who more frequently target younger children and are themselves younger parents.[396] In the early and mid-1990s, when the sexual abuse decline started, the members of the prime sexual-abuser-recruitment pool of men age 25 and older would have been unaffected by the *Roe* decision, as they would have been born well before the ruling. The offenses of younger men and younger parents (e.g., physical abuse and neglect) should have been at the leading edge of a decline related to a ripple from fertility changes started in 1973.

These anomalies do not rule out a role for a wanted-child effect. The wanted-child effect may have been operating in conjunction with other factors that explain some of the anomalies we have highlighted. Moreover, the detailed quantitative analyses conducted on this issue illustrate the level of empirical inquiry that might be undertaken for many of the hypotheses discussed in this chapter. Nonetheless, the doubts about this hypothesis make it somewhat questionable as a sufficient explanation for the phenomena we are trying to explain.

Economic Prosperity

The 1990s were a time of increasing prosperity in the United States. There was considerable job growth, hourly wages rose, and considerable social and occupational mobility occurred.[397] Notably, the percentage of children living in poverty declined, and, maybe most important, many people who had been chronically unemployed or underemployed were able to work or work more. The graph of the unemployment rate has a drop that looks very similar in the 1990s to the trend for sexual abuse substantiations. Criminologists have endorsed prosperity as a likely candidate in the crime decline,[355,358] and Land[372] cites it as a probable factor in the broad improvement of child trends.

One appeal of an explanation linked to the prosperity of the 1990s is that the effects might have been broad and fairly simultaneous for large groups of people. If economic prospects are looking up, everyone may be feeling more positive. Increasing opportunities create a greater stake in conformity[398] and more costs to deviance, since rule breakers may miss out on the rising tide. Large segments of the population, including both the young and the old, may have more to do. A wide variety of stresses may decline and interpersonal relationships may improve, both inside and outside the family. Prosperity might have been responsible for reductions in crime committed by adults and by children, crime in rural and urban areas, and crime within the family as well as outside the family. One might expect those who are newly employed, like young adults, to be those most dissuaded from crime and maltreatment, but it is easy to imagine that these positive prospects might have also affected young people not in the labor market at nearly the same time through increased optimism.

At least one observer, though, has discounted the prosperity of the 1990s as a factor in the overall crime decline,[373] arguing that historical studies generally show a small relationship between unemployment and crime, and that whatever effect occurs is almost exclusively related to property crime and not violent crime. It is our sense, however, that the topic has not been sufficiently studied to draw a firm conclusion, and that the impacts of different boom times may be different and may have differential effects on different kinds of crime and social problems.

One puzzle in regard to the prosperity explanation, of course, is the salience of the declines in sexual assault and sexual abuse. Sexual abuse has conventionally been one of the child welfare problems that we have believed to be least associated with social class and economic deprivation.

Studies have not shown systematically higher rates of sexual abuse in deprived families or systematically higher perpetration rates among disadvantaged adults, at least not to the same extent as one finds deprivation to be associated with problems such as teen pregnancy, domestic violence, and violent crime. In fact, one important question is why, if prosperity is the main explanation, the rates of neglect did not decline while sexual abuse stayed the same rather than vice versa.

Nonetheless, it may be true that prosperity, and particularly the prosperity of the 1990s, was a factor in the decline of sexual abuse. The prosperity of the 1990s may have strongly benefited the marginal middle class, in particular underemployed men or employed men unhappy with their jobs. As employment problems are a risk factor for offending,[399, 400] some of the men in this category at risk to molest may have gotten new work or become busier with their work during this time, had much less free time on their hands to spend around children, and encountered exciting possibilities in their work and professional lives that they had not had before. Maybe young people themselves had more to do that took them out of risky environments. Maybe some of the prosperity of the 1990s acted in ways that were more specifically associated with the occurrence of sexual abuse.

Obviously, if the prosperity of the 1990s was a key factor in the decline of child victimization and crime, one test of that hypothesis may be to note what happened when the prosperity slowed in the early 2000s. We should presumably have seen a concomitant plateau or rise in incidence of crime and victimization. Interestingly, the newest data from the early 2000s show some moderations but mostly continued declines. These occurred at a time when the unemployment rate was going up again. That is at least one hopeful sign that the declines will not be easily reversed by deteriorating economic fortunes, but it does not lend reinforcement to the idea that prosperity played a role in producing the declines.

Incarceration and Incapacitation

In analyzing the crime decline of the 1990s, almost all analysts are in agreement that the dramatically increased number of incarcerated offenders was a major factor.[17,358,373] It was an indicator that started to change, as it should have, in advance of the drop. It is also a factor that has stood up to statistical analyses. Some detailed quantitative studies have suggested that one-third to one-half of the general crime decline was due to growth in the prison population.[401]

However, one problem with the incarceration hypothesis in regard to child victimization is that many of the offenses children suffer are not typically punished by incarceration. The youth who beat up and steal from other youth do not often end up incarcerated, even in youth facilities. Physically abusive parents only rarely end up in prison. So these offender populations, unlike the general criminal offender population, were not thinned as a result of increased imprisonment.

One type of youth victimization, though, that may have been affected by increased incarceration is sexual abuse. According to Bureau of Justice Statistics data, there was a tripling in the number of child sex offenders incarcerated in state prisons between 1986 and 1997, up from 19,000 to over 63,000,[402] and it was almost certainly quite a bit higher by 2005. High-frequency offenders are more likely to get incarcerated, so potentially small increases in incarceration of high-volume offenders can have large effects on the overall offense rate. Large increases in incarceration could possibly have even more dramatic effects. But even with sexual abuse, a problem with the incarceration theory is that some classes of child molesters, such as incestuous abusers, are much less likely to be incarcerated than others. Curiously, based on available data, it would appear that intrafamily abuse has declined as much as other child molesting, if not more.[350] Adolescent perpetrators are a group encompassing as much as a third of all sexual abusers, but they also are less likely than adults to be incarcerated, even though such incarcerations have also increased.[6] Offenses by adolescent sexual abusers appear to have declined in CPS data as much as offenses by adults.[350] Increased incarceration may have possibly resulted in a general deterrent effect on all offenders. But then the effects of incarceration become difficult to distinguish from some of the other theories, which also posit mechanisms that would generally deter offending. In any case, if incarceration is a key mechanism, it should have its greatest effect on the classes of individuals most likely to be incarcerated. So even in the case of sexual abuse, other factors must be at work, and incarceration does not explain why the declines have occurred across the board.

Agents of Social Intervention, Police, and Others

In analyzing the general crime decline, another factor that has been widely debated is the role of increased policing. Funds were made available in the 1990s through various mechanisms, but in particular the Omnibus Crime Bill of 1994 allowed the hiring of tens of thousands of additional police. The stated goal was 100,000 new officers, but Uniform Crime Reports data suggest the increase for the decade was 50,000 to 60,000, or roughly a 14% increase.[373] Politicians eager to take credit for the crime decline have pointed to the putative success of this and related measures. But some observers have dismissed the policing hypothesis, arguing that the decline began well before the federal money for new officers began to flow into local government coffers. It also might superficially seem as though increased policing is not a very potent explanation for something like the decline in physical abuse. While more police patrolling the streets might deter gangs and property crime, do they really keep men from sexually abusing their daughters or mothers from scalding their babies?

But if the increased-policing hypothesis is thought of as an increase in more generalized agents and mechanisms of social intervention, then a broad range of juvenile victimizations might indeed have been affected by this buildup. For example, along with increases in the number of police, there were increases in the number of social workers, child protection workers, and people engaged in various child safety and child abuse prevention activities.[403] The new police activities in place by the early 1990s included not just community patrols but also specialized domestic violence units with a mandate to intervene aggressively in violent families,[293] specialized sexual assault officers to work in the investigation and prosecution of sexual abuse inside and outside of families,[404, 405] and specialized school resource officers trained to reduce the quantity of youth-on-youth victimization.[406] This diversification of police activity was accompanied by a diversification of prosecutorial activity, as district attorneys took on domestic violence, sexual abuse, and in some cases even juvenile crime. The mental health profession also increased the number of its professionals who were working consciously in social control activities such as facilities for delinquent youth, offender treatment programs in prisons and in the community, and anticrime activities through work with victims.[407]

The presence of these new agents of social control could well have curbed child victimization through a number of mechanisms. These agents were increasingly visible, in both the media and the community, and this presence may have deterred many offenders or would-be offenders. Aggressive youth might be less likely to bully others knowing a police officer is just down the hall. Reading about arrests of child molesters in the news, other molesters may have become less confident that they could get away with a sexual encounter with a child. The new agents also undoubtedly had many cautionary encounters with offenders that may have terminated or reduced offending patterns. The batterer may have been chastened by a police visit to the home. Some of these new agents worked directly with victims, such as victim advocates. Some provided education and valuable prevention information to schoolchildren and parents. This education may have protected children considerably. Some of these agents empowered victims simply through their presence and activism. These agents may have helped victims become more independently resistant to victimization.

In one of the few studies relevant to this explanation, researchers found that domestic homicide rates fell more rapidly in cities with the greatest growth in legal advocacy and other services for victims of domestic abuse.[408] Domestic violence and child victimization are closely related, and similar effects from services and advocacy may apply. Thus, if we think of the 1980s and early 1990s as a time when agents of social intervention, not just police, increased in number, diversity, and approach to a variety of offenses, this makes a plausible explanation for why there might have been declines not just in conventional crime but also in forms of child abuse, child molestation, and youth-on-youth offenses.

One important question about the agents-of-intervention explanation is how it accounts for a decline that got started only in the early 1990s. Some of the expansion of agents of social intervention dates far back to the 1970s and 1980s, when, for example, many new child protection workers were hired and many new domestic violence units were established. It may have been that the first effect of these new agents was to inflate statistics. In fact, some believe that a growth of these agents was what accounts for the big increases in substantiated child maltreatment in the 1970s and 1980s as well as a big spike in police-identified juvenile crime in the 1980s. The theory here is that more juvenile crime was reported because officials were available to crack down on it, and various kinds of domestic assaults (including adolescents threatening their parents) were defined as criminal under new domestic violence policies.[409]

The agents-of-social-intervention explanation may also account for why sexual abuse fell earlier and faster than physical abuse, and why both fell when neglect did not. Although effort is hard to allocate, most observers believe that more intensive prevention and intervention activities were directed at sexual abuse, which typically mobilized members of both law enforcement and child welfare professions.[410] Observers generally agree that despite the large number of cases identified, few law enforcement personnel are involved in neglect intervention or prevention.[295] Nonetheless, the agents-of-social-intervention explanation does not account exactly for why, in the early 1990s, awareness efforts stopped being the main driver in the child abuse statistics and why a real underlying decline either became evident or gained momentum. But it is an explanation that is plausible to the many professionals now working in various fields to prevent and respond to child victimization.

Other Possible Reasons for Juvenile Victimization Declines

The declines in juvenile victimization, and the numerous improvements in child well-being during the same time period, provide an opportunity to consider explanations that go beyond those typically discussed in relation to crime trends. Below, we discuss three hypotheses that have not received much attention: arguments that values have shifted, that a generational change occurred, and that the dissemination of psychiatric medication has had a broad ameliorative impact.

Changing Norms and Practices

It is hard to know to what extent the increasing numbers of social intervention agents were the cause of changes in social norms and public awareness, or whether they were simply a reflection of such changes. But when attempting to explain the broad changes that have been occurring, it would probably be a mistake to attribute them all to the activities of the agents without taking the broader normative shifts into account. Some of this shift needs to be attributed to a broad range of opinion leaders—

activists and volunteers in the fields of education, politics, mental health, social science, journalism, and elsewhere—drawing attention to juvenile victimization issues. At the same time, the population was becoming more educated in general and more exposed to the points of view of activists and professionals. All of this may have contributed to changing norms and attitudes about what is acceptable behavior and what kinds of child safety standards adults need to maintain—norms affecting both potential abusers and those who provide supervision.

As a result of this process, the public has in the last two decades become aware of various types of child victimization that they were less aware of a generation ago. Sexual abuse, of course, is perhaps the most dramatic example of a change in awareness: a problem that was rarely discussed has become one that is frequently the topic of news and educational programs, not to mention major Hollywood films (e.g., *Mystic River*) and best-selling books (e.g., *Bastard Out of Carolina*). But physical abuse, domestic violence, school bullying, and sexual harassment, to name a few, have also received considerable exposure. It is plausible that this greater awareness has resulted in more protective action by families and others who work with children.

Parents may now be more cautious about who they allow to be with their children and under what circumstances. Increased awareness of potential dangers may have affected the choices that women with young children make when they look for new husbands or boyfriends or when they decide on forming a family. Aware people, including aware children, may be quicker to short-circuit and report victimizations.[51]

The awareness has changed the norms. Behaviors that were once tolerated, ignored, or treated as minor—for example, bullying or parents hitting children—have come to be seen as more serious and damaging.[16] This may deter potential offenders from engaging in these behaviors and may make observers more likely to act to stop them when they occur.

The awareness may also have affected the socialization processes of children, leading to less offending behavior. For example, there is generally believed to be some level of intergenerational transmission for aggressive and sexually abusive behavior. As access to mental health services has increased,[411, 412] many childhood victims from previous generations have sought and received some professional help that may have forestalled the repetition of such behaviors in the subsequent generation. But beyond professional help, many survivors of childhood victimization have probably gotten cultural help. Physical and sexual abuse and bullying are topics about which one can learn a considerable amount from the media, friends, and other members of one's social network in the course of growing up. To the extent that victims of physical abuse and sexual abuse do not grow up in a climate of silence or embarrassment about these problems, such experiences may not induce quite the same feelings of shame, guilt, or stigma as they have in the past. The corrosive effects of such experiences may well have been diminished by this more open social environment, leading to less intergenerational transmission. So it is plausible that cultural, educational, and normative factors may have played a role in the declines.

A pattern that one might expect from the changing-norms-and-practices explanation is that measures of real victimization (and other problems) might be going down at the same time that official reports of victimization might actually be going up, owing to the new awareness and concern. Some observers believed this was the case when parent surveys showed declining support for corporal punishment and less violence toward children during the time that the official child abuse reports were rising.[16, 413] Patterns of the early and later 1990s, however, showed more parallel rises and falls in both self-report and official data on some victimizations, such as conventional crime.

Dissipation of the Side Effects of the Cultural Revolution of 1960s

Another cultural-change explanation for the decline contends that we are simply returning to a more historically normal level of social deviance after a period of unusual change.[414] It has been widely recognized that an enormous cultural revolution occurred starting in the 1960s. Aspects of this revolution have been referred to variously as the women's movement, the sexual revolution, the civil rights movement, the Vietnam War protest, and the counterculture. It was marked by an expansion of people's sense of what might be possible, a questioning of established norms, and a delegitimatizing of established institutions such as governments, corporations, and organized religion.

For many of the people it touched, the revolution raised aspirations, undermined oppressive social arrangements, and inspired positive social changes. But it had side effects. For example, it may have created resentment among those who felt left out or unable to take advantage of new opportunities. It may have delegitimatized institutions and social forces that had had some stabilizing effects on certain people, such as traditional religious beliefs and police authority. It may have been particularly troublesome for people who needed to rely strongly on external authority and traditional norms to regulate and control their impulses, in contrast to people who had good internal gyroscopes and could experiment with developing new personal moralities and codes of conduct. Specifically, some people may have interpreted the sexual revolution to mean that all sexual prohibitions, including that against sex with children, were outdated. Some people may have understood the civil rights movement to mean that they were justified in obtaining extralegal restitution for injustices. And some people took the counterculture to mean there was value to the expression of all impulses, including aggressive or sexual ones, whatever the circumstances.[415]

The side effects of the Cultural Revolution may have been behind an increase in criminal and sexually irresponsible behavior. Some of the crime increase in the 1970s, for example, may be a reflection of this phenomenon. But perhaps after 30 years the generation most affected by that revolution has largely aged out of the side effects, the influence of the attitudes that they spawned has dissipated, and the culture has better integrated the changes. A trend supportive of this explanation comes from the Catholic-clergy sexual abuse cases, which show a big rise in the 1960s as this group of authority- and tradition-oriented men tried to cope with the changing culture. The number of cases takes a dramatic drop in the mid-1980s, by which time the clergy and the culture at large had perhaps better integrated the changes.[416] This explanation could account for why rates for a variety of other deviant behaviors and social problems first deteriorated and then improved.

This hypothesis is reasonable for explaining why there was first a boom and then a bust in social problems. But it is an explanation that might be expected to produce differing trends for differing cohorts. So, for example, one might expect that there would have been more continuing levels of deviance by older cohorts as younger cohorts, unaffected by the Cultural Revolution, emerged on the scene. But that is not what the pattern looks like. The deviance by both older and younger cohorts seems to have declined in roughly equal measure. Deviance does decline as people age, meaning that older cohorts have less deviance in all eras. But if a generational change is going on, the relative changes for different age groups should be different.

For this hypothesis to work, then, it would have to argue that somewhat different mechanisms were at work at nearly the same time on different cohorts. That is, the 1960s generation aged out of their deviance at around the same time that the influence of the values of that era waned on the younger cohorts. Another problem is the dramatic character of the downturn. Behaviors and attitudes influenced by generational change tend to be slower to shift. So the "dissipation of the Cultural Revolution" explanation is not fully satisfying.

Psychopharmacology

Another interesting, but generally overlooked, possible explanation for the declines is suggested by the particular timing of their onset in the early and mid-1990s. A technological revolution taking shape around and just prior to that time involved the broad introduction and dissemination of several new classes of psychiatric medication. Prozac (fluoxetine hydrochloride) arrived on the market in 1987, and within 5 years 4.5 million Americans had taken it—the fastest acceptance ever for a psychiatric drug.[417] Along with its descendents, it spurred a sea change in the medical community's and the public's approach to depression, anxiety, and related mental health problems. Large segments of the population are now being treated pharmacologically by primary care physicians, and many of the patients are people who perhaps would never have sought treatment from a psychiatric or mental health professional, particularly men and the less well educated. Data show that the percentage of the population being treated for depression in a given year jumped from 0.7% in 1987 to 2.3% in 1997, and by the end of the period much of that treatment involved drugs.[417, 418]

At the same time, the percentage of youth being treated with psychiatric medication also increased dramatically.[419, 420] One epidemiological analysis suggested that by 1996 fully 6% of young people under the age of 20 had been using prescribed psychotropic medication during the last year, a two- to threefold increase from the previous decade, with the growth concentrated particularly in the period since 1991.[418] Stimulants (such as methylphenidate or Ritalin) were the most common drugs in usage, and antidepressants were close behind. There was an estimated 292% increase between 1990 and 1995 in the rate of school-age children diagnosed with attention-deficit/hyperactivity disorder and prescribed stimulants, with the rise particularly concentrated between 1992 and 1993.[421] By 1998, over 2.3 million office visits per year were for such diagnosis and stimulant-prescription purposes among children ages 5 to 18.[422]

How would the psychopharmacology revolution have made an impact on child victimization, child welfare, and crime in general? There could have been several vectors of influence. First, it certainly seems plausible that when you alleviate chronic depression, discouragement, and despair among a large segment of the population, you might have fewer individuals acting out aggressively and sexually. Second, if you help youth control their impulsive behaviors, as methylphenidate seems to, you may have less delinquency and less risk-taking behavior putting young people in danger of victimization. As young people feel more in control of themselves, they may be less alienated and less drawn to delinquent subgroups and delinquent activities. The psychiatric medications may help improve family life and reduce interpersonal stress, leading to more effective parenting, less child maltreatment, and better supervision. Some of the antidepressant drugs even depress libido, which may be an important factor in the decline of sexual abuse and sexual assault. So psychiatric drugs could have had broad effects on a variety of crimes, both offending and victimization, as well as on other social problems, including running away, risky sexual behavior, and suicidal behavior, for which at least one study suggests time trend benefits.[423]

The psychopharmacology explanation is clearly among the most compelling potential explanations for an onset of decline in the early to mid-1990s. Something dramatically new happened just prior to the decline and affected at least some portion of the at-risk population. It is even more plausible than the economic-prosperity explanation, since much of the prosperity did not trickle down to at-risk individuals until after the crime and victimization declines had already started.[358] Where the psychopharmacology explanation may fail is in accounting for the demographic breadth and universality of the declines. Drugs almost certainly did not disseminate uniformly or simultaneously to all segments of society; they would have reached certain accessible groups and localities before others.[419] When data are available on geography and ethnicity, they do not show smaller declines in groups that one might expect to reflect diminished access to pharmaceuticals. Another puzzle is why the drugs didn't have an even greater ameliorative effect on child neglect, since much neglect is thought to be a function of depressed parents. Another problem is why, if more youth were getting helpful prescription drugs to deal with mood issues, the use of illegal drugs didn't decline as well. Nonetheless, the medication explanation seems like a plausible candidate worthy of further empirical investigation.

Taking Stock: Where Does This Review Leave Matters?

Most important, we believe the evidence for the existence of a decline in youth victimization is extremely strong. It is a reality deserving of much more attention and discussion. Something positive is going on in the social environment. Not only is there encouragement to be drawn from this development, there are also important lessons to be learned. If something is working, it is incumbent on us to find out what and to try to do more of it or expand its impact in some way. For these reasons, we should be highlighting the trends identified here and encouraging as many interested people as possible to search for an understanding of exactly what has been and is going on.

Next, we need to formulate plans to investigate some of the most promising of the explanations, to gather confirmatory or disconfirmatory empirical evidence about them. Based on the arguments and evidence we have reviewed, the explanations of economic prosperity, increased numbers of agents of social intervention, and use of psychiatric pharmacology merit particular investigation. A wide variety of research strategies are warranted. Analyses can be done, for example, using smaller geographic units, such as counties, to see if such factors as changes in economic conditions or prescription levels are associated with the timing and magnitude of changes in child maltreatment and crime victimization. Even prospective intervention designs can be undertaken to see if policies based on providing income enhancements to maltreating families, offering psychiatric medications to abusers or increasing the numbers of child welfare and law enforcement specialists in some areas actually make a difference.

The search for additional explanations needs to be prolonged. The ones reviewed here are certainly not exhaustive. Suggestions have also been made about the possible ameliorative effects of the reduction of environmental lead, increased access to higher education, and the development of the Internet.[424]

International comparisons are also an important source of information for both generating and confirming hypotheses on the declines. Canada, for example, also witnessed a decline in crime during the period when U.S. crime rates were dropping,[424] but since Canada did not expand its prison population or its police force, Canadian analysts have been skeptical that these two factors widely cited by U.S. analysts were actually that consequential. The Canadian National Incidence Study actually documented large increases in overall child maltreatment, physical abuse, neglect, and emotional maltreatment, but stable or declining sexual abuse rates, during the 1990s.[360] However, some Canadian observers believe that most or all of this increase was due to an expansion of abuse categories so that they included children exposed to domestic violence and other family problems.[425]

Ultimately, we think it very unlikely that one particular explanation will account for all of the declines. It is much more likely that the declines are the product of multiple ameliorative factors, and even that different kinds of child victimization have responded to different sets of factors. Thus, economic factors may be responsible for declines in property crime victimization, while psychopharmacology may have had the biggest impact on sex offenses. Factors may have had interacting and mutually reinforcing effects; for example, the adoption of new values may be more rapid in an optimistic environment created by economic progress. There may have also been "tipping point" effects[426] as a certain number of cumulating positive changes occurred that resulted in a sudden, rapid cascade of improvement. The cascade may have occurred, for example, in the growth of people invested in the idea of protecting children from assaults and sexual abuse—certainly a noble and appealing idea. Or the cascade may have been in the idea that one could get in a lot more trouble or lose status acting in violent or abusive ways, especially toward a child. If the change resulted from interactions or self-propagating cascades, providing the evidence for the interaction of various mechanisms and problems will certainly be a challenging research undertaking.

Policy Implications

What are some of the policy implications of these hypotheses if evidence in their favor should become stronger? An obvious implication, not lost on child protection activists and professionals, is that social and technological developments beyond their own narrow sphere of effort may act to leverage (or in theory impede) the objectives they seek with a power even greater than those that they can exert. This kind of influence has long been acknowledged with regard to economics, insofar as most child protection professionals have tended to promote poverty reduction as a component of child safety enhancement. But perhaps more attention should also be paid to other potentially transformative forces such as technology and its ramifications for drug treatment, behavioral management, genetic screening, contraception, family communications, and parenting education. While child protection professionals may not have expertise in these areas, they may have the ability to promote the dissemination and adapt the uses of technologies so that they have faster and more pervasive impacts on reducing child victimization. The fact that little or no research exists on child maltreatment among children or parents using psychiatric medication does suggest that child protection professionals have been slow to envision such a connection. The child protection field may need mechanisms enabling it to better monitor and integrate information from a wide variety of other fields where social, organizational, and technological change may be occurring.

This analysis also suggests renewed attention to the possible connections between economic forces and child maltreatment. While child advocates are in wide agreement that prosperity and antipoverty measures help protect children, there really is not sufficient understanding of what specific economic forces and economic policies result in greater child safety. For example, based on knowledge at the time, child advocates had great qualms about the potential for the welfare reform legislation of 1996 to increase child maltreatment, particularly neglect, because of its work requirements directed at poor mothers and other burdens.[427–429] But for the most part, analysts have been unable to identify any increase in child maltreatment or broader deterioration of child well-being as a result of the 1990s welfare reform.[430,431] This raises the question of whether there are specific kinds of employment opportunities, tax incentives, transfer payments, housing subsidies, or income streams with more or specific effects on various kinds of child safety and child welfare outcomes.[432] If more of the specific mechanisms by which prosperity improves child safety can be discovered, then some targeted programs may be able to continue progress or stave off deterioration even in the event of future economic downturns.

Another policy matter worthy of consideration is how the child welfare improvements detailed in this chapter should be handled in the public and political forums. Some advocates and practitioners have worried that drawing attention to the declines will prompt politicians and policymakers to cut funding and withdraw support, claiming that it is no longer needed. They point to the possibility of this feeding the trends of antigovernment political rhetoric and concerns about growing governmental fiscal exigencies. It is true that rising social-problem rates have been effective in some places and times in promoting and sustaining public and political attention.[29] But the opposite dynamic—the idea that good news means bad news—does not have much precedent. The decline in crime, for example, has received considerable attention but has not inspired calls for reductions in police or prison funding. Advocates in the teenage pregnancy field have actually been quite public in promoting the declines as arguments for continuing efforts. It can be argued that policymakers like to see a return on their investment and often get discouraged when it appears that nothing works. In any case, the era of continually rising numbers of child maltreatment and crime victimization cases is clearly over.

In our view, child welfare advocates should draw attention to the declines in child maltreatment and other forms of child victimization as evidence of an encouraging trend whose momentum should be maintained and accelerated. By almost any standard, levels of child victimization, even after the declines, are still disturbingly high. New issues such as clergy abuse and the increased availability of child pornography have continued to surface. Media attention to child victims has a strong foundation in current journalistic practice and public interest, and it is not going to disappear anytime soon. In the context of continuing education about the size and seriousness of the existing problems, it would seem to make sense to draw greater attention to the declines. We are actually quite baffled about why recent epidemiological reports on child maltreatment have given so little attention to the issue.[9]

In short, we see the declines in child maltreatment and child victimization as an important issue for discussion by researchers, practitioners, and policymakers—people who need to collaborate to understand what is going on and why and what the policy and practice implications are. If we can answer these questions, we may be much closer to extending or even accelerating these trends, and that is a prospect virtually everyone would celebrate.

TABLE 7.1. Description of Data Sources for Trends in Child Victimization

National Child Abuse and Neglect Data System (NCANDS)	Data on trends in sexual and physical abuse were drawn from NCANDS. NCANDS is overseen by the U.S. Department of Health and Human Services (USDHHS) and collects annual data on abused and neglected children known to state child welfare agencies. State agencies submit data to NCANDS on child abuse investigations, victims, and perpetrators. The number of participating states has increased since the program was initiated in 1990, with all but a few states submitting data since the mid-1990s. For most years of data collection, states have submitted statistics to NCANDS in aggregate, but an increasing number are submitting case-level data. Data on victims, perpetrators, and type of victimization (sexual abuse, physical abuse, neglect, etc.) are available only for cases where abuse was verified (substantiated or indicated) following a child protection investigation.

TABLE 7.1. *(continued)*

National Crime Victimization Survey (NCVS)	Trend data on sexual assaults and other crimes against teenagers 12 to 17 years old and trends in domestic violence were drawn from the NCVS. The NCVS is a self-report survey conducted annually by the U.S. Department of Commerce's Bureau of the Census on behalf of the U.S. Department of Justice's Bureau of Justice Statistics. Approximately 55,000 U.S. households with a total of 100,000 individuals ages 12 and older are surveyed each year. The survey collects information about the characteristics of victimizations, including victim and perpetrator demographics, the incident location, and a description of the incident.
Minnesota Student Survey	Additional self-report information about sexual and physical abuse victimization trends is available through the Minnesota Student Survey. This survey is a voluntary, anonymous, self-administered questionnaire that asks students about a range of experiences including substance use, sexual behavior, and school climate. Two survey questions ask about sexual abuse victimization and one asks about familial physical abuse. The survey has been administered to 6th, 9th, and 12th grade students in Minnesota five times: in 1989, 1992, 1995, 1998, and 2001. Approximately 90% to 99% of Minnesota's school districts have participated in the survey each year, involving more than 100,000 students. For trend analyses, data are limited to the approximately 69% of Minnesota's school districts that participated in the survey in all 5 years. A weighting procedure was used to adjust for differences in student participation rates across districts. For more information about the Minnesota Student Survey's methodology, see Harrison, Fulkerson, and Beebe (1997), or Minnesota Department of Children, Families & Learning (2001).
Supplementary Homicide Reports (SHR)	Data on homicides against children and infants were drawn from the FBI's Supplementary Homicide Reports (SHR), which is a part of the Uniform Crime Reporting (UCR) program. Under the UCR program, law enforcement agencies submit information to the FBI monthly on criminal offense, arrest, and law enforcement personnel statistics. The UCR program collects only those data that come to the attention of law enforcement through victim reports or observation. Supplemental data about homicide incidents are submitted through the SHR monthly with detail on location, victim, and offender characteristics. These reports include information on the age, race, and sex of victims and offenders, and on the victim/offender relationship, weapon use, and circumstance of the crime.

Chapter 8

The Juvenile *Victim* Justice System: A Concept for Helping Victims

This chapter introduces the concept that there is a large "justice system" that responds to juvenile victims. This juvenile *victim* justice system is a complex set of agencies and institutions that goes far beyond the child protection system as it is conventionally perceived. It includes police, prosecutors, criminal and civil courts, children's advocacy centers, victim services, and mental health agencies. The system has a structure and sequence, but its operation, despite the thousands of cases it handles every year, is not as widely recognized and understood as the operation of the more familiar juvenile *offender* justice system.

The juvenile victim justice system is not as widely recognized in part because it is a fragmented system, suffering many of the fragmentation problems outlined in Chapter 1. It has not been conceptualized as a whole or implemented by a common set of statutes in the way that the juvenile offender system has. Many of the agencies that handle juvenile victims are part of other systems, not designed with juvenile victims primarily in mind. But increasingly, as policies about juvenile victims evolve and more professionals specialize in this area, the relevance of thinking about a juvenile victim justice system has grown. This systemic concept can help change policy and practice to make the system more responsive to child victims and further the system's missions of protecting children and achieving justice. Other practical benefits in such areas as victim assistance, information management, and system design are discussed below.

This chapter describes the major elements of the justice system for juvenile victims and what is known about the flow of cases through this system. Like that for processing juvenile offenders, it is a system governed at the state level and implemented somewhat differently in each community, so there are wide variations in practices and procedures across the country. But there are important commonalities among these systems that can be described in a schematic way.

Juvenile Victimization: Crime and Child Maltreatment

One of the central complexities of the juvenile victim justice system is that it encompasses two distinct subsystems: the criminal justice system and the child protection system. These systems are typically thought of as separate, but their interaction in cases involving juvenile victims is considerable and increasing.

Officially, the two systems concern what many people take to be two different issues: crime and child maltreatment. But these domains overlap considerably. The crime domain, when it comes to juvenile victims, includes all the offenses customarily seen as violent, such as homicides and physical and sexual assaults. But it also includes sex offenses not necessarily involving force or assault, such as incest and statutory rape; property crimes such as theft; and criminal neglect. Across these crime categories, the justice system places no restriction on the nature of the perpetrator, be it a family member, a stranger, an adult, or a juvenile.

In contrast, the child maltreatment domain—the concern of the child protection system—is usually limited by statute to perpetrators who occupy a caretaking relationship to the child victim and thus tend to be adult family members or other caretakers. Child maltreatment is divided into the categories of physical and sexual abuse, neglect, and emotional maltreatment.

Direct overlap between the two systems is primarily in the areas of physical and sexual abuse, which are generally considered both child maltreatment and crimes because they involve assaults. Episodes of neglect and emotional maltreatment may or may not be crimes, depending on the acts and the state's statutes.

The concept of child maltreatment rarely includes property crimes, even when committed by caretakers and family members. Those concerned with crimes against children also generally ignore property crimes, in part because they seem so much less serious than the violent crimes and sex offenses that dominate this literature. Nonetheless, law enforcement agencies receive reports every year of hundreds of thousands of property crimes against juveniles,[433] which research suggests have significant negative psychological impact on their victims.[434] These crimes need to be considered to understand the response of the justice system to juvenile victims.

It has become increasingly clear that the mission of the child protection system can be accomplished effectively only through coordination with the criminal justice system. It has also become evident that the criminal justice system cannot provide true justice without ensuring the current and future protection of the child victims whose cases it processes. So concerns about justice for and protection of juvenile victims have increasingly led professionals from each of the separate systems to look at the operations of their systems in combination.

We have constructed a chart (see Fig. 8.1) to portray graphically the operation of what we are calling the juvenile victim justice system. Following Figure 8.1 from left to right, the reader can see each step in the case-flow process for both the child protection and the criminal justice components. At each step, we review the research evidence, where it exists, for the proportion of cases (and therefore child victims) following a particular path. We then discuss the implications of this case flow for understanding and improving the response to child victims. For the sake of simplicity, many less typical actions that can occur in the system are omitted from Figure 8.1.

Reported and Unreported Victimization

The gateway to the juvenile victim justice system is a report to an authority, which for the most part means either the police or the child protection system. Extrapolation from data in the National Incident Based Reporting System (NIBRS) suggests that in 2004 about 1.3 million violent crimes against children were reported to the police nationwide. These crimes were predominantly assaults (77%), plus some sex offenses (20%). There were also about 500,000 property crimes against juveniles reported, mostly (77%) larceny/theft.[433]

The National Child Abuse and Neglect Data system (NCANDS) records about 3 million referrals annually to child protection authorities for suspicion of child maltreatment, of which the majority, 58%, are for neglect by children's caretakers. An additional 21% are for physical abuse, and 11% for sexual abuse.[435] It is not known how much overlap there is in these figures—that is, how many individual cases involve reports to both police and child protection. However, the police reports are quite skewed toward older children (71% of the victims of violent crime are 12 years or older), whereas Child Protective Services (CPS) cases are made up predominantly of younger children (74 % under age 12). This suggests that the two victim populations have relatively modest overlap.

The reports to the CPS system come primarily (55%) from professionals,[435] who are legally mandated under state law to report suspicions of child maltreatment. The largest category of professional reporters comprises teachers and educational professionals, followed by criminal justice and human service professionals. Direct reports from victims and families make up only 18% of the total.

Reports to police about juvenile victimization, in contrast, tend to come from victims and families themselves. For violent victimizations of children, 29% come from the victims themselves and another 30% from

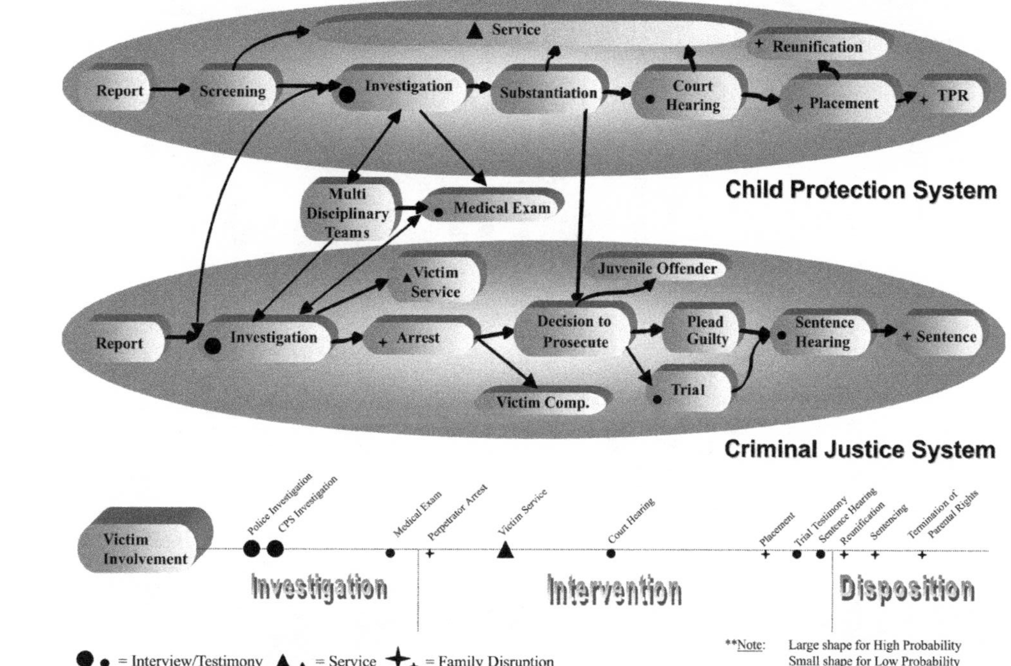

FIGURE 8.1. The juvenile victim justice system.

another member of the victim's household.[258] For property crimes, the proportion coming from victims or their households is even higher. Reports to police from officials such as school authorities and CPS workers are relatively infrequent—21% for violent crimes and 14% for property crimes—much less than the proportion of reports from such officials to CPS. As might be expected, compared to adult victimizations, juvenile victimizations are reported more by family members and other officials and less by the victims themselves.

Beyond these reported cases, it is widely recognized that an enormous amount of crime and maltreatment against children never comes to the attention of police or child welfare authorities. According to the National Crime Victimization Survey (NCVS), only 28% of the robberies and simple and aggravated sexual assaults occurring to juveniles ages 12 to 17 years old became known to police. This reporting rate for offenses against juveniles is substantially lower than for offenses against adults. Moreover, since the youngest children in the NCVS (the 12-year-olds) have the lowest reporting rates, police are even less likely to find out about crimes against children under the age of 12.[72] Crimes are more likely to be reported to the police when they involve injuries, adult or multiple offenders, or families who have had prior experience with police or been advised to report to them.[278] The involvement of school authorities may inhibit reporting to the police, since many schools try to handle these episodes on their own.

Child maltreatment is also widely underreported to authorities, although the data are less precise about how much so. The National Incidence Study of Child Abuse and Neglect[80] found that only 28% of cases known to professionals in the community could be traced to any investigation conducted by the local CPS. The percentages were higher for physical and sexual abuse (48% and 42% respectively) than for neglect (18%). These statistics can be taken as a crude measure of underreporting by professionals, but it is not clear to what extent these professionals simply did not report or, rather, made reports that were screened out by CPS officials.[80] In addition, a considerable amount of child maltreatment is not even known to professionals.

In summary, millions of children enter the juvenile victim justice system annually through reports to police (mostly by victims and their families) and CPS (mostly by professionals). However, there appear to be millions of additional children whose victimizations are not reported, and many others whose victimizations remain secrets from everyone.

The Child Protection System

The operation of the juvenile victim justice system varies considerably according to whether the initial report is made to the police or the child protection system. Thus this section describes the processes separately, starting with a report to the child protection system and following with a report to the police. The path for the child protection system is portrayed in the top of Figure 8.1, with the steps in the process depicted in the figure in chronological order from left to right.

Screening

It is important to recognize that, because state law requires professionals to report suspicions of child abuse, the calls coming in to the child protection system (called *reports*) may concern a child who has not truly been victimized. These reports of child maltreatment are often cited as statistics regarding maltreated children (as in, "3 million abused children reported each year"), but this is not necessarily so. Child protection agencies screen out many calls very quickly because they concern suspicions that are judged to be unfounded, contain too little or unreliable information, or concern situations that do not fall within the agency's jurisdiction. As an overall national average, about 62% of reports are accepted for investigation or assessment.[361] State agencies vary considerably in what they are willing and able to investigate, with some accepting (or screening in) only very serious and specific allegations, and others conducting at least a minimal inquiry on a much broader range of reports.[436] One study found that cases involving sexual abuse, allegations of drug use, families on welfare, and direct evidence of maltreatment were more likely to be taken on, and cases involving custody disputes were more likely to be screened out.[437]

Child Maltreatment Investigation

The first objectives of the CPS investigation are to assess the case and take whatever steps are necessary to ensure the child's safety. Because children may be in danger, child protection investigations need to be timely. State laws require a response within a fixed time. Among states that report investigation response time, the average is about 64 hours or three days, but it varies from five hours to over two weeks in different states.[435] At the investigation stage, workers may authorize a medical examination and an evaluation by mental health or other experts.

Investigations are not always part of the child protection process. More than a dozen states have adopted an innovative two-track system in which cases involving less serious allegations and lower levels of risk are not opened for investigation at all; instead they are assessed by child protection workers for the possibility of needed services. Only serious allegations are formally investigated. In states with such systems, a large majority of the screened-in reports of maltreatment (71% in Missouri, 73% in Virginia) are being handled on this "assessment only" track.[438]

In cases in which investigations are initiated, investigators have the authority to take the child into custody on an emergency basis. In Connecticut, for example, child protective workers may remove children immediately and hold them for up to 4 days, typically with the help of the police, if the children have a serious physical illness or injury or are in immediate danger from their surroundings or from being unattended.

Referral to Police and Prosecutors

Referrals of child protection reports to police and prosecutors occur primarily at the investigation stage. Some state laws, in fact, require automatic referral of certain types of maltreatment allegations to police or prosecutors at some stage of the CPS investigation. In other places, referral to police and prosecutors is more discretionary. Child protection workers involve police when they need investigative help or as soon as they confirm evidence that a criminal law has been violated. Referral to police is most consistent and immediate when cases involve allegations of sexual abuse, child death, or physical abuse that involves particularly serious injury, brutality, or callousness.

Sometimes police conduct independent investigations. Sometimes investigations are conducted jointly by child protection workers and police—what have been termed *multidisciplinary teams*—and some jurisdictions have even experimented with turning CPS investigation activities over to the police entirely.[439] Nationally, police are involved in more sexual abuse investigations (45%) than investigations of physical abuse (28%) or neglect (20%).[440] There is great variability, however, among jurisdictions, given the dramatic differences in state laws and levels of interagency cooperation.

Medical Examination

A medical examination can provide crucial evidence to substantiate crime or child maltreatment. It also can assess children's medical needs and assist recovery by reassuring children about their bodies and providing them with an opportunity to talk with a trusted authority. Many states and jurisdictions have specialized child-abuse medical diagnostic units to perform these exams. The percentage of reported children who receive medical exams varies greatly across studies, but such exams probably occur in 10% to 25% of all cases.[290,441–443]

These exams can disclose previous similar or related injuries, can check whether injury details are consistent with the history given by caretakers or reporters, and can sometimes differentiate accidents and disease conditions from injuries that are likely to have been inflicted.[444] Injuries and aspects of genital physiology, semen, and hair can also help confirm sexual abuse and the identity of the perpetrator. On the other hand, often abuse can neither be confirmed nor disconfirmed by a medical examination. In examinations subsequent to allegations of sexual abuse, definitive physical findings are established in only about one-quarter of cases.[445,446]

Substantiation of Child Maltreatment

The primary outcome of a child maltreatment investigation is a determination by the investigator of whether maltreatment occurred; such a determination generally requires a preponderance of evidence as its standard of proof. The most common term for this is *substantiation*, but other terms such as *confirmation* or *support* are also used. In some states (referred to as three-tiered states), there is another category, *indicated*, which means that evidence is consistent with child maltreatment but is not strong enough to substantiate allegations.

Substantiation rates nationwide are estimated to be 29% of all reports (this includes both substantiated and indicated reports).[435] These rates vary somewhat by type of maltreatment and, more dramatically, by state. For example, in Massachusetts, allegations were supported in 52% of investigations in 1999, while in New Hampshire only 9% were substantiated.[435] Historically, as the number of reports has risen, these rates have declined. This change could be a reflection of increasing conservatism in substantiation standards, an increase in reporting of less serious situations, or a sign of limitations in investigative resources in CPS agencies.

When reports of child maltreatment are not substantiated, it can be for a variety of reasons, including failure of the family or other informants to cooperate with the investigation, lack of sufficient evidence about the allegation, discovery that the allegation falls outside the jurisdiction or authority of the agency, or even sometimes an inability of the agency to adequately investigate owing to time or manpower constraints. The number of willfully false or malicious allegations is generally shown to be quite small.[447–449] The few states that keep a tally of intentionally false allegations find that they have been made in well under 1% of all investigations.[435] Some observers have noted that a form of plea bargaining sometimes operates in the substantiation process, whereby reports are unsubstantiated or made for a less serious form of maltreatment (e.g., neglect rather than sexual abuse) in exchange for a commitment to accept services or other interventions.

Provision of Services

An important goal of the child protection system is to prevent future episodes of maltreatment among the children served. One of the main avenues for this is preventive or remedial services such as counseling, parent education, and family support. According to state data, an average of 5 weeks elapses between the start of investigation and the provision of services. About 55% of maltreated children receive services documented through the child protection system, although, once again, the variability among states ranges from 100% down to only 15%.[435] Although there is widespread concern that the child protection system does not do an adequate job of providing services, it cannot be said confidently that the 45% of maltreated children without CPS-documented services all needed services or all failed to get them. For example, informal and familial solutions to child maltreatment situations (e.g., a parent moving in with grandparents) may be deemed adequate solutions from the CPS point of view. Children and families may also receive services from non-CPS sources such as family service or mental health agencies. In fact, referral to services may occur at almost every juncture in Figure 8.1, including from the criminal justice system, but arrows have been omitted for the sake of simplicity.

Court Hearing

Families with a substantiated child maltreatment finding proceed to a formal court hearing only when child protective workers believe there is cause to remove the child on more than an emergency basis or a need to take custody of the child for some other reason. Court services are actually initiated for about one-fourth of the substantiated victims of child maltreatment.[435]

There has been a recognition that child victims involved in these court proceedings need someone who can represent their needs and point of view other than the state agency bringing the child protection action. These representatives are typically called *court-appointed special advocates* or *guardians ad litem*. According to reports from a limited number of states, about 80% of child victims are provided with such representatives.

Out-of-Home Placement

Removal of a child from the home is certainly the most serious intervention taken by the child protection system. Approximately 170,000 children were removed in 1999, or about 21% of those with a substantiated finding of child maltreatment. Rates for individual states tend to vary between 15% and 22%.[435] The rate of child removal is about 6% of the total number of children investigated for suspicion of child maltreatment, and less than 4% of those reported. Some additional children are allowed to remain in their homes, but only with supervision.

When removed, children are placed in a variety of different settings. Three-fourths of children in foster care are in foster families, one quarter with their relatives and one half with nonrelatives.[450] About 10% are placed in institutions and another 8% in group homes (these breakdowns include some children in foster care for reasons other than child maltreatment). Some children are removed from the home on an emergency basis during the investigation, but the typical removal is for a longer period and involves action by the court. The median length of stay in foster care is 16.5 months, although this statistic applies to all children in foster care, not just those placed there owing to child maltreatment. Children being cared for by relatives tend to stay for longer periods of time because the placement is generally viewed as a permanent one.[451]

Reunification

Most children placed in foster care do return to their families. In 1999, the percentages of children exiting foster care to reunite with their families ranged from 31% in Illinois to 85% in Idaho, with the median at 66%. A majority of the reunifications in most states occurred within 12 months of children's removal from the home.[451] Some children, however, need to reenter foster care following reunification because of further maltreatment or risk of maltreatment.

Termination of Parental Rights

In the most serious cases of child maltreatment, the state moves to terminate parental rights and places a child for adoption. In 2000, parents of 64,000 children, or about 11% of all those in foster care, had their parental rights terminated.[450] Not all terminations occurred simply because of child maltreatment. Moreover, because the mean time to termination is 22 months, it is not accurate to calculate terminations as a percent of substantiated maltreatment for the same year, since most terminations are from maltreatment cases recorded for prior years. However, based on a crude annual estimate of 800,000 substantiated victims of child abuse and neglect, the rate of terminations per substantiated child maltreatment victims is about 8%.

A Summary of the Juvenile Victim Justice System

The child protection system's primary goal is to insure child safety, but it also aims to facilitate delivery of services. On average, about 60% of reports to CPS are accepted for investigation. Nationally, about 29% of investigations lead to substantiation, though this rate varies greatly by state. CPS can initiate a number of interventions during or as a result of investigation, including medical examinations, referral to criminal justice, and service delivery by CPS and other agencies. Removing children on an emergency basis or as a result of a court hearing is fairly rare, and nationally most children who are removed are later reunified with their families.

The Criminal Justice System

In addition to referrals from the child protection system, the criminal justice system receives many reports of child victimization from victims, families, and other institutions such as schools. Since the mandate of the criminal justice system is crime and not simply child maltreatment, the mix of child victim cases coming to the attention of the criminal justice system is different from those in the child protection system. Most of these criminal justice system cases (about 70%) involve a nonfamily perpetrator, and a little over half are youth-on-youth offenses.[70] Very few concern simple neglect or emotional abuse. As mentioned earlier, the majority of these victims—78%—are teens.[70] The criminal justice system also receives an estimated 400,000 to 500,000 reports per year involving juveniles who are victims of property crimes.[433]

The path for child victim cases entering the criminal justice system is portrayed in the bottom half of Figure 8.1. Again, the steps in the process are depicted in chronological order from left to right. Unfortunately, many of the studies of case processing within the criminal justice system from the victim's point of view are limited to cases of sexual assault, sexual abuse, or other serious offenses. Much less is known about the experience in the justice system of juvenile victims who experience simple assault, crimes by other youth, and property victimizations.

Criminal Justice Investigation

It is standard practice for police to investigate reports of juvenile victimization, but there is little research on the numbers, percentages, or circumstances related to police investigations. For this chapter, we analyzed data from 12- to 17-year-old victims in the NCVS, a national study that interviews crime victims. In the wake of a police report, police made contact with juvenile victims in 92% of violent and 79% of property crimes. They actually took a report (that is, collected information about the crime) in 63% of violent and 72% of the property crimes in which they made contact with the victim.

If reports to and investigations by police lead to a suspicion of child maltreatment, police are mandated to report this to CPS. Although we are not aware of any data on how often this actually happens, it is supposed to be standard practice, as police are mandated reporters by law.

Arrest

An arrest occurs when police find probable cause that a person has committed the crime that has come to their attention and are able to locate and apprehend that person. However, police make an arrest in only a minority of the juvenile-victim crimes that do come to their attention. Our analysis of the NCVS revealed that offenders are arrested in 28% of violent crimes and only 4% of the property crimes against juveniles that become known to the police. (The arrest rate is a bit higher—32%—using police-record data for all juvenile-victim violent crime cases from the FBI's NIBRS system.) Juvenile-victim crimes have somewhat lower arrest rates than adult-victim crimes with regard to physical assaults, but higher arrest rates for sexual assaults.[452] The overall low arrest rates reflect the limited resources that police have; the absence of information in many cases about who the offenders are, particularly in property crimes; and the fact that many crimes are judged to be relatively minor in nature.

Arrests are more common in juvenile victimizations that involve more serious offenses, such as sexual assaults and aggravated assaults, or that involve a weapon.[452] Arrests are less likely when the perpetrator is a stranger, which reflects the greater difficulty in locating the offender in order to complete an arrest.

An important feature of juvenile victimization that affects arrests and other aspects of criminal justice activity is the fact that a relatively large number of offenders against juveniles, somewhat more than 50%, are other juveniles.[70] Offenses committed by other juveniles are handled by the institutions and procedures of the juvenile offender justice system. The procedures in this system are somewhat less formal and less public than those of the criminal justice system for crimes by adults, but they do include analogues to trials, called *adjudicatory hearings*, and sentencing, called *disposition hearings*, at which victims may testify, as well as other features such as victim-offender mediation. (To keep Figure 8.1 relatively simple, we have excluded the specific steps of the juvenile offender justice system, but a diagram of that system is available in Snyder and Sickmund.[409]) Unfortunately, even though there is a large amount of research literature on juvenile justice, the experience of juvenile victims whose offenders are processed in this system—for example, how many victims provide testimony in hearings—has been the subject of very little specific study.

Victim Compensation

Most states have systems for compensating victims of crime for costs such as medical care, counseling, home and auto repair, and replacement of stolen items. Victims need to file applications, which are acted upon by victim-compensation boards. Victims may file claims at any point in the criminal justice process, although many are referred to such resources by police. The arrest or conviction of an offender is not required for compensation to be awarded.

Of all recipients of compensation nationally in 2003, 22% were child abuse victims,[453] and over $37 million was provided for services for child abuse victims. Interestingly, over half of this amount was used in California, which has an active record of using victim compensation to support psychotherapy for child victims. There are no data, however, on what percentage of eligible children apply. Nationally, over 45,000 claims were approved for victims 17 years old and under, although there is a widespread perception that many victims fail to find out about the availability of victim compensation funds.

Decision to Prosecute

Either in conjunction with an investigation or after an arrest has been made, cases are referred to the prosecutor. The decisions about prosecution, which the prosecutor manages, vary considerably from jurisdiction to jurisdiction. In virtually all jurisdictions, the prosecutor evaluates the strengths and weaknesses of the case and the likelihood of success before deciding to proceed, sometimes after talking with victims and other witnesses. In addition, in many jurisdictions, prosecutors bring the cases before a judge in a preliminary hearing and/or before a grand jury to determine if there is probable cause to take the case to trial. In both cases, children may testify. If probable cause is not established, the case is dismissed.

Offenders may be arrested before or after the decision to prosecute. If police have made an arrest, cases are almost always forwarded to prosecutors for decision.[454,455] Once the cases are referred for prosecution, the proportion of child victim cases that move on to actual prosecution varies widely. Across 14 studies reviewed by Cross, Walsh, Jones, and Simone,[456] the proportion of cases in which charges were brought against the perpetrator ranged from 28% to 94%, with a median of 64%. Rates differ considerably across prosecutors' offices not only because of the resources they have to devote and the priority they give to juvenile-victim cases but also because of differences in which cases are referred to prosecutors and the point at which cases are screened out. Prosecution is less likely when child victims are under the age of 7, when children are related to the perpetrator, or when they have suffered less severe offenses.[457] These variables probably relate both to the availability of evidence and to children's capacity to talk about the abuse and testify in court. Cases accepted by prosecutors can later be dismissed by the grand jury, the judge, or the prosecutors themselves, but in Cross et al.'s[456] sample an average of 80% of cases were carried forward without dismissal.

Pleading Guilty Versus Going to Trial

If a case is accepted by the prosecutor and not dismissed, a disposition will be reached either by a guilty plea or by a trial. Once a child victim case is carried forward without dismissal, the likelihood that the offender will plead guilty is high. According to a review of 20 studies of prosecution of child abuse, an average of 81% of offenders against children pleaded guilty to at least some charge,[456] which is the same as the percentage of general violent offenders and very close to the 76% of general sexual assaulters who plead guilty. This consistency in rates reflects the fact that prosecutors go forward only with cases they believe to be fairly strong and in which they feel they will be able to exert considerable leverage in negotiating charges and sentences. Still, in about 19% of cases, prosecutors fail to obtain a plea and the case goes to trial.

Sentencing

Across 15 studies of prosecution of child abuse, the median incarceration rate was 53% of convicted offenders, although these rates varied from 24% to 96%.[456] There has been considerable media concern about whether offenders against juveniles receive unusually lenient sentences. An analysis of sentences from a national sample of offenders incarcerated in state correctional facilities found that some of the disparities in sentencing were explained by the fact that offenders against juveniles are less likely to be recidivists, less likely to use weapons, and less likely to be strangers to their victims—factors that are associated with longer sentences. There were still some sentencing disparities related to victim age even after controlling for such variables, but they all related to offenders against adolescents, who did tend to receive shorter sentences. There was no evidence of a leniency bias in favor of those offending against younger children.[402]

A Summary of the Criminal Justice System

Police investigate most reported juvenile victim crimes, but they make an arrest in only a minority. Prosecutors are referred to the vast majority of these cases once an arrest is made, but the proportion accepted by prosecutors varies from about one-half to three-fourths. If we generalize primarily from the experience with sexual assault crimes, we find that cases tend to be dropped based on concerns about evidence and children's testimonial capacities. Eighty percent of cases carried forward, however, end in guilty pleas. Sentences for offenders against young juvenile victims are not systematically lighter than sentences in comparable adult-victim cases, but they may be lighter for offenders against adolescents. Anecdotally, juvenile victims are thought to be a sizable proportion of those who receive victim compensation awards, but many victims may still not be aware of these funds.

The Impact of the Juvenile Victim Justice System on Victims

As can be seen in the previous sections, cases involving juvenile victims may pass in a bureaucratic sense through a number of procedures that are part of this juvenile victim justice system. But importantly, not all of these procedures necessarily have an immediate or direct impact on the juvenile victim. For example, an offender may be charged, plead guilty, be sentenced, and enter prison without the victim having to see anyone, appear anywhere, or even necessarily know about the events. (This is not typical, but it is theoretically possible in cases in which there is considerable physical evidence or there are other eyewitnesses to provide evidence and where the perpetrator cooperates with authorities.)

Identifying the components of the system that have the most frequent and most consequential impact on victims is an important part of conceptualizing the juvenile victim justice system. Three particular impacts are salient: (1) interviews and appearances that a child victim must make before officials, (2) family or life activity disruptions that are the consequence of institutional decisions within the justice system, and (3) direct therapeutic or reparative services that the child victim receives. These impacts can be charted in terms of both their sequencing and their likelihood of occurrence, and this is an important adjunct to the overall understanding of the operation of the juvenile victim justice system. They have been represented in the system diagram at the bottom of Figure 8.1 on a scale of victim involvement with the following shape codes: a diamond for interview or testimony, a star for family or life-activities disruption, and a triangle for service. The shapes appear larger when the probability of the relevant event is high and smaller when it is only moderately common or less so.

The impact of the juvenile victim justice system is not confined to these three types of events. Some of the most consequential impacts of these processes may involve simple information that a victim receives, sometimes quite indirectly. For example, the victim may be told or find out that the prosecutor refused to press charges or that a perpetrator's attorney called the victim a liar, and this may be extremely distressing. But these events and impacts are more difficult to classify and situate.

Interviews and Testimony

Of all the events occurring in this process that have an impact on a victim, the one with the highest probability of taking place is an investigative interview. If the victimization is reported to police, a police officer will likely interview the juvenile. If the victimization is reported to child protection, a CPS worker will almost always talk to the child, unless the child is very young. An interview with a police officer occurs in 92% of juvenile-victim violent crimes reported to the police, according to the NCVS, and an investigation, which typically involves a child interview, occurs in 60% of child maltreatment reports recorded by NCANDS. In some cases, there will be more than one investigative interview, which can occur as investigators gather additional evidence or when another agency becomes involved (CPS referral to police or vice versa). Analyzing prosecutor case data from 1988 to 1991, Smith and Elstein[458] found that law enforcement interviewed children in 96% of cases, and CPS in 46%. When both police and social workers conducted interviews, however, 64% of the time these were separate rather than joint interviews, and children would typically have to "tell their story" again.

Trying to reduce the number of duplicative investigative interviews and their possible negative impact on victims is one of the issues most explicitly behind the development of multidisciplinary teams and children's advocacy centers. It has also been an important motive behind the effort to more routinely videotape investigative interviews. The nationwide development of several hundred children's advocacy centers and other multidisciplinary team programs during the 1990s may well have reduced the amount of duplicative interviewing, although more confirmation of this is needed.

As part of the investigation, some victimized children (one estimate, cited earlier, is 22% of violent-crime victims passing through the criminal justice system) will receive a medical exam. Victims of sexual abuse and physical abuse involving injury are more likely to receive such exams. Such exams can be stressful, but one study found it equivalent to providing testimony in juvenile court—twice as stressful as talking to a social worker but not nearly as stressful as testimony in criminal court.[459]

Child victims may be interviewed at a number of subsequent junctures. Prosecutors may decide to interview children again even after the police investigation while making the decision about whether to prosecute and trying to assess the strength of the testimony. As part of the process, a child may be asked to testify at a preliminary or grand jury hearing. Studies have reported that 12% to 31% of children in prosecuted cases testify at pretrial proceedings.[233,458,460,461] If an actual trial is held, a child may testify again, often in conjunction with some prior meetings with the prosecutor. However, because so many cases are plea-bargained, relatively few children have to testify in trial court. Only between 5% and 15% of cases involve a child victim's testimony at a trial or a court hearing.[233,290,460–463] Finally, there are sometimes voluntary opportunities for a victim to provide testimony at a sentencing hearing.

Juvenile Services

Juvenile victims may be affected by the provision of services. One of the specific goals of CPS investigations is to provide services to promote the well-being of victimized children. As indicated earlier, about 55% of maltreated children are referred for services. Children may also be referred to services by police or prosecutors as part of criminal justice system processing, but there is little systematic documentation about this referral pathway, and it is probably not as frequent a referral as with CPS. Some specific child maltreatment services have well-established beneficial impacts. For example, cognitive-behavioral therapy that specifically teaches sexually abused children and their families how to cope with the effects has shown advantages over standard care in several studies.[136,464,465]

Family Disruption

The juvenile victim justice system can have a major impact on child victims when it results in family disruption—that is, a major change in living circumstances or the household configuration. At an early point in the process, one form of disruption may occur if a child protection worker uses emergency power to remove an endangered child from his or her home. A disruption may also occur if police arrest and hold a parent suspected of a crime against the child. At later stages in the child protection process, a child may be removed from the home by the court, either temporarily for foster care placement or subsequently as part of the termination of parental rights. Reunifications are frequently part of this process once initial removal has occurred, and they can create other disruptions. The sentencing of an intrafamilial abuser to time in prison may also disrupt the family. Although all these events may have major impacts on children, they occur in only a minority of child victimization cases.

How the System Concept Can Help

This chapter has described in general terms the operation of the juvenile victim justice system and what is known about the case flow in that system. The notion that there is a system that often contributes to, but sometimes detracts from, the justice, safety, and physical and psychological well-being of juvenile victims has important implications. The following highlights some of these:

- More people need to understand the operation of the juvenile victim justice system in its entirety. Agency administrators and line workers need to know more about the workings of the other agencies in the system, and policy makers and researchers need better knowledge of the system as a whole. Such knowledge is important for planning policy and for managing individual cases, so that the decisions made in one part of the system can take into account actions that may occur in other parts.
- Juvenile victims need the assistance of professionals who can orient, guide, and support them and their families through their involvement in the juvenile victim justice system. Professionals in children's advocacy centers or serving as court-appointed special advocates and guardians ad litem play such roles, but often only for certain limited aspects of the system process. It makes sense for the support to be much more comprehensive and continuous.
- More consideration needs to be given to ways to integrate and rationalize the system as a whole. In recent years, considerable effort has been devoted to coordinating certain aspects of the juvenile victim justice system—for example, by conducting joint investigations or developing multidisciplinary teams for sharing information and decision making. Even more dramatic forms of integration might be possible. For example, the application of criminal sanctions and decision making about child custody and service provision, and even the awarding of compensation funds to victims,

might be centralized and handled by a single judicial institution. The goals of such integration would obviously be to expedite the processes, coordinate the decisions, and minimize the impact on victims. Where separation between components of the system is necessary (e.g., between criminal justice and support interactions with families), better methods are required for assessing which cases belong where and for moving cases between parts of the system as needs change.

- There is a need for more and improved exchange of information among components of the system. A child can be involved with up to six or seven agencies and a dozen or more professionals over the course of an intervention, which can last several years. Information from one part of the system can have an impact on decisions made in other parts. The criminal investigation of an alleged perpetrator living in the home, for instance, may have a bearing on the child protection system's decision of whether to place children outside the home. The need for confidentiality sets limits, yet information sharing between agencies often falls short because it is a secondary priority for busy professionals focused on their primary mission. Whitcomb and Hardin,[466] for example, found that communication between criminal and civil court staff on simultaneous proceedings regarding the same child was often minimal or nonexistent, which increases the risk that contradictory decisions would be made by the two courts. Where communication is present, it tends to occur in early phases and is often not maintained throughout the child's contact with the system. Case review and case-tracking systems are steps in the right direction, but there is no central repository of information. New methods, or perhaps even new technology, need to be developed to ensure adequate information flow.
- There is a need, for policy purposes, to identify and prioritize the most important stages and transitions of the system. For example, the concern about child victims in criminal court concentrated policy attention for a long time on ways to mitigate children's stress over having to testify in criminal cases. But a systems-level analysis has demonstrated that only a small percentage of juvenile victims actually face the prospect of testifying in criminal court. By contrast, issues related to the stressfulness and efficacy of CPS interviews or medical examinations have the potential to impact many more children. At some other levels, answering questions about why arrests are not made in so many child victim cases or what techniques lead to guilty pleas holds the potential to bring far more justice for child victims than increased knowledge of effective trial procedures.
- Greater attention needs to be paid to the fact that the juvenile victim justice system can be the entry point for needed services for

thousands of victimized children. Agencies that provide services to children and families tend to think about their referral sources simply as other individuals and agencies, and the identification of a need for service as something that happens case by case. However, when those referral patterns are considered as part of a larger system involving large numbers of children with service needs, new realities come into focus. For example, the demand on some children to talk about their victimization in many different places and to many different people over an extended period of time suggests the need for system-wise human service professionals to provide support to children throughout the process. The fact that many child victims with service needs related to trauma or inadequate care come through the system at predictable junctures suggests new places, time points, and programming for addressing children's needs.

- More systematic and comprehensive information needs to be collected about the operation of the system and interrelationships among the components. There are tremendous gaps in information, and virtually no data-collection effort that covers the entirety of the system. Several steps are needed. Pilot studies that track juvenile victims through all the steps and stages need to be undertaken. Data elements need to be added to current information systems that track interrelationships within the system. Thus, for example, the police data gathered in the NIBRS could record whether a crime was referred to police from CPS. CPS data might record whether an arrest was made. In addition, although it raises serious privacy concerns, if victims could be recorded in different systems with some common identifier, it might be possible to track victims through various databases to uncover the pathways through the systems.
- Efforts need to be made to comprehensively characterize and summarize how the juvenile victim justice system operates in different communities. Some key dimensions need to be delineated so that systems can be compared and contrasted. For example, comparative study might be able to establish the criteria for systems that are integrated versus fragmentary, victim oriented, and so forth.

Initiatives such as these may help create a justice system that is more responsive to the needs of the thousands of juvenile victims who encounter it every year.

Chapter 9

Proposals

Many encouraging initiatives are underway to combat child victimization, from federal legislation about Internet crime to home-visitation programs for new parents. So much is going on, in fact, that a whole book should be devoted to a review of these activities. In this chapter we do not undertake any such broad review; instead, we touch on just a few topics.

Reforming the Child Protection System

There is widespread agreement that the child protection system in the United States has a great many flaws. Joining the chorus of its critics takes no great courage, so, before doing so, it is only fair to make several points on behalf of the system and its accomplishments.

Accomplishments of the System

The child protection system has certainly managed to sensitize and orient an enormous number of professionals and citizens to the problems of child abuse and child victimization. It is fair to say that the United States has a professional class and citizenry more attentive to this problem than almost any other country in the world. While the formal child protection system is not exclusively responsible for this public awareness, it certainly has participated in and helped foster it.

The system, since its inception in the 1970s, has evolved in a variety of important and positive directions that suggest a certain amount of adaptiveness that many bureaucracies lack. Although established to deal primarily with the battered-child syndrome characteristic of physical abuse, the system both helped to uncover the problem of child sexual abuse and evolved to respond to it, even though sexual abuse posed many different challenges than did the forms of child mistreatment that it was originally organized to confront. Among its changes, the system has become much more capable of participating in multidisciplinary practice, especially in conjunction with law enforcement.

Finally, although the child protection system may not always act efficiently, almost all observers agree that it has rescued a considerable number of endangered children over the years. The available research does suggest that seriously maltreated children removed from dangerous homes do fare better than children allowed to return to and continue to live in such circumstances.[467] The child protection system cannot conclusively be credited with the declines in physical and sexual abuse outlined in Chapter 7, but it is possible that these improvements have some connection to its activities.

Acknowledged Problems in the System

In spite of such accomplishments, the child protection system has few admirers. It is generally seen as cumbersome, inefficient, unfocused, and bureaucratic. Some of the more specific criticisms are the following:

- The child protection system has serious workforce problems. It has a hard time recruiting ambitious and educated professionals, and it experiences a high rate of turnover and burnout.
- The system suffers from a generally negative reputation among other professionals and the public in general. This poor reputation inhibits the reporting of abuse and justifies a certain reluctance to cooperate and collaborate.
- The resources of the system are disproportionately devoted to the process of investigation—that is, to determining whether abuse occurred or not, rather than remediation and help for families and children.
- The system is vulnerable to disruptive, defensive policy gyrations, particularly in response to high-profile cases. When a child dies while in the custody of a previously identified abuser, the policy pendulum swings in one direction. When a child is removed unjustly or suffers harm while in state custody, the pendulum swings the other way. Such fluctuations do not make for good policy.
- There is little evaluation and accountability in a system of such size and authority. Very little of the policy of the child protection system is based on research-tested practice, and very little ongoing evaluation and few solid statistical indicators exist to allow the system to judge whether it is working well or not.

A variety of reform propositions have been tendered as starting places for the improvement of the child protection system.[468] Some have argued that the investigative function should be greatly reduced or transferred to law enforcement, and experiments have been undertaken in this direction.[439,469] Others have argued for child protection to be more explicitly medicalized and integrated as a branch of the public-health system, as it is in places such as England and the Netherlands.[470] The current crisis in our medical care financing system and the absence of a real state-sponsored public-health system make this an unlikely solution in the United States.

What is much more likely is a flurry of incremental changes to the child protection system. I suggest a number of directions for reforms that seem plausible, modest, and feasible.

Learning from Law Enforcement

It has always seemed that, even though we do not want child protection officials to act like police, they could learn a lot from the police. The police and child protection services share many common challenges. They are both arms of a sometimes coercive state authority. They are charged with rooting out and preventing antisocial behavior. They have an adversarial relationship with some of the people they deal with. They work in dangerous and unpleasant circumstances. They confer daunting authority, responsibility, and discretion on individuals of relatively modest education and social-class position. In spite of these challenges, law enforcement has managed to attain a fairly high level of legitimacy and public confidence. Child protection has fallen quite short by comparison—but this shouldn't be seen as inevitable. The activities that child welfare workers engage in—the protection and rescue of endangered children—could earn much of the same respect that crime fighting has.

Here are five components of police success that might be better emulated by child protection:

1. **Build the charisma of child protection**. Even though police spend most of their time in dull pursuits, writing motor vehicle citations, taking reports of thefts, and dispersing unruly teenagers, this is not their image. Police are perceived as crime fighters, homicide investigators, highly skilled marksmen, masters of technology, and defenders of neighborhoods. By contrast, the child protection authorities have done a poor job of conveying the charismatic aspects of their work. Just as in police work, the brilliant investigations, timely rescues, grateful victims, and reformed offenders are relatively rare, but they exist, and the public—and even the professional community—has rarely been exposed to these inspiring stories in the way that it has with the crime-fighting police. Some of this has to do with the extreme confidentiality that cloaks child welfare work, but surely there are ways to convey these inspirational stories to the public so that the importance and heroism of child protection could be better appreciated.

2. **Establish a professional child protection corps.** Law enforcement has devised a successful formula for the creation of a corps of relatively disciplined, well-trained, and committed professionals who inspire public confidence, using as raw materials individuals who are not particularly highly educated or well paid (compared, say, to the professionals in the public-health or education arenas). They have done this by giving the corps a distinct persona that its members can identify with. They build loyalty through high standards and rigorous training procedures. They maintain a clear hierarchy and career path that inspire commitment and ambition. They have highly publicized review boards to maintain accountability and weed out unprofessional behavior.

   The child protection system could move more toward this model. The system could give workers a more identifiable persona—for example, a distinctive sweater or jacket that workers could wear or an insignia they could display on their cars. They could establish more rigorous and visible child protection academies. They could create publicized honors for professional child protection heroism. Better defined career hierarchies could be developed. This would probably have to be combined with pay increases and improved working conditions, but in the end, child protection, even at higher salaries, should be a cheaper public service than police protection with its sometimes expensive technology and infrastructural expenditures.
3. **Develop positive community outreach.** One of the key public-relations dilemmas that police in the United States have successfully finessed is to persuade the public to see them as "good guys," even while much of what they do is keep people in line. (In other countries, such as France, police have been less adept at promoting this image.) An important component of this success is that police combine their social control functions—ticket writing, corralling of drunks, etc.—with highly visible positive community service functions, such as leading drug education programs in schools, offering community notification about ex-offenders, and other public safety campaigns.

   By contrast, the child protection system is publicly identified almost exclusively by its child abuse investigation function, even though these agencies may be doing other things. This means they are identified almost exclusively as people who take children away from their parents or make threats to do so. It might help considerably to inspire a more positive view if state child protection workers were more publicly involved in activities such as teaching positive parenting skills and child safety in schools and elsewhere, engaging in media campaigns, and providing seasonal reminders about child welfare.

4. **Offer neighborhood-based child protection**. Police have built their legitimacy in part through a strong local, community presence. Community policing has actually been rediscovered in recent years as an effective crime-prevention tool after some years of greater specialization and bureaucratization. People like seeing the police in the community, having informal interactions with them, and knowing where they can be accessed. Child protection might well benefit from such a decentralized community presence as well. Modern technology has made obsolete the need for a highly centralized child welfare office. Community-based child protection workers who could be seen as resources for parenting and child safety information might help out considerably to improve the reputation of the institution and perhaps even the appeal of the job.
5. **Apply a broader definition of child protection**. The police force is a multifunction agency, with a broad spectrum of services. Officers respond to crime, traffic problems, and psychiatric emergencies, to name just few items in their portfolio. They are trained in an enormous variety of crisis situations.The child welfare system might benefit from accommodating a broader spectrum of child welfare functions and capabilities. These functions could include parent education, home visiting, and school-based educational programs on parenting and child safety. Specialized workers could undertake these different functions, as is the case in some police departments, but they would be perceived as emanating from the same agency. This would both allow the institution to take a more holistic approach to child protection and leaven the social control functions with community service functions as proposed earlier.

Evidence-Based Practice

Neither police nor child protection does a very good job of subjecting its practice to formal evaluation. Law enforcement perhaps has a bit more to show, and can boast of some large-scale formal evaluations of practices such as mandatory domestic-violence arrests, community policing, and road blocks.[471] By contrast, practically no portion of conventional child protection practice has been subjected to formal evaluation. To see what large-scale evidence-based practice looks like, one needs to turn to the public-health system, where evaluation is an integral part of the evolution of professional practice.

It is noteworthy that in public health, the need for evaluation is accepted and valued by staff at all levels. Ordinary family practice physicians do not object to research, as many child protection workers or even police officers would, on the grounds that research and evaluation distract from and interfere with the more important priorities of saving lives, protecting children, and catching criminals. This is because of their training, which orients them to evaluation, and also because they have seen how evaluation improves practice.

In the long term, the true legitimacy of and public confidence in the child welfare system will need to be based on scientific evidence of its utility and efficacy. The public and policy makers will need to know definitively that children really are better off as a result of the actions of child protection workers. They will need to know that the costs of the system and the intrusions into family life sanctioned by the system have large, demonstrable payoffs. Until this happens, the system will have credibility problems and will be mired in politics. Only when administrators can point to studies that say "What we are doing is working" will they be able to combat the backlash from the inevitable political frenzy that occurs in the wake of a child who dies or a parent who is mistakenly accused.

Several initiatives could lead to a more evidence-based child welfare system. For one, the federal government and private foundations could collaborate to establish a National Center for Child Protection System Research and Evaluation that could fund large-scale and systematic evaluations of core elements of child protection practice. Second, states could be encouraged to experiment and innovate with regard to core components of child protection practice, on the condition that the innovations be subjected to careful, independent evaluation. Core components that could be subject to evaluation include the breadth and operation of mandatory reporting, the criteria for substantiation, and the standards and practices surrounding the removal of children or the termination of parental rights.

Multiprofessional Collaboration and Child Protection "Deputies"

One of the more successful recent innovations in child protection practice has been the introduction of multiprofessional collaboration. This collaboration has improved the standing of the child protection system among allied professionals and has led to more integrated and less bureaucratic responses to endangered children. The collaboration that has been best developed in the last decade is that between child protection and law enforcement agencies. Communities have seen the development of collaborative investigations, information and decision-making protocols, and agencies such as children's advocacy centers that bring representatives of different professions and institutions together under one roof.

Other forms of collaborative practice need to be developed as well. One thing that might be useful to the child protection system is the devolution of investigatory, monitoring, and intervention responsibilities to other community professionals under a system of what might be called "registered reporters," "designated professionals," or "child protection deputies."

One of the barriers that consistently divide members of the child protection system and other community professionals is the inflexibility of the mandatory reporting system. Professionals are required to report even suspicions of child maltreatment, without any confidence that something positive will result. In making the report, they know they may be jeopardizing their own relationship with the child or family and perhaps compromising their own capacity to influence or intervene. Many professionals believe they are better positioned to act and even more competent than state child protection authorities. Yet they are required to cede authority to the system while at the same time putting their own personal relationship with clients at risk. It is this conflict, perhaps more than any other, that breeds disrespect, resentment, and criticism toward child protection. It also leads many professionals to wantonly disregard their mandatory reporting obligations, further widening the divide between the system and the community, because professionals cannot be honest about their practice with child protection officials. This makes it hard for them to work together.

A Devolution of Responsibility

One solution to the above problem would be for the child protection system to concede to the obvious expertise and abilities of certain community professionals. Well-trained and experienced professionals in fields such as mental health, school counseling, and pediatrics may be able to use their judgment and embedded relationships with some families to produce superior outcomes than could be achieved through the system of centralized reporting, investigation, and referral. It is at least worth an experiment.

The key to the success of some devolution of responsibility is to make sure that the "child protection deputies" are indeed well trained and capable in the diagnosis of child abuse and intervention. It is also important that they have clear recognition of the limitations of their abilities and know when state intervention is really required.

States, under this proposal, could create a special status that community professionals could apply for. To qualify, professionals would need to show that they have had sufficient training and experience with regard to child maltreatment. In addition, these professionals might need to participate in some special training so that everyone inside and outside the state system is on the same page. Once certified, these professionals would be relieved of the responsibility of making mandatory reports for certain clearly defined kinds of child maltreatment. (Cases involving clear-cut criminal acts, serious injury to a child, and many sexual offenses might be excluded.) Perhaps they would still need to file a report on the case for statistical and monitoring purposes, but the report would lack identifying information about the specific child and family.

Would professionals be willing to register for such status? Some might do so simply to be relieved of the interference they believe reporting obligations pose in their therapeutic relationships with families. Others, representing schools and hospitals, for example, might do so to assist a range of other professionals working in those institutions. One major potential benefit for the child protection system from this devolution of responsibility to "child protection deputies" might be a reduction in caseload. The centralized child protection system would have fewer cases requiring investigation, but at the same time more time and effort would go into the training and monitoring of the deputies.

Such devolution of responsibility would, of course, raise legitimate concerns. Would community professionals, in fact, be competent and responsible—perhaps even more effective than state officials? Or would some use their new dispensation to abdicate their reporting responsibilities? Evaluation might lead the way to training and selection practices that would maximize the former and minimize the latter. Would such a system undermine the notion of mandatory reporting, which has been the cornerstone of the child protection ethic in this country for a generation? Administered properly, devolution of responsibility might change little about the mandatory reporting ethic, or it might give it new legitimacy by curtailing the perceived irrationality of the system.

It may be time to modify or experiment with the mandatory reporting system, anyway. One of the main objectives of the mandatory reporting laws was to apprise professionals in all walks of life about their affirmative responsibility to identify and do something about child maltreatment when they encountered it. The requirement forced professionals of all sorts to learn about child maltreatment and plan for what to do. But it may be that this awareness and its associated practices are now strongly institutionalized in most professions and do not need the mandatory reporting laws as they are currently framed in order to be perpetuated. The mandatory reporting laws are a one-size-fits-all garment, and in a professional world with considerably more knowledge and skill regarding child maltreatment, it may be time to tailor an approach to the specific knowledge, abilities, and resources of differently situated professionals.

Broad-Spectrum School-Based Victimization Prevention

There are many reasons that advocates of victimization prevention have chosen schools as a preferred locale for their prevention efforts. Considerable victimization occurs in and around schools, so the topic is relevant. Large numbers of young people assemble in schools, so delivery of programs is cheap and efficient. School personnel know a lot about effective education, and students are used to learning in that environment, so prevention education modalities are familiar and appropriate there.

Encouragingly, victimization prevention has proved successful in the school environment. Many school-based programs have produced evaluation results showing that they can change attitudes and behaviors regarding aggression and bullying.[472–476] But there have also been at least a few true randomized, controlled trials—the gold standard for evaluation research—that have shown school-based victimization prevention programs to be effective, too.[477]

One of these programs is the Safe Dates dating-violence-prevention program, developed at the University of North Carolina. It is a curriculum of 10 45-minute sessions taught by health and physical education teachers, and it includes a poster contest and a play performed by students. A total of 1,885 students were randomly assigned to receive the program through their schools, and there was less dating-violence perpetration and victimization among the students who had participated in the program at four different follow-up intervals.[478]

Another school-based prevention program deemed effective in a randomized trial is the Second Step program, targeted at bullying and assaults among elementary and middle school children. Second Step involves 30 instructional sessions, each 35 minutes in duration, involving role playing and videos with an emphasis on empathy, impulse control, problem solving, and anger management. Second- and third-grade classes in 12 schools were randomly assigned to program and control conditions, with a result of lower levels of aggression among students involved in the program even 6 months after its completion.[479]

These studies and many others suggest that the concept of school-based prevention of violence and victimization can work. However, school-based prevention does have its drawbacks. One concern is whether it is really applicable to all forms of child victimization. For example, one might have doubts that a school-based program could help prevent the physical abuse of infants and young children by caretakers, given that most school-age children are somewhat removed from the prospect of parenthood. Nonetheless, some parenting education, often called "family life skills," is being offered at the high school level. As far as we know, its effectiveness at preventing child maltreatment has not been evaluated.

Others have raised concerns about whether school-based programs can be effective in preventing sexual abuse in particular,[480–482] even though considerable effort has gone into this approach.[54] The doubters base their skepticism on several issues. For one, they consider sexual abuse to be a cognitively complicated concept that may be too difficult to convey via group instruction. Second, they are concerned that the highly charged emotional and moral issues surrounding sexuality, and the issues they raise for students and families, may make it hard to ensure quality instruction on this topic. They also have qualms about the morality of the approach, arguing that it puts the onus of preventing sexual abuse on the children themselves rather than on the adults in the community, where it belongs. Finally, some have contended that it is based on a flawed premise: that children are capable of foiling the intentions of motivated child molesters.[483] The argument is that this is a difficult or impossible expectation.

These objections, while plausible, are not compelling, especially in light of the declining rates of sexual abuse in recent years and the positive empirical evidence that has accrued in support of school-based prevention efforts in general. For example, sexual abuse may be cognitively complicated, and some forms of noncoercive sexual abuse that are accompanied by extensive grooming and affection may be difficult for children to identify. But many forms of sexual abuse are relatively easy for children to identify—because they are coercive, unpleasant, and attempted by awkward and anxious offenders—and many of the safety rules about touching and about the special nature of private parts are clear-cut and intuitive. These programs do not necessarily need to work with all forms of sexual abuse and all offenders to have some efficacy.

Moreover, other types of victimization, such as bullying, have cognitively complicated elements as well—for example, being openly disliked does not always equal bullying, and kids do get hit "by accident." Nonetheless, there are some programs that have been proven effective at reducing bullying.[472,479] It may be that school-based programs about sexual abuse do indeed have limited effectiveness with very young children, but it is not unreasonable to expect that children older than 8 years, who are at the beginning of an age period in which sexual abuse becomes more likely,[484] will be able to acquire and use the key concepts of sexual abuse prevention.[485] The fact that many studies show that children absorb the concepts taught in sexual abuse prevention education undercuts the notion that it is too cognitively complicated for children.[486]

The argument about the immorality of placing the burden of prevention on children has carried a lot of weight with many child advocates, who naturally do not want to be seen as oppressors. But it is not an argument that withstands a great deal of scrutiny. This objection can be applied to the prevention of any problem for which adults bear some responsibility. According to such logic, it is immoral to teach children pedestrian safety, because the problem is bad drivers. It is immoral to teach children nutritional health, because the problem is corporate marketing to children. This is a well-intended argument offered in an attempt to make sure that we take a broad approach to prevention and do not leave the responsibility *solely* to children. But especially in cases where we know that child safety measures can make a difference, it actually becomes immoral *not* to rely to some extent on children's own prevention capacities. So, for example, protecting kids on bicycles should really be the responsibility of adults, who should drive more safely, but we know that bicycle helmets save lives, and it would be immoral to deprive children of that advantage. In fact, children, if asked, almost certainly would want to have whatever information and resources might help them stay safe, even if everyone agreed that preserving their safety shouldn't be solely their responsibility.

Skeptics of sexual abuse prevention education also like to point to studies of sex offenders who dismiss the possibility that they would have been deterred or dissuaded by actions children might have taken. Some of the research on offenders indeed shows many of them to be full of guile and quite persistent in their overtures.[487] Nonetheless, there are limitations to the conclusions one can draw from such evidence. For one thing, convicted offenders, or adults in general, may be reluctant to acknowledge the influence children's actions have on their own behavior, and so they minimize the ability of their victims to foil their advances. In addition, offenders may not be entirely conscious of the factors that go into their victim selection, and so they minimize the subtle behaviors and awareness that actually protect some children. Moreover, convicted offenders may not be representative of all offenders. For example, younger, inexperienced, and intrafamilial offenders, who are not represented as much in these samples, may be more easily put off by what children do. Testimonials by offenders that prevention advice won't work are no more persuasive about its efficacy than are survivors' assertions about how much they believe prevention education might have helped.

The evidence that sexual abuse prevention education might be effective is not yet strong, but it is suggestive. At least one study has found that groups of young people exposed to prevention education have lower rates of sexual abuse victimization.[488] Evaluations show that children acquire concepts and may be able to put them in action.[486,489] It is certainly premature to abandon this particular strategy, and more experimentation and evaluation are warranted.

Unfortunately, when it comes to evaluation, sexual abuse prevention is a hard outcome to confirm because victimization base rates are relatively low. This means that one may have to train and study a very large population of children in order to detect a statistically significant advantage for the program. Moreover, the methodology for reliably gathering information from children is fraught with problems, not the least of which is the possibility that prevention education may make it more likely that children in the treatment group will disclose their abuse to authorities or researchers. Nonetheless, it is premature to conclude that prevention education is hopeless or ineffective. The evidence for school-based victimization prevention in general, and sexual abuse prevention in particular, is strong enough to warrant more research, including studies large enough and sophisticated enough to detect an effect.

Those urging a public-health approach to sexual abuse and other victimization prevention certainly have a strong point about the importance of a broad spectrum of approaches that include more education directed at adults and organizations.[490,491] But a public-health approach should supplement school-based prevention, not be seen as an alternative to it. Ironically, some people who have criticized school-based sexual abuse prevention education as unproven have proposed other strategies that are at best highly experimental, such as community-wide appeals through advertisements to offenders to stop their offending and get help.[487] This is a strategy worthy of some consideration and evaluation, but there is as yet little evidence that this strategy can be broadly effective. It is one thing—and a very positive one—to argue for expanded efforts and a greater variety of prevention approaches. It is another thing, and quite dangerous in my view, to urge the abandonment of a strategy with some promising evidence in favor of other strategies with little evidence.

Establishing the effectiveness of school-based prevention programs is, unfortunately, just a first step. An even bigger and more serious problem facing school-based victimization prevention is getting these programs widely adopted. Schools are an effective venue, but, maybe for that reason, they are an exclusive venue. Schools see an overwhelming number of educational and social policy agendas dropped on their doorstep. In schools, the victimization prevention agenda faces stiff competition.

This is where the fragmented nature of the child victimization field is such a big liability. School officials concerned about victimization are confronted with an assemblage of competing prevention curricula. Some target dating violence, others bullying, others sexual harassment, others sexual abuse. The developers of all of these programs emphasize their generic content, and most programs do indeed cover a variety of victimizations. But almost all of them also give particular emphasis to one kind of victimization. One can easily imagine why school principals or superintendents may simply decide to adopt no curriculum or to allow instructors to cherry-pick content from various curricula in a cafeteria-style approach.

What is needed is for those in the victimization field to come together on a comprehensive, integrated, and developmental curriculum to prevent child victimization at every age. This is no different from the way in which writing or mathematics is now taught, with the understanding that learning is a continuous and cumulative process. To accomplish this goal, victimization prevention educators need to figure out several things. First, they need to identify the core generic prevention skills that are relevant to all forms of victimization prevention. These may include skills such as boundary setting, self-assertion, empathy, negotiation, and seeking help. Then, they need to identify an appropriate developmental sequence for the introduction of these skills, as well as for the victimization-specific content. What do first-graders need to hear about bullying, violence, and so on, and what do fifth-graders need to hear? The developmental content needs to be based on both the kinds of victimization likely at different age levels and the capabilities and limitations of children relative to acquiring the knowledge and putting it into practice.

Very importantly, educators need to construct an approach that provides an adequate introduction to and sufficient training opportunity for all types of victimization. They need to package this efficiently, keeping in mind that school administrators are unlikely to sacrifice much precious time for new, nonacademic endeavors. The tightly integrated package needs to achieve broad-spectrum results while intruding minimally on the curriculum. This may mean careful studies of what concepts to present and reinforce, and at which times. These integrated developmental curricula exist for math and reading, and they need to be developed for victimization as well.

Prevention in Youth-Serving Organizations

Most youth-serving organizations have tight resources and big agendas organized around everything from sports to music to religious education. Child victimization is a particularly grim topic that, at best, seems a burden and, at worst, turns off staff and volunteers, and even young people. Organizations have often handled the issue only when faced with serious liability and/or public relations issues. But the expectation from the public, insurance providers, and the legal system that organizations provide strong protections against victimization is only going to grow. It makes sense for these organizations to start providing such protections in advance of any crises, and for educators and organizational consultants to encourage them to take such steps.

Because public relations and legal liability were prominent motivators, the initial prevention emphasis in youth-serving organizations—ranging from the Catholic Church to the Boy Scouts—was on sexual abuse. But these organizations are also important venues where children can be protected from and educated about other kinds of victimization, including physical abuse, bullying, sexual harassment, and Internet predation, all of which can occur at times within the organization.

Many organizations have hoped for a quick fix, which in most cases translates into background checks on employees and volunteers, a process that fortunately has become cheaper, quicker, and more readily accomplished in recent years. But background checks for criminal records are an extremely limited form of protection, for two generally well-recognized reasons. First, most adults who victimize children do not have prior criminal records that indicate such a tendency. Second, many of those who pose a risk to children in organizations, including other children and family members of staff and participants, are not subject to background checks. So, in cases where background checks lull organizations into a sense of having "done their duty," the background checks may actually be counterproductive.

Youth-serving organizations need to adopt a comprehensive strategy for protecting children.[492] The strategy needs to encompass a thorough review of victimization threats and to protect against victimization in four specific organizational processes, described below.

Hiring and Volunteering

While a lot of the emphasis has been put on background checks, what is likely to be more effective is what might be called "foreground checks." *Foreground* means that the topic needs to be brought to the "fore" in recruitment and hiring. Organizations need to articulate their child protection agenda early and often in the course of recruitment and screening. They can do this by informing applicants about the importance of child protection, explaining the steps that they take to ensure it and eliciting comments and information from applicants relevant to this issue. It is true that few applicants will voluntarily disclose information that suggests their unsuitability, but an emphasis on the issue has two other positive benefits. First, it may discourage unsuitable candidates because they won't want to work or volunteer in an environment where they sense a high level of scrutiny. Second, it helps teach prospective employees and volunteers that child protection will be an important part of the agenda during their involvement in the organization.

Training

More child protection information and practice needs to be embedded in the training that individuals receive to work in organizations providing services to children. Some of this training is straightforward. Employees and volunteers need to know how to identify the different forms of child victimization. They need to understand their responsibilities when they identify suspected episodes, including children who are being victimized by persons unconnected with the organization. Their responsibilities need to include specific directives to reach outside the organization itself under some circumstances, such as when they have mandatory child maltreatment reporting obligations.

Employees and volunteers also need training in how to handle their own impulses. This component is missing even from much of the professional training provided to teachers and counselors. Many individuals new to working with children are unprepared for the challenges posed by sexualized children or those who have crushes on them, or who are provocative and uncooperative. Many individuals also do not anticipate how their own life conditions—for example, depressions, romantic rejections, or drug usage—can easily lead to potential violations of the boundaries between them and the children, including sexual and aggressive behaviors. In some cases employees and volunteers need to be taught specific behavioral techniques for dealing with these situations, possibly including scripted behaviors that can be rehearsed in advance.

Supervision

Youth-serving organizations need detailed, clear, and specific guidelines on acceptable behavior for both adults and youth. These organizations often have guidelines to promote orderliness and cooperation but lack guidelines that prevent abuse, victimization, and boundary violations. These guidelines should cover the circumstances under which adults are allowed to be alone with children; the kinds of touching that are acceptable; and how sleeping, toileting, and other private activities are to be handled. The guidelines also need to cover reporting practices, such as when staff should report violations of these guidelines to supervisors. This is a very hard practice to cultivate, since staff and volunteers usually feel considerable loyalty toward one another. But in the area of child protection, it is important for organizations to emphasize the staff's responsibility for preventing laxness in other volunteers and employees.

Child/Family/Client Empowerment

Prevention education, or *target hardening*, entails the empowerment of the children and their families to resist and report victimizations that occur at the hands of other adults and children who are part of the organization. It also means imparting skills and awareness that children and families can use to prevent victimizations from arising in the first place. There are many ways for this empowerment to be brought about. For instance, some organizations give youth and families pamphlets to read or videos to watch. Some conduct classes or educational sessions for children. It probably helps to have some of the staff and volunteers purvey this information; the more interaction that occurs between staff and children regarding these issues, the easier it may be to talk about the topics, and the more important they will seem.

Establishing a comprehensive child protection approach is a challenge for many youth-serving organizations, which may lack resources and expertise. In recent years, some organizations have tried to borrow from the materials and resources of other organizations that have invested more time and effort in the development of their approaches.

Child protection advocates could take a number of steps to promote the diffusion of these prevention activities into more youth-serving organizations. One step would be to develop more generic materials that could be used or adapted by the organizations. Another might be to establish a clearinghouse or resource center where the organizations could access and review existing materials, guidelines, and training programs. Child protection advocates might also establish a process for reviewing and rating these materials so that, in the tradition of the Underwriters Laboratory or *Consumer Reports*, there would be a sense of which resources were thought by experts to be of higher quality.

Concerns about legal liability and public transparency have created a demand for a method of auditing the performance of youth-serving organizations in the child protection domain. Thus, for example, in the wake of the clergy abuse scandal, the U.S. Conference of Catholic Bishops (USCCB) instituted a process of auditing the dioceses about their compliance with the child protection guidelines issued by the USCCB. Likewise, it may become important for child protection advocates to establish guidelines for this type of auditing, so as to ensure that it is done in a fair, dispassionate, and thorough fashion.

All signs point to continuing growth in organizations interested in promoting child protection activities. The task for those concerned about child victimization is to make sure these activities are as comprehensive and as high in quality as possible. The experience of the D.A.R.E. program in the domain of drug abuse prevention shows how difficult and disappointing the results can be when an ineffective approach dominates the market, and how hard it is to reverse course once this has happened. Child protection advocates should try to ensure, through research, that this kind of development is not repeated in the field of victimization prevention.

Conclusion

The child protection field has a lot to be proud of. It is fair to say that child advocates have transformed the landscape in America concerning the welfare of children. Issues of child victimization and safety have been in the limelight for at least three decades, and there is every sign that they will remain there. Indeed, the awareness of crime and abuse against children has a persistence that belies the comments of many pundits about the typically short shelf life of social-problem concerns. Yet the field has been more effective in raising awareness than it has been at transforming that awareness into demonstrably effective action and policy. When policymakers decide that, yes, they want to prevent child abuse, or stop youth homicide, or make schools bully-free zones, it is not as if they have a set of proven remedies to turn to. The field has been much better at drawing attention to the issues than at figuring out what needs to be done to resolve them. In spite of many exhortations to implement one solution or another, there is a tremendous amount that remains unknown about what works and what doesn't.

The biggest challenge that the field faces is how to move from exhortation—where we spend our efforts alerting and alarming people about the problem—to implementation. Implementation is hard. For one thing, it makes allies and adversaries. As an example, people who agree that child abuse is a terrible problem can become adversaries when asked if it is better to invest in neonatal home visitation or in parent–child interaction training.

Implementation also requires research, critical thinking, and the willingness to abandon treasured strategies that have turned out to be ineffective—all challenging undertakings. Fortunately, the motivation to take on these hard jobs does not need to come just from within. The climate of public policy is becoming more demanding, a fortunate shift in our view. The standards for advocates and program proponents in all these fields are rising; in some cases they are doing so slowly and fitfully, but they are rising nonetheless. Child protection advocates may not always be inclined to embrace the standards, but they will be increasingly required to implement them.

This is more good news for children. Children will benefit most when we have strong and effective programs for protecting them from victimization. But the transition to implementation can be slow or fast depending on how readily it is embraced. Let us hope the time is ripe for all concerned about child victimization to band together and promote comprehensive, conceptually sound, and empirically tested remedies for a scourge in the lives of our children.

Notes

Chapter 1

*The problem referred to here concerns the counting of what are called "series victimizations" in the NCVS, or repeated crimes at the hands of the same individual(s), such as in cases of spousal assault or school bullying. When such crimes exceed six in one measurement period, NCVS generally counts them as a *single* victimization (because the agency considers it impossible to characterize all the episodes). Juveniles experience a disproportionate number of these series victimizations. The following shows the contrast between juveniles ages 12–17 and young adults ages 18–24, first under the conventional NCVS rules that count a

Series Counted as One Victimization

	Juvenile	Young Adult
Rape/SA	2.1	3.1
Robbery	4.9	5.4
Aggravated Assault	8.9	11.5
Simple Assault	39.2	32.2

Series Counted as Actual Number of Victimizations

	Juvenile	Young Adult
Rape/SA	5.3	6.1
Robbery	8.1	6.8
Aggravated Assault	19.3	15.1
Simple Assault	69.8	52.5

series as just one victimization and then under rules that count the actual number of victimizations reported by the respondents.

†The annual rate of serious *intrafamilial* violent assault for children was 67 per 1,000 for teens, according to the Developmental Victimization Survey, compared to the overall violent victimization rate shown in the NCVS of 84 per 1,000.[2,8]

§This takes the percentage of violent crimes committed against children in the jurisdictions covered by the National Incident Based Reporting System and multiplies it by the total number of violent crimes nationally.

Chapter 2

*Figure 2.5 shows the percentage of each age cohort experiencing any victimization or any specific type of victimization, but it does not show the total frequency of victimizations. However, taking victimization frequency—which is roughly the same at all ages—into account does not change the shape of the lines shown in the figure.

Chapter 3

*These protection processes are different from and should not be confused with the protection processes described in the stress process model. The latter concern how stressful events are translated into mental health and life-course difficulties. In our terms, protection processes are personal capabilities that allow children to ward off victimization and victimizers.

References

1. Wells, L. E., & Rankin, J. H. (1995). Juvenile victimization: Convergent validation of alternative measurements. *Journal of Research in Crime, 32*(3), 287–307.
2. Baum, K. (2005). Juvenile victimization and offending, 1993–2003. Washington, DC: Office of Justice Programs, U.S. Department of Justice.
3. Garofalo, J., Siegel, L., & Laub, J. (1987). School-related victimizations among adolescents: An analysis of National Crime Survey (NCS) narratives. *Journal of Quantitative Criminology, 3*, 321–338.
4. Planty, M. (2003). An examination of adolescent telescoping: Evidence from the National Crime Victimization Survey. *58th Annual AAPOR Conference.* Nashville, TN: American Association for Public Opinion Research.
5. Bureau of Justice Statistics. (2006). *Criminal offender statistics.* Retrieved June 9, 2006, from http://www.ojp.usdoj.gov/bjs/crimoff.htm.
6. Snyder, H. N., & Sickmund, M.(2006). Juvenile offenders and victims: 2006 National Report. Washington, DC: U.S. Department of Justice, Office of Justice Programs, Office of Juvenile Justice and Delinquency Prevention.
7. Straus, M. A., Gelles, R. J., & Steinmetz, S. K. (1980). *Behind closed doors.* Newbury Park, CA: Sage.
8. Finkelhor, D., Ormrod, R. K., Turner, H. A., & Hamby, S. L. (2005). The victimization of children and youth: A comprehensive national survey. *Child Maltreatment, 10*(1), 5–25.
9. U.S. Department of Health and Human Services. (2006). Administration on Children, Youth and Families. *Child Maltreatment 2004.* Washington, DC: U.S. Government Printing Office.
10. Hodges, E. V. E., Malone, M. J., & Perry, D. G. (1997). Individual risk and social risk as interacting determinants of victimization in the peer group. *Developmental Psychology, 33*(6), 1032–1039.
11. Lauritsen, J. L., Sampson, R. J., & Laub, J. H. (1991). The link between offending and victimization among adolescents. *Criminology, 29*, 265–292.

12. Lauritsen, J. L., Laub, J. H., & Sampson, R. J. (1992). Conventional and delinquent activities: Implications for the prevention of violent victimization among adolescents. *Violence and Victims*, *7*(2), 91–108.
13. Fagan, F., Piper, E. S., & Cheng, Y. (1987). Contributions of victimization to delinquency in inner cities. *Journal of Criminal Law and Criminology*, *78*, 586–613.
14. Cuevas, C., Finkelhor, D., Turner, H. A., & Ormrod, R. K. (in press). Juvenile delinquency and victimization: A theoretical typology. *Journal of Interpersonal Violence*.
15. Straus, M. A. (1995). Trends in cultural norms and rates of partner violence: An update to 1992. In S. Stith & M. A. Straus (Eds.), *Understanding partner violence: Prevalence, causes, consequences, and solutions* (pp. 30–33). Minneapolis: National Council on Family Relations.
16. Straus, M. A., & Mathur, A. (1996). Social change and the trends in approval of corporal punishment by parents from 1968 to 1994. In D. Frehsee, W. Horn, & K. D. Bussman (Eds.), *Family violence against children: A challenge for society* (pp. 91–105). New York: Walter deGruyter.
17. Rosenfeld, R. (2004). The case of the unsolved crime decline. *Scientific American*, *290*(2), 82–89.
18. Fairbanks, M., Maullin & Associates, & The Tarrance Group (1996). *Polling data*. Woodland Hills, CA: California Wellness Foundation.
19. Soler, M. (2001). *Public opinion on youth, crime, and race: A guide for advocates*. Retrieved February 23, 2006, from http://www.buildingblocksforyouth.org/advocacyguide.pdf.
20. Mennel, R. M. (1982). Attitudes and polices toward juvenile delinquency in the United States: A historiographical review. In M. Tonry & N. Morris (Eds.), *Crime and justice: An annual review of research* (pp. 191–224). Chicago: University of Chicago Press.
21. Platt, A. (1974). The child-saving movement and the origins of the juvenile justice system. In R. Quinney (Ed.), *Criminal justice in America* (pp. 362–383). Boston: Little, Brown.
22. Masson, J. M. (1984). *The assault on truth: Freud's suppression of the seduction theory*. New York: Farrar, Straus & Giroux.
23. Margolin, G., & Gordis, E. B. (2000). The effects of family and community violence on children. *Annual Review of Psychology*, *51*, 445–479.
24. Jenkins, P. (1998). *Moral panic: Changing concepts of the child monster in modern America*. New Haven, CT: Yale University Press.
25. Finkelhor, D. (1984). *Child sexual abuse: New theory and research*. New York: Free Press.
26. Finkelhor, D., Hotaling, G. T., & Sedlak, A. (1990). *Missing, abducted, runaway and thrownaway children in America: First report*. Washington, DC: Juvenile Justice Clearinghouse.
27. Sedlak, A. J., Finkelhor, D., Hammer, H., & Schultz, D. J. (2002). *National estimates of missing children: An overview* (p. 12). Washington, DC: Office of Juvenile Justice and Delinquency Prevention.
28. Best, J. (1990). *Threatened children: Rhetoric and concern about child-victims*. Chicago: University of Chicago Press.
29. Vossekuil, B., Reddy, M., Fein, R., Borum, R., & Modzeleski, W. (2000). *U.S. Secret Service Safe School initiative: An interim report on the*

prevention of targeted violence in schools (pp. 1–9). Washington, DC: U.S. Secret Service, National Threat Assessment Center.

30. Brooks, K., Schiraldi, V., & Ziedenberg, J. (1999). *School house hype: Two years later* (pp. 1–25). Washington, DC: Center of Juvenile Crime and Justicep.
31. Nelson, B. J. (1983). *Making an issue of child abuse: Political agenda setting for social problems*. Chicago: University of Chicago Press.
32. Forst, M. L., & Blomquist, M. (1991). *Missing children: Rhetoric and reality*. New York: Lexington Books.
33. Cooper, S. W., Kellogg, N. D., & Giardino, A. P. (2006). *Child sexual exploitation quick reference: For health care, social service, and law enforcement professionals*. St. Louis, MO: G. W. Medical Publishing.
34. Ross, D. M. (1996). *Childhood bullying and teasing: What school personnel, other professionals, and parents can do*. Alexandria, VA: American Counseling Association.
35. Ross, D. M. (2003). *Childhood bullying, teasing, and violence: What school personnel, other professionals, and parents can do*, 2nd ed. Alexandria, VA: American Counseling Association.
36. Rickert, V., Vaughan, R., & Wiemann, C. (2002). Adolescent dating violence and date rape. *Adult and Pediatric Psychology*, *14*(5), 495–500.
37. Gorman-Smith, D., & Tolan, P. H. (1998). The role of exposure to community violence and developmental problems among inner-city youth. *Development and Psychopathology*, *10*(1), 101–116.
38. Fantuzzo, J., & Mohr, W. (1999). Prevalence and effects of child exposure to domestic violence. *The Future of Children*, *9*(3), 21–32.
39. Heinz, J., Ryan, G., & Bengis, S. (1991). The system's response to juvenile sex offenders. In G. D. Ryan & S. L. Lane (Eds.), *Juvenile sexual offending: Causes, consequences, and correction* (pp. 185–198). Lexington, MA: Lexington Books.
40. Lynch, M., & Cicchetti, D. (1998). An ecological transactional analysis of children and contexts: The longitudinal interplay among child maltreatment, community violence, and children's symptomatology. *Development and Psychopathology*, *10*, 235–257.
41. Perry, D. G., Hodges, E. V. E., & Egan, S. K. (2001). Determinants of chronic victimization by peers: A review and new model of family influence. In J. Juvonen & S. Graham (Eds.), *Peer harassment in school: The plight of the vulnerable and victimized* (pp. 73–104). New York: Guilford Press.
42. Finkelhor, D., & Asdigian, N. L. (1996). Risk factors for youth victimization: Beyond a lifestyles theoretical approach. *Violence & Victims*, *11*(1), 3–20.
43. Finkelhor, D., Turner, H. A., & Ormrod, R. K. (2006). Kid's stuff: The nature and impact of peer and sibling violence. *Child Abuse & Neglect*, *30*(12), 1401–1421.
44. Greven, P. (1990). *Spare the child: The religious roots of punishment and the psychological impact of physical abuse*. New York: Alfred A. Knopf.
45. Strassberg, Z., Dodge, K. A., Pettit, G. S., & Bates, J. E. (1994). Spanking in the home and children's subsequent aggression toward kindergarten peers. *Development and Psychopathology*, *6*, 445–461.
46. Straus, M. A. (1994). *Beating the devil out of them: Corporal punishment in American families*. New York: Lexington Books.

47. Jaffe, P. G., Wolfe, D. A., & Wilson, S. K. (1990). *Children of battered women*. Newbury Park, CA: Sage.
48. Wolak, J., & Finkelhor, D. (1998). Children exposed to partner violence. In J. L. Jasinski & L. M. Williams (Eds), *Partner violence: A comprehensive review of 20 years of research* (pp. 73–112). Thousand Oaks, CA.Sage.
49. Kilpatrick, D. G. (1990). *Violence as a precursor of women's substance abuse: The rest of the drugs-violence story*. Presented at the 98th Annual Convention of the American Psychological Association, Boston, MA.
50. Nader, K., Pynoos, R., Fairbanks, L., & Frederick, C. (1990). Children's PTSD reactions one year after a sniper attack at their school. *American Journal of Psychiatry*, *147*, 1526–1530.
51. Wolak, J., Mitchell, K. J., & Finkelhor, D. (2007). Unwanted and wanted exposure to online pornography in a national sample of youth Internet users. *Pediatrics*, *119*(2), 247–257.
52. Finkelhor, D., & Ormrod, R. K. (2001). *Child abuse reported to the police* (pp. 1–8). Washington, DC: Office of Juvenile Justice and Delinquency Prevention.
53. Hashima, P., & Finkelhor, D. (1999). Violent victimization of youth versus adults in the National Crime Victimization Survey. *Journal of Interpersonal Violence*, *14*(8), 799–820.
54. Finkelhor, D., & Dziuba-Leatherman, J. (1995). Victimization prevention programs: A national survey of children's exposure and reactions. *Child Abuse & Neglect*, 19(2), 129–139.
55. Finkelhor, D., Hamby, S. L., Ormrod, R. K., & Turner, H. A. (2005). The JVQ: Reliability, validity, and national norms. *Child Abuse & Neglect*, *29*(4), 383–412.
56. Finkelhor, D., Ormrod, R. K., & Turner, H. A. (2007). Poly-victimization: A neglected component in child victimization trauma. *Child Abuse & Neglect*, *31*, 7–26.
57. Finkelhor, D., Ormrod, R. K., Turner, H. A., & Hamby, S. L. (2005). Measuring poly-victimization using the JVQ. *Child Abuse & Neglect*, *29*(11), 1297–1312.
58. Hanson, R. F., Self-Brown, S., Fricker-Elhai, A. E., Kilpatrick, D. G., Saunders, B.E., & Resnick, H. S. (2006). The relations between family environment and violence exposure among youth: Findings from the national survey of adolescents. *Child Maltreatment*, *11*(1), 3–15.
59. Christoffel, K. K. (1990). Violent death and injury in US children and adolescents. *American Journal of Diseases of Children*, *144*, 697–706.
60. Christoffel, K. K., Anzinger, N. K., & Amari, M. (1983). Homicide in childhood: Distinguishable pattern of risk related to developmental levels of victims. *American Journal of Forensic Medicine and Pathology*, *4*(2), 129–137.
61. Crittenden, P. A., & Craig, S. E. (1990). Developmental trends in the nature of child homicide. *Journal of Interpersonal Violence*, *5*, 202–216.
62. Jason, J. (1983). Child homicide spectrum. *American Journal of Diseases of Children*, *137*, 578–581.
63. Jason, J., Carpenter, M. M., & Tyler, C. W. (1983). Underrecording of infant homicide in the United States. *American Journal of Public Health*, *73*(2), 195–197.
64. Sedlak, A. J. (1991). *National incidence and prevalence of child abuse and neglect: 1988—Revised report*. Rockville, MD: Westat.

65. Federal Bureau of Investigations. (1992). *Crime in the United States, 1991: Uniform crime reports*. Washington, DC: U.S. Department of Justice.
66. Bureau of Justice Statistics. (1992). *National crime survey*. Washington, DC: U.S. Department of Justice.
67. Kanazawa, S., & Still, M. C. (2000). Why men commit crimes (and why they desist). *Sociological Theory*, *18*, 434–447.
68. Greenberg, D. F. (1985). Age, crime, and social explanation. *American Journal of Sociology*, *91*, 1–21.
69. Grogger, J. (1998). Market wages and youth crime. *Journal of Labor Economics*, *16*(4), 756–791.
70. Finkelhor, D., & Ormrod, R. K. (2000). *Characteristics of crimes against juveniles* (pp. 1–11). Washington, DC: Office of Juvenile Justice and Delinquency Prevention.
71. Elliott, D. S., Huizinga, D., & Menard, S. (1989). *Multiple problem youth: Delinquency, substance use, and mental health problems*. New York: Springer-Verlag.
72. Finkelhor, D., & Ormrod, R. K. (1999). *Reporting crimes against juveniles (Juvenile Justice Bulletin)* (pp. 1–7). Washington, DC: U.S. Department of Justice, Office of Juvenile Justice and Delinquency Prevention.
73. Finkelhor, D., & Wells, M. (2003). Improving national data systems about juvenile victimization. *Child Abuse & Neglect*, *27*(1), 77–102.
74. Boney-McCoy, S., & Finkelhor, D. (1995). Prior victimization: A risk factor for child sexual abuse and for PTSD-related symptomatology among sexually abused youth. *Child Abuse & Neglect*, *19*(12),1401–1421.
75. Boney-McCoy, S., & Finkelhor, D. (1996). Is youth victimization related to trauma symptoms and depression after controlling for prior symptoms and family relationships? A longitudinal, prospective study. *Journal of Consulting and Clinical Psychology*, *64*(6), 1406–1416.
76. Eth, S., & Pynoos, R. S. (1985). *Post-Traumatic Stress Disorder in children: Progress in psychiatry*. Washington, DC: American Psychiatric Press.
77. Terr, L. (1990). *Too scared to cry*. New York: HarperCollins.
78. Catalano, S. M. (2004). *Criminal victimization, 2003* (pp. 1–12). Washington, DC: U.S. Department of Justice.
79. U.S. Department of Health and Human Services, Administration on Children, Youth and Families. (2004). *Child maltreatment 2002: Reports from the states to the National Child Abuse & Neglect Data System*. Washington, DC: U.S. Government Printing Office.
80. Sedlak, A. J., & Broadhurst, D. D. (1996). *Third national incidence study of child abuse and neglect*. Washington, DC: U.S. Department of Health and Human Services.
81. Axelrod, A., & Markow, D. (2001). *Hostile hallways: Bullying, teasing, and sexual harassment in school*. Washington, DC: American Association of University Women Educational Foundation.
82. Hammer, H., Finkelhor, D., & Sedlak, A. J. (2002). *Children abducted by family members: National estimates and characteristics* (p. 12). Washington, DC: Office of Juvenile Justice & Delinquency Prevention.
83. Fox, J. A. (2005). *Uniform crime reports [United States]: Supplementary homicide reports, 1976–2003 [Computer file] ICPSR04351-v1* (pp. 11–22). Ann Arbor, MI: Inter-University Consortium for Political and Societal Research.

84. Nansel, T. R., Overpeck, M., Pilla, R. S., Ruan, W. J., Simons-Morton, B., & Scheidt, P. C. (2001). Bullying behaviors among U.S. youth: Prevalence and association with psychosocial adjustment. *Journal of the American Medical Association*, *285*(16), 2094–2100.
85. Straus, M. A., Hamby, S. L., Finkelhor, D., Moore, D., & Runyan, D. K. (1998). Identification of child maltreatment with the Parent-Child Conflict Tactics Scales: Development and psychometric properties data for a national sample of American parents. *Child Abuse & Neglect*, *22*(4), 249–270.
86. Daro, D. (1999). *Public opinion and behaviors regarding child abuse prevention: 1999 survey*. Chicago: Prevent Child Abuse America.
87. Crandall, J. (2002). *Most say spanking's OK by parents but not by grade-school teachers* [telephone poll data]. Retrieved February 10, 2006, from http://abcnews.go.com/sections/us/DailyNews/spanking_p011021108.html.
88. Finkelhor, D. (2007). Commentary: Prevention of sexual abuse through educational programs directed toward children. *Pediatrics, 120*, 640–645.
89. Finkelhor, D., Hammer, H., & Sedlak, A. J. (2002). *Non-family abducted children: National estimates and characteristics* (p. 16). Washington, DC: Office of Juvenile Justice & Delinquency Prevention.
90. Douglas, E., & Finkelhor, D. (2006). *Childhood sexual abuse fact sheet*. Retrieved June 6, 2006, from http://www.unh.edu/ccrc/factsheet/pdf/CSA-FS20 .pdf.
91. Olweus, D. (1991). Bully/victim problems among schoolchildren: Basic facts and effects of a school based intervention program. In D. J. Pepler & K. H. Rubin (Eds.), *The development and treatment of childhood aggression* (pp. 411–448). Hillsdale, NJ: Lawrence Erlbaum.
92. Lauritsen, J. L. (2003). *How families and communities influence youth victimization*. Washington, DC: Office of Juvenile Justice and Delinquency Prevention.
93. Turner, H. A., Finkelhor, D., & Ormrod, R. K. (2007). Family structure variations in patterns and predictors of child victimization. *American Journal of Orthopsychiatry,* 77(2), 282–295.
94. Singer, S. I. (1981). Homogeneous victim-offenders populations: A review and some research implications. *Journal of Criminal Law & Criminology*, *72*(2), 779–788.
95. Arata, C. M. (2002). Child sexual abuse and sexual revictimization. *Clinical Psychology*, 9(2), 135–164.
96. Finkelhor, D., Ormrod, R. K., & Turner, H. A. (2007). Revictimization patterns in a national longitudinal sample of children and youth. *Child Abuse & Neglect*, *31*(5), 479–502.
97. Cohen, L. E. (1981). Modeling crime trends: A criminal opportunity perspective. *Journal of Research in Crime and Delinquency*, *17*, 140–159.
98. Gottfredson, M. R. (1986). Substantive contributions of victimization surveys. *Crime and Justice: An annual review of research*, *7*, 251–287.
99. Hindelang, M. S., Gottfredson, M., & Garofalo, J. (1978). *Victims of personal crime*. Cambridge, MA: Ballinger.
100. Miethe, T. D., & Meier, R. F. (1994). *Crime and its social context: Toward an integrated theory of offenders, victims, and situations* (p. 209). Albany, NY: State University of New York Press.
101. Jensen, G. F., & Brownfield, D. (1986). Gender, lifestyles, and victimization: Beyond routine activity theory. *Violence and Victims*, *1*, 85–99.

102. Sparks, R. F. (1982). *Research on victims of crime*. Washington, DC: Government Printing Office.
103. Finkelhor, D., Ormrod, R. K., & Turner, H. A. (in submission). The developmental epidemiology of childhood victimization. *Journal of Interpersonal Violence*.
104. Olweus, D. (1993). Bullies on the playground: The role of victimization. In C. H. Hart (Ed.), *Children of playgrounds: Research perspectives and applications* (pp. 85–128). Albany, NY: State University of New York Press.
105. Smith, P. K., Bowers, L., Binney, V., & Cowie, H. (1993). Relationships of children involved in bully/victim problems at school. In S. Duck (Ed.), *Learning about relationships* (pp. 184–205). Newbury Park, CA: Sage.
106. National Research Council. (1993). *Understanding child abuse and neglect*. Washington, DC: National Academies Press.
107. Mullick, M., Miller, L. J., & Jacobsen, T. (2001). Insight into mental illness and child maltreatment risk among mothers with major psychiatric disorders. *Psychiatric Services*, *52*(4), 488–492.
108. Walsh, C., MacMillan, H., & Jamieson, E. (2002). The relationship between parental psychiatric disorder and child physical and sexual abuse: Findings from the Ontario Health Supplement. *Child Abuse & Neglect*, *26*, 11–22.
109. Berdie, J., Berdie, M., Wexler, S., & Fisher, B. (1983). *An empirical study of families involved in adolescent maltreatment*. San Francisco: URSA Institute.
110. Garbarino, J. (1989). Troubled youth, troubled families: The dynamics of adolescent maltreatment. In D. Cicchetti & V. Carlson (Eds.), *Child maltreatment: Theory and research of the causes and consequences of child abuse and neglect* (pp. 685–706). New York: Cambridge University Press.
111. Libby, P., & Bybee, R. (1979). The physical abuse of adolescents. *Journal of Social Issues*, *35*, 101–126.
112. Schellenbach, C. J., & Guerney, L. F. (1987). Identification of adolescent abuse and future intervention prospects. *Journal of Adolescence*, *10*(1), 1–12.
113. Finkelhor, D. (1993). Epidemiological factors in the clinical identification of child sexual abuse. *Child Abuse & Neglect*, *17*, 67–70.
114. Finkelhor, D. (1994). Current information on the scope and nature of child sexual abuse. *The Future of Children*, *4*(2), 31–53.
115. Hough, M. (1987). Offenders' choice of targets: Findings from victim surveys. *Journal of Quantitative Criminology*, *3*, 355–369.
116. Kaplow, J. B., & Widom, C. S. (2007). Age of onset of child maltreatment predicts long-term mental health outcomes. *Journal of Abnormal Psychology*, *116*(1), 176–187.
117. Manly, J. T., Kim, J. E., Rogosch, F. A., & Cicchetti, D. (2001). Dimensions of child maltreatment and children's adjustiment: Contribution of developmental timing and subtype. *Development & Psychopathology*, *13*, 759–782.
118. Davis, L., & Siegel, L. J. (2003). Posttraumatic stress disorder in children and adolescents: A review and analysis. *Clinical Child and Family Psychology Review*, *3*(3), 135–154.
119. Caffo, E., Forresi, B., & Lievers, L. S. (2005). Impact, psychological sequelae and management of trauma affecting children and adolescents. *Current Opinion in Psychiatry*, *18*(4), 422–428.
120. Thornberry, T. P., Ireland, T. O., & Smith, C. A. (2001). The importance of timing: The varying impact of childhood and adolescent maltreatment on multiple problem outcomes. *Development & Psychopathology*, *13*, 957–979.

121. Cook, A., Blaustein, M., Spinazzola, J., & van der Kolk, B. (2003). *Complex trauma in children and adolescents*. Los Angeles: National Child Traumatic Stress Network.
122. Widom, C. S. (1999). Posttraumatic stress disorder in abused and neglected children grown up. *American Journal of Psychiatry*, *156*, 1223–1229.
123. Bolger, K. E., & Patterson, C. J. (2001). Developmental pathways from child maltreatment to peer rejection. *Child Development*, *72*(2), 549–568.
124. Bolger, K. E., Patterson, C. J., & Kupersmidt, J. B. (1998). Peer relationships and self-esteem among children who have been maltreated. *Child Development*, *69*(4), 1171–1197.
125. Eckenrode, J., Laird, M., & Doris, J. (1993). School performance and disciplinary problems among abused and neglected children. *Developmental Psychology*, *29*, 53–62.
126. Lansford, J. E., Dodge, K. A., Pettit, G. S., Bates, J. E., Crozier, J., & Kaplow, J. B. (2002). A 12-year prospective study of the long-term effects of early child physical maltreatment on psychological, behavioral, and academic problems in adolescence. *Archives of Pediatrics & Adolescent Medicine*, *156*, 824–830.
127. Shonk, S. M., & Cicchetti, D. (2001). Maltreatment, competency deficits, and risk for academic and behavioral maladjustment. *Developmental Psychology*, *37*(1), 3–17.
128. Mills, C. (2004). *Problems at home, problems at school—The effects of maltreatment in the home on children's functioning at school: An overview of recent research*. London: National Society for the Prevention of Cruelty to Children (NSPCC).
129. Veltman, M. W. M., & Browne, K. D. (2001). Three decades of child maltreatment research. *Trauma, Violence, and Abuse*, *2*(3), 215–239.
130. Aston-Jones, G., Valentino, R. J., Van Bockstaele, E. J., & Meyerson, A. T. (1994). Locus coeruleus, stress, and PTSD: Neurobiological and clinical parallels. In M. M. Murburg (Ed.), *Catecholamine function in posttraumatic stress disorder: Emerging concepts* (pp. 17–62). Washington, DC: American Psychiatric Press.
131. Teicher, M., Anderson, S., Polcari, A., Anderson, C., Navalta, C., & Kim, D. (2003). The neurobiological consequences of early stress and childhood maltreatment. *Neuroscience and Biobehavioral Reviews*, *27*, 33–44.
132. Kendall-Tackett, K. (2003). *Treating the lifetime health effects of childhood victimization*. Kingston, NJ: Civic Research Institute.
133. Donnelly, C. L., & Amaya-Jackson, L. (2002). Post-traumatic stress disorder in children and adolescents: Epidemiology, diagnosis and treatment options. *Pediatric Drugs*, *4*(3), 159–170.
134. Schwarz, E. D., & Perry, B. D. (1994). The post-traumatic response in children and adolescents. *Psychiatric Clinics of North American*, *17*, 311–326.
135. Cloitre, M., Koenen, K., Cohen, L. R., & Han, H. (2002). Skills training in affective and interpersonal regulation followed by exposure: A phase-based treatment for PTSD related to childhood abuse. *Journal of Consulting and Clinical Psychology*, *70*, 1067–1074.
136. Cohen, J. A., Berliner, L., & Mannarino, A. P. (2000). Treating traumatized children: A research review and synthesis. *Trauma Violence & Abuse*, *1*(1), 29–46.
137. DeRosa, R., Pelcovitz, D., Kaplan, S. J., Rathus, J., Ford, J., Layne, C., et al. (2003). *Group treatment for adolescents with complex PTSD manual*. Durham,

NC: North Shore University Hospital, Adolescent Trauma Treatment Development Center, National Child Traumatic Stress Network.
138. Herman, J. L. (1992). Complex PTSD: A syndrome in survivors of prolonged and repeated trauma. *Journal of Traumatic Stress*, *5*(3), 377–391.
139. Adorno, T. W. (1950). *The authoritarian personality*. New York: Harper.
140. Aboud, F. E. (1993). The developmental psychology of racial prejudice. *Transcultural Psychiatric Research Review*, *30*(3), 229–242.
141. Oskamp, S. (1991). *Attitude and opinion*, 2nd ed. Englewood Cliffs, NJ: Prentice-Hall.
142. March, J. S., & Amaya-Jackson, L. (1993). Post-Traumatic Stress Disorder in children and adolescents. *PTSD Research Quarterly*, *4*(4), 1–2.
143. Dodge, K. (1980). Social cognition and children's aggressive behavior. *Child Development*, *51*, 162–170.
144. Kendall-Tackett, K. A., Williams, L. M., & Finkelhor, D. (1993). Impact of sexual abuse on children: A review and synthesis of recent empirical studies. *Psychological Bulletin*, *113*, 164–180.
145. Letourneau, E. J., Schoenwald, S. K., & Sheldow, A. J. (2004). Children and adolescents with sexual behavior problems. *Child Maltreatment*, *9*(1), 49–61.
146. Putnam, F. (2003). Ten year research update review: Child sexual abuse. *Journal of the American Academy of Child and Adolescent Psychiatry*, *42*(3), 269–278.
147. Finkelhor, D., & Browne, A. (1985). The traumatic impact of child sexual abuse: A conceptualization. *American Journal of Orthopsychiatry*, *55*(4), 530–541.
148. McLeer, S. V., Deblinger, E., Atkins, M. S., Foa, E. B., & Ralphe, D. L. (1988). Post-Traumatic Stress Disorder in sexually abused children. *Journal of American Academy of Child and Adolescent Psychiatry*, *27*, 650–654.
149. Pynoos, R., Nader, K., Frederick, C., Gonda, L., & Stuber, M. (1987). Grief reactions in school age children following a sniper attack at school. *Israeli Journal of Psychiatry & Related Sciences*, *24*, 53–63.
150. Terr, L. C. (1979). Children of Chowchilla: A study of psychic trauma. *Psychoanalytic Study of Children*, *34*, 547–623.
151. Finkelhor, D., & Dziuba-Leatherman, J. (1994). Victimization of children. *American Psychologist*, *49*(3), 173–183.
152. Gershoff, E. T. (2002). Corporal punishment by parents and associated child behaviors and experiences: A meta-analytic and theoretical review. *Psychological Bulletin*, *128*(4), 539–579.
153. Beck, M. (1993). The sad case of Polly Klaas. (Kidnapped girl found dead in Cloverdale, California). *Newsweek*, December 13, p. 39.
154. Berstein, A. (1995). Should you be told that your neighbor is a sex offender? *Ms.*, *6*, 24–27.
155. Oxenhandler, N. (1993). Polly's face. *The New Yorker*, November 29, 94–97.
156. Steinbock, B. (1995). A policy perspective. (Megan's Law: Community notification of the release of sex offenders). *Criminal Justice Ethics*, *14*(2), 4–9.
157. Toobin, J. (1994). The man who kept going free. *The New Yorker,* March 7, pp. 38–50.
158. Thorne, B. (1993). *Gender play: Girls and boys in school*. New Brunswick, NJ: Rutgers University Press.

159. Finkelhor, D., Asdigian, N. L., & Dziuba-Leatherman, J. (1995). The effectiveness of victimization prevention programs for children: A follow-up. *American Journal of Public Health*, *85*(12), 1684–1689.
160. Best, R. (1983). *We've all got scars*. Bloomington, IN: Indiana University Press.
161. Maccoby, E. E., & Jacklin, C. N. (1974). *The psychology of sex differences*. Stanford, CA: Stanford University Press.
162. Friedrich, W. N., Grambasch, P., Damon, L., Hewitt, S. K., Koverola, C., Lang, R., et al. (1992). Child Sexual Behavior Inventory: Normative and clinical comparisons. *Psychological Assessment*, *4(*3), 303–311.
163. Browning, C. R., & Laumann, E. O. (1995). Sexual contact between children and adults: Tracking the long-term effects. *American Sociological Review*, *62*(4), 540–561.
164. Finkelhor, D., & Baron, L. (1986). Risk factors for child sexual abuse. *Journal of Interpersonal Violence*, *1*(1), 43–71.
165. Putnam, F. W. (1991). Dissociative disorders in children and adolescents: A developmental perspective. *Psychiatric Clinics of North America*, *14*(3), 519–532.
166. Putnam, F. (1997). *Dissociation in children and adolescents: A developmental perspective*. New York: Guilford.
167. Isquith, P. K., Levine, M., & Scheiner, J. (1993). Blaming the child: Attribution of responsibility to victims of child sexual abuse. In G. S. Goodman & B. L. Bottoms (Eds.), *Child victims, child witnesses: Understanding and improving testimony* (pp. 203–228). New York: Guilford.
168. Cicchetti, D. (1989). How research on child maltreament has informed the study of child development: Perspectives from developmental psychopathology. In D. Cicchetti & V. Carlson (Eds.), *Child maltreatment: Theory and research on the causes and consequences on child abuse and neglect* (pp. 377–431). New York: Cambridge University Press.
169. Crittenden, P. M. (1988). Distorted patterns of relationship in maltreating families: The role of internal representational models. *Journal of Reproductive & Infant Psychology*, *6*, 183–199.
170. Egeland, B., & Sroufe, L. A. (1981). Developmental sequelae of maltreatment in infancy. *New Directions for Child Development*, *11*, 77–92.
171. Maccoby, E. E. (1983). Social-emotional development and response to stressors. In N. Garmezy & M. Rutter (Eds.), *Stress, coping, and development in children* (pp. 217–234). New York: McGraw-Hill.
172. Smetana, J. G. (1993). Understanding of social rules. In M. Bennett (Ed.), *The development of social cognition: The child as psychologist* (pp. 111–141). New York: Guilford.
173. Kinsey, A. C., Pomeroy, W. B., Martin, C.E., & Gebhard, P. H. (1953). *Sexual behavior in the human female*. Philadelphia: W. B. Saunders.
174. Hewitt, S. K., & Friedrich, W. N. (1991). *Preschool children's responses to alleged sexual abuse at intake and one-year follow up*. Paper presented to the American Professional Society on the Abuse of Children, San Diego, CA.
175. Browne, A., & Finkelhor, D. (1986). The impact of child sexual abuse: A review of the research. *Psychological Bulletin*, *99*(1), 66–77.
176. Eder, D. (1985). The cycle of popularity: Interpersonal relations among female adolescents. *Sociology of Education*, *58*, 154–165.
177. Orbach, I., Gross, Y., Glaubman, H., & Berman, D. (1986). Children's perception of various determinants of the death concept as a function of intelligence, age, and anxiety. *Journal of Clinical Child Psychology*, *15*(2), 120–126.

178. Schowalter, J. E. (1975). Parent death and child bereavement. In B. Schoenberg, I. Gerber, A. Wiener, A. H. Kutscher, D. Peretz, & A. C. Carr (Eds.), *Bereavement: Its psychosocial aspects* (pp. 172–179). New York: Columbia University Press.
179. Kohlberg, L. (1976). Moral stages and moralization: The cognitive-developmental approach. In T. Lickona (Ed.), *Moral development and behavior: Theory, research and social issues* (pp. 31–53) New York: Holt, Rinehart & Winston.
180. Ferguson, T. J., & Rule, B. G. (1988). Children's evaluations of retaliatory aggression. *Child Development, 59*, 961–968.
181. Olthof, T., Ferguson, T. J., & Luiten, A. (1989). Personal responsibility antecedents of anger and blame reactions in children. *Child Development, 60*, 1328–1336.
182. Zelazo, P. D., Helwig, C. C., & Lau, A. (1996). Intention, act, and outcome in behavioral prediction and moral judgment. *Child Development, 67*(5), 2478–2492.
183. Janoff-Bulman, R., & Lang-Gunn, L. (1988). Coping with disease, crime and accidents: The role of self-blame attributions. In L. Y. Abramson (Ed.), *Social cognition and clinical psychology* (pp. 116–147).New York: Guilford.
184. Bass, E., & Davis, L. (1988). *The courage to heal: A guide for women survivors of child sexual abuse*. New York: Harper & Row.
185. Dalenberg, C. J., & Jacobs, D. A. (1994). Attributional analyses of child sexual abuse episodes: Empirical and clinical issues. *Journal of Child Sexual Abuse, 3*(3), 37–50.
186. Lamb, S. (1986). Treating sexually abused children: Issues of blame and responsibility. *American Journal of Orthopsychiatry*, 56, 303–307.
187. Hazzard, A., Celano, M., Gould, J., Lawry, S., & Webb, C. (1995). Predicting symptomatology and self-blame among child sex abuse victims. *Child Abuse & Neglect, 19*(6), 707–714.
188. Celano, M. P. (1992). A developmental model of victims' internal attributions of responsibility for sexual abuse. *Journal of Interpersonal Violence, 7*(1), 57–69.
189. Blanchard, E. B., Hickling, E. J., Mitnick, N., & Taylor, A. E. (1995). The impact of severity of physical injury and perception of life threat in the development of post-traumatic stress disorder in motor vehicle accident victims. *Behavior Research & Therapy*, 33(5), 529–534.
190. Pynoos, R. S., Steinberg, A. M., & Wraith, R. (1995). A developmental model of childhood traumatic stress. In D. Cicchetti & D. Cohen (Eds.), *Manual of developmental psychopathology, vol. 2: Risk, disorder, and adaptation* (pp. 72–95). New York: John Wiley.
191. Green, B. L., Korol, M., Grace, M. C., Vary, M. G., Leonard, A. C., Gleser, G. C. et al. (1991). Children and disaster: Age, gender, and parental effects on PTSD symptoms. *Journal of the American Academy of Child and Adolescent Psychiatry, 30*(6), 945–951.
192. Foa, F. B., & Kozak, M. J. (1986). Emotional processing of fear: Exposure to corrective information. *Psychological Bulletin, 99*, 20–35.
193. Pitman, R. K. (1988). Post-Traumatic Stress Disorder, conditioning, and network theory. *Psychiatric Annals, 18*(3), 182–189.
194. Michael, T., & Ehlers, A. (2007). Enhanced perceptual priming for neutral stimuli occurring in a traumatic context: Two experimental investigations. *Behaviour Research and Therapy, 45*, 341–358.

195. Foa, E. B., Steketee, G., & Rothbaum, B. O. (1989). Behavioral/cognitive conceptualization of post-traumatic stress disorder. *Behavior Therapy*, *20*, 155–176.
196. Pynoos, R., & Nader, K. (1988). Children who witness the sexual assault of their mothers. *Journal of the American Academy of Child and Adolescent Psychiatry*, *27*(5), 567–572.
197. Kliewer, W., Sandler, I., & Wolchik, S. (1994). Family socialization of threat appraisal and coping: Coaching, modeling, and family context. In F. N. Klaus Hurrelmann (Ed.), *Social networks and social support in childhood and adolescence: Prevention and intervention in childhood and adolescence* (pp. 271–291). Berlin: Walter de Gruyter.
198. Smetana, J. G., Kelly, M., & Twentyman, C. T. (1984). Abused, neglected, and non-maltreated children's conceptions of moral and social-conventional transgressions. *Child Development*, *55*, 277–287.
199. Dodge, K. A., Bates, J. E., & Pettit, G. S. (1990). Mechanisms in the cycle of violence. *Science*, *250*(4988), 1678–1683.
200. Weiss, B., Dodge, K. A., Bates, J. E., & Pettit, G. S. (1992). Some consequences of early harsh discipline: Child aggression and a maladaptive social information processing style. *Child Development*, *63*, 1321–1355.
201. Slaby, R. G., & Guerra, N. G. (1988). Cognitive mediators of aggression in adolescent offenders: 1. Assessment. *Developmental Psychology*, *24*, 580–588.
202. Russell, D. H. (1984). The prevalence and seriousness of incestuous abuse: Stepfathers vs. biological fathers. *Child Abuse & Neglect*, *8*, 15–22.
203. Cicchetti, D., & Lynch, M. (1993). Toward an ecological/transactional model of community violence and child maltreatment: Consequences for children's development. *Psychiatry*, *56*, 96–118.
204. Cicchetti, D., Ganiban, J., & Barnett, D. (1991). Contributions from the study of high-risk populations to understanding the development of emotion regulation. In J. Garber & K. A. Dodge (Eds.), *The development of emotion regulation and dysregulation* (pp. 15–48). New York: Cambridge University Press.
205. van der Kolk, B. A., & Fisler, R. E. (1994). Childhood abuse and neglect and loss of self-regulation. *Bulletin of the Menninger Clinic*, *58*(2), 145–168.
206. Rieder, C., & Cicchetti, D. (1989). Organizational perspective on cognitive control functioning and cognitive-affective balance in maltreated children. *Developmental Psychology*, *23*(3), 382–393.
207. Hilgard, J. R. (1970). *Personality and hypnosis: A study of imaginative involvement*. Chicago: University of Chicago Press.
208. Parker, J. G., Rubin, K. H., Price, J. M., & DeRosier, M. E. (1995). Peer relationships, child development, and adjustment: A developmental psychopathology perspective. In D. Cicchetti & D. J. Cohen (Eds.), *Developmental, psychopathology: Risk, disorder, and adaptation* (pp. 96–161). New York: John Wiley.
209. Cicchetti, D., Lynch, M., Shonk, S., & Monly, J. T. (1992). An organizational perspective on peer relations in maltreated children. In R. D. Parke & G. W. Ladd (Eds.), *Family-peer relationships: Modes of linkage* (pp. 345–384). Hillsdale, NJ: Lawrence Erlbaum.
210. Rutter, M. (1988). Epidemiological approaches to developmental psychopathology. *Archives of General Psychiatry*, *45*, 486–495.
211. McCann, L., Sakheim, D. K., & Abrahamson, D. J. (1988). Trauma and victimization: A model of psychological adaptation. *The Counseling Psychologist*, *16*(4), 531–594.

212. Mowbray, C. T. (1988). Post-traumatic therapy for children who are victims of violence. In F. M. Ochberg (Ed.), *Post-traumatic therapy and victims of violence* (pp. 196–212). New York: Brunner/Mazel.
213. Saarni, C. (1993). Socialization of emotion. In M. Lewis & J. M. Haviland (Eds.), *Handbook of emotions* (pp.435–446). New York: Guilford.
214. Lonigan, C. J., Shannon, M. P., Taylor, C. M., Finch, A. J., & Sallee, F. R. (1994). Children exposed to disaster: II. Risk factors for the development of post-traumatic symptomatology. *Journal of the American Academy of Child and Adolescent Psychiatry*, *33*(1), 94–105.
215. Pynoos, R., Goenjian, A., Tashjian, M., Karakashian, M., Manjikian, R., Manoukian, G. et al. (1993). Post-traumatic stress reactions in children after the 1988 Armenian earthquake. *British Journal of Psychiatry*, *163*, 239–247.
216. Pynoos, R., Sorenson, S., & Steinberg, A. (1993). Interpersonal violence and traumatic stress reactions. In L. Goldberger & S. Breznitz (Eds.), *Handbook of stress: Theoretical and clinical aspects* (pp. 573–590). New York: Free Press.
217. Shirk, S. R. (1988). The interpersonal legacy of physical abuse of children. In M. B. Straus (Ed.), *Abuse and victimization across the life span* (pp. 57–81). Baltimore, MD: Johns Hopkins University Press.
218. O'Donnell, D. A., Schwab-Stone, M. E., & Muyeed, A. Z. (2002). Multidimensional resilience in urban children exposed to community violence. *Child Development*, *73*(4), 1265–1282.
219. Perkins, D., & Jones, K. (2004). Risk behaviors and resiliency within physically abused adolescents. *Child Abuse & Neglect*, *28*(5), 547–563.
220. Conte, J., & Schuerman, J. (1987). Factors associated with an increased impact of child sexual abuse. *Child Abuse & Neglect*, *11*, 201–211.
221. Everson, M. D., Hunter, W. M., Runyan, D. K., Edelsohn, G. A., & Coulter, M. L. (1989). Maternal support following disclosure of incest. *American Journal of Orthopsychiatry*, *59*, 197–207.
222. Gomes-Schwartz, B., Horowitz, J. M., Cardarelli, A. P., & Sauzier, M. (1990). The aftermath of child sexual abuse: 18 months later. In B. Gomes-Schwartz, J. M. Horowitz, & A. P. Cardarelli (Eds.), *Child sexual abuse: The initial effects* (pp. 132–152).Newbury Park, CA: Sage.
223. Toth, S. L., & Cicchetti, D. (1993). Child maltreatment: Where do we go from here in our treatment of victims. In D. Cicchetti & S. L. Toth (Eds.), *Child abuse, child development, and social policy* (pp. 399–437). Norwood, NJ: Ablen.
224. Runyan, D. K., Hunter, W. M., Everson, M. D., De Vos, E., Cross, T., Peeler, N. et al. (1992). *Maternal support for child victims of sexual abuse: Determinants and implications*. Chapel Hill, NC: Chapel Hill and Educational Development Center, University of North Carolina.
225. Osofsky, J. D., Wewers, S., Hann, D. M., & Fick, A. C. (1993). Chronic community violence: What is happening to our children? *Psychiatry*, *56*, 36–45.
226. Schwartz, D., Dodge, K. A., & Coie, J. D. (1993). The emergence of chronic peer victimization in boys' play groups. *Child Development*, *64*(6), 1755–1772.
227. Nightingale, N. N. (1993). Juror reactions to child victim witnesses. *Law and Human Behavior*, *17*(6), 679–694.
228. Bottoms, B. L. (1993). Individual differences in perceptions of child sexual assault victims. In G. S. Goodman & B. L. Bottoms (Eds.), *Child victims,*

child witnesses: Understanding and improving testimony (pp. 229–261). New York: Guilford.

229. Kendall-Tackett, K. (1992). Professionals' standards of "normal" behavior with anatomical dolls and factors that influence these standards. *Child Abuse & Neglect, 16*(5), 727–733.
230. Ceci, S. J., & Bruck, M. (1993). Suggestibility of the child witness: A historical review and synthesis. *Psychological Bulletin, 113*(3), 403–439.
231. Cross, T. P., De Vos, E., & Whitcomb, D. (1994). Prosecution of child sexual abuse: Which cases are accepted? *Child Abuse & Neglect, 18*(8), 663–677.
232. Whitcomb, D., Runyan, D. K., De Vos, E., Hunter, W. M., Cross, T., Everson, M. D., et al. (1991). *Final report: Child victim as witness research and development program.* Chapel Hill, NC: Education Development Center, University of North Carolina.
233. Goodman, G. S., Taub, E. P., Jones, D. P., England, P., Port, L. K., Rudy, L., et al. (1992). Testifying in criminal court: Emotional effects on child sexual assault victims. *Monographs of the Society for Research in Child Development, 57*(5), 142–229.
234. Runyan, D.K., Everson, M. D., Edelsohn, G. A., Hunter, W. M., & Coulter, M. L. (1988). Impact of legal intervention on sexually abused children. *Journal of Pediatrics, 113*, 647–653.
235. Oates, R. K., Lynch, D., Stern, A. E., O'Toole, B. I., & Cooney, G. (1995). The criminal justice system and the sexually abused child: Help or hindrance? *Medical Journal of Australia, 162*, 126–130.
236. Deblinger, E., McLeer, S. V., Atkins, M. S., Ralphe, D., & Foa, E. (1989). Post-traumatic stress in sexually abused, physically abused and nonabused children. *Child Abuse & Neglect, 13*, 403–408.
237. Eron, L. D., Gentry, J. H., & Schlegel, P. (1994). *Reason to hope: A psychosocial perspective on violence and youth.* Washington, DC: American Psychological Association, p. 492.
238. Reiss, A. J., & Roth, J. A. (1993). *Social issues.* In A. J. Reiss, J. A. Roth (Eds.), Panel on the Understanding and Control of Violent Behavior, & National Research Council, *Understanding and Preventing Violence* (vol. 3, p. 464). Washington, DC: National Academies Press.
239. Lindesay, J. (1991). Fear of crime in the elderly. *International Journal of Geriatric Psychiatry, 6*(2), 55–56.
240. Mawbry, R. I. (1986). Fear of crime and concern over the crime problem among the elderly. *Journal of Community Psychology, 14*(3), 300–306.
241. Finkelhor, D., & Strapko, N. (1992). Sexual abuse prevention education: A review of evaluation studies. In D. Willis, E. Holden, & M. Rosenberg (Eds.), *Child abuse prevention* (pp. 150–167). New York: John Wiley.
242. Cicchinelli, L. (1986). *Directory of child sexual abuse treatment programs*, ed. S.S.R.a.E. Division. Denver, CO: Denver Research Institute, University of Denver.
243. Keller, R. A., Cicchinelli, L. F., & Gardner, D. M. (1989). Characteristics of child sexual abuse treatment programs. *Child Abuse & Neglect, 13*, 361–368.
244. Grusznski, R. J., Brink, J. C., & Edleson, J. L. (1988). Support and education groups for children of battered women. *Child Welfare, 5*, 431–444.
245. Peled, E., & Davis, D. (1995). *Groupwork with children of battered women: A practitioner's guide.* Thousand Oaks, CA: Sage.

246. Cohen, J. A., Deblinger, E., Mannarino, A. P., & Steer, R. (2004). A multi-site, randomized controlled trial for children with sexual abuse-related PTSD symptoms. *Journal of the American Academy of Child and Adolescent Psychiatry*, *43*(4), 393–402.

247. Kolko, D. J., & Swenson, C. C. (2002). *Assessing and treating physically abused children and their families: A cognitive behavioral approach*. Thousand Oaks, CA: Sage.

248. Egeland, B. (1991). A longitudinal study of high-risk families: Issues and findings. In R. H. Starr & D. A. Wolfe (Eds.), *The effects of child abuse & neglect* (pp. 33–56). New York: Guilford.

249. Loeber, R., & Farrington, D. P. (1995). Longitudinal approaches in epidemiological research of conduct problems. In F. C. Verhulst & H. M. Koot (Eds.), *The epidemiology of child and adolescent psychopathology* (pp. 309–336). Oxford, UK: Oxford University Press.

250. Straus, M. A., & Gelles, R. J. (1990). How violent are American families? Estimates from the National Family Violence Resurvey and other studies. In M. A. Straus & R. J. Gelles (Eds.), *Physical violence in American families: Risk factors and adaptations to violence in 8,145 families* (pp. 95–112). New Brunswick, NJ: Transaction.

251. Goodwin, M. P., & Roscoe, B. (1990). Sibling violence and agnostic interactions among middle adolescence. *Adolescence*, *25*, 451–467.

252. Roscoe, B., Goodwin, M., & Kennedy, D. (1987). Sibling violence and agonistic interactions experienced by early adolescents. *Journal of Family Violence*, *2*(2), 121–137.

253. Duncan, R. D. (1999). Peer and sibling aggression: An investigation of intra- and extra- familial bullying. *Journal of Interpersonal Violence*, *14*, 871–886.

254. Kilpatrick, D. G., Saunders, B. E., & Smith, D. W. (2002). *Youth victimization: Prevalence and implications*. Washington, DC: U.S. Department of Justice,National Institute of Justice.

255. Marcus, R. F. (2005). Youth violence in everyday life. *Journal of Interpersonal Violence*, *20*(4), 442–447.

256. Bennett, L., & Fineran, S. (1998). Sexual and severe physical violence among high school students—Power beliefs, gender, and relationship. *American Journal of Orthopsychiatry*, *68*(4), 645–652.

257. Katz, J. (1988). *Seductions of crime: Moral and sensual attractions in doing evil*. New York: Basic Books.

258. Ormrod, R. K. (2002). *Reports to police by source: NCVS-2000*. Durham, NH: University of New Hampshire.

259. Clement, M. (1997). *The juvenile justice system: Law and process*. Newton, MA: Butterworth–Heinemann.

260. Houlihan, L. (2005). Mothers rally against bullies: Schoolchildren crossed off 'hit list.' Melbourne *Herald Sun*, p. 7.

261. Cervantes, N. (2003). Easy targets: Despite state-mandated policies against harassment, schoolyard bullying still is a problem. *The Buffalo News*, June 25, A1.

262. West, N. (2001). Kids harassing kids. *New Hampshire Sunday News*, July 15, p. A1.

263. (1999). Strategic ways to squash sibling squabbles. *Jet*, *96*(22), 1–20.

264. (1996). Clive Soley: Education at comprehensive rife with bullying had helped him cope with life. *The Guardian*, January 25, p. 5.

265. Shaw, J. A., Applegate, B., & Schorr, C. (1996). Twenty-one month follow-up of school-age children exposed to Hurricane Andrew. *Journal of the American Academy of Child and Adolescent Psychiatry*, *35*(3), 359–364.
266. Astor, R. A. (1995). School violence: A blueprint for elementary school interventions. *Social Work in Education*, *17*(2), 101–115.
267. Wiehe, V. R. (1997). *Sibling abuse: Hidden physical, emotional and sexual trauma*, 2nd ed. Thousand Oaks, CA: Sage.
268. Myers, J. E. B. (2004). *A history of child protection in America*. Philadelphia: Xlibris.
269. Eisenberg, M. E., & Aalsma, M. C. (2005). Bullying and peer victimization: Position paper of the Society for Adolescent Medicine. *Journal of Adolescent Health*, *36*(1), 88–91.
270. Fottrell, D. (2000). *Revisiting children's rights—10 years of the UN Convention of the Rights of Children*. The Hague/Boston, MA: Kluwer Law International.
271. Harlow, C. W. (1985). *Reporting Crimes to the police*. Washington DC: Bureau of Justice Statistics, U.S. Department of Justice.
272. Bachman, R. (1998). The factors related to rape reporting behavior and arrest: New evidence from the National Crime Victimization Survey. *Criminal Justice and Behavior*, *25*(1), 8–30.
273. Conaway, M. R., & Lohr, S. L. (1994). A longitudinal analysis of factors associated with reporting violent crimes to the police. *Journal of Quantitative Criminology*, *10*(1), 23–39.
274. Greenberg, M. S., & Ruback, R. B. (1992). Self-Reports: Surveying crime victims. In M. S. Greenberg (Ed.), *After the crime: Victim decision making* (pp. 151–179). New York: Plenum.
275. Kaukinen, C. (2002). The help-seeking decisions of violent crime victims: An examination of the direct and conditional effects of gender and the victim-offender relationship. *Journal of Interpersonal Violence*, *17*(4), 432–456.
276. Finkelhor, D., & Dziuba-Leatherman, J. (1994). Children as victims of violence: A national survey. *Pediatrics*, *94*(4), 413–420.
277. Kilpatrick, D. G., & Saunders, B. E. (1999). *Prevalence and consequences of child victimization: Results from the national survey of adolescents*. Charleston, SC: U.S. Department of Justice.
278. Finkelhor, D., & Wolak, J. (2003). Reporting assaults against juveniles to the police: Barriers and catalysts. *Journal of Interpersonal Violence*, *18*(2), 103–128.
279. Paine, M. L., & Hansen, D. J. (2002). Factors influencing children to self-disclose sexual abuse. *Clinical Psychology Review*, *22*, 271–295.
280. Davis, R. C., Lurigio, A. J., & Skogan, W. G. (1999). Services for victims. *International Review of Victimology*, *6*, 101–115.
281. Kilpatrick, D., Best, C., Saunders, B., & Veronen, L. (1988). Rape in marriage and dating relationships: How bad is it for mental health? *Annals of the New York Academy of Sciences*, *528*, 335–344.
282. Kidd, R. F., & Chayet, E. F. (1984). Why do victims fail to report? The psychology of criminal victimization. *Journal of Social Issues*, *40*(1), 39–50.
283. Bachman, R. (1993). Predicting the reporting of rape victimizations: Have rape reforms made a difference? *Criminal Justice and Behavior*, *20*(3), 254–270.

284. Fleury, R. E., Sullivan, C. M., Bybee, D. I., & Davidson, W. S. (1998). Why don't they just call the cops? Reasons for differential contact among women with abusive partners. *Violence and Victims*, *13*(4), 333–346.
285. Coulter, M., & Chez, R. (1997). Domestic violence victims support mandatory reporting: For others. *Journal of Family Violence*, *12*(3), 349–357.
286. Sauzier, M. (1989). Disclosure of child sexual abuse: For better or for worse. *Psychiatric Clinics of North America*, *12*(2), 455–469.
287. Freedy, J. R., Resnick, H. S., Kilpatrick, D. G., Dansky, B. S., & Tidwell, R. P. (1994). The psychological adjustment of recent crime victims in the criminal justice system. *Journal of Interpersonal Violence*, *9*(4), 450–468.
288. Besharov, D. (1990). Gaining control over child abuse reports. *Public Welfare*, *48*(2), 34–40.
289. Besharov, D. J. (1993). Overreporting and underreporting are twin problems. In R. J. Gelles & D. R. Loseke (Eds.), *Current controversies on family violence* (pp. 257–272). Newbury Park, CA: Sage.
290. Berliner, L., & Conte, J. (1995). The effects of disclosure and intervention on sexually abused children. *Child Abuse & Neglect*, *19*(3), 371–384.
291. Sas, L. D., Hurley, P., Hatch, A., Malla, S., & Dick, T. (1993). *Three years after the verdict: A longitudinal study of the social and psychological adjustment of child witnesses referred to the child witness project*. London, Ontario, Canada: London Family Court Clinic.
292. Harshbarger, S. (1987). Prosecution is an appropriate response in child sexual abuse cases. *Journal of Interpersonal Violence*, *2*(1), 108–112.
293. Sherman, L. W., Schmidt, J. D., & Rogan, D. P. (1992). *Policing domestic violence: Experiments and dilemmas*. New York: Free Press.
294. Wilson, C., Vincent, P., & Lake, E. (1996). *An examination of organizational structure and programmatic reform in public child protective services*. Olympia, WA: Washington State Institute for Public Policy.
295. Cross, T., Finkelhor, D., & Ormrod, R. K. (2005). Police involvement in child protective services investigations. *Child Maltreatment*, *10*(3), 224–244.
296. Davis, R. C., & Henley, M. (1990). Victim service programs. In A. J. Lurigio, W. G. Skogan, & R. C. Davis (Eds.), *Victims of crime: Problems, policies, and programs* (pp. 157–171). Newbury Park, CA: Sage.
297. Skogan, W. G., Davis, R. C., & Lurigio, A. J. (1990). *Victims' needs and victim services: Final report to the National Institute of Justice*. Washington, DC: Northwestern University/Center for Urban Affairs.
298. Friedman, K., Bischoff, H., Davis, R. C., & Person, A. (1982). *Victims and helpers: Reactions to crime*. Washington, DC: U.S. Government Printing Office.
299. McCormack, R. J. (1991). Compensating victims of violent crime. *Justice Quarterly*, *8*(3), 329–346.
300. Boney-McCoy, S., & Finkelhor, D. (1995). The psychosocial impact of violent victimization on a national youth sample. *Journal of Consulting and Clinical Psychology*, *63*(5), 726–736.
301. Kopiec, K., Finkelhor, D., & Wolak, J. (2004). Which juvenile crime victims get mental health treatment? *Child Abuse & Neglect*, *28*, 45–59.
302. Miller, T. R., Cohen, M. A., & Wiersema, B. (1996). *Victim costs and consequences*. Washington, DC: National Institute of Justice.
303. Kolko, D. J., Selelyo, J., & Brown, E. J. (1999). The treatment histories and service experiences of physically and sexually abusive families: Description, correspondence, and correlates. *Child Abuse & Neglect*, *23*, 459–476.

304. Kinard, E. M. (1999). *Services for maltreated children: Variations by maltreatment characteristics*. Presented at the 6th International Family Violence Research Conference, Durham, NH.
305. Garland, A. F., Landsverk, J. L., Hough, R. L., & Ellis-MacLeod, E. (1996). Type of treatment as a predictor of mental health service use for children in foster care. *Child Abuse & Neglect*, *20*(8), 675–688.
306. Oates, R. K., O'Toole, B. I., Lynch, D. L., Stern, A., & Cooney, G. (1994). *Stability and change in outcomes for sexually abused children*. Sydney, Australia: Sydney University, Department of Paediatrics and Child Health.
307. Trupin, E. W., Tarico, S., Low, B. P., Jemelka, R., & McClellan, J. (1993). Children on child protective service caseloads: Prevalence and nature of serious emotional disturbance. *Child Abuse & Neglect*, *17*, 345–355.
308. Horowitz, L. A., Putnam, F. W., Noll, J. G., & Trickett, P. K. (1997). Factors affecting utilization of treatment services by sexually abused girls. *Child Abuse & Neglect*, *21*(1), 35–48.
309. Berliner, L., & New, M. (1997). *Mental health service use by adult victims of crime*. Presented at the ISTSS Annual Meeting: Linking Trauma Studies to the Universe of Science and Practice,Montreal, Quebec, Canada.
310. Burns, B. J., Costello, E. J., Angold, A., Tweed, D., Stangl, D., Farmer, E. M. Z. et al. (1995). Children's mental health service use across service sectors. *Health Affairs*, *14*(3), 147–159.
311. Cunningham, P. J., & Freiman, M. P. (1996). Determinants of ambulatory mental health services use for school-age children and adolescents. *Health Services Research*, *31*(4), 409–427.
312. Leaf, P. J., Alegria, M., Cohen, P., Goodman, S. H., Horwitz, S. M., Hoven, C. W. et al. (1996). Mental health service use in the community and schools: Results from the four-community MECA study. *Journal of the American Academy of Child and Adolescent Psychiatry*, *35*(7), 889–897.
313. Offord, D. R., Boyle, M. H., Szatmari, P., Rae-Grant, N. I., Links, P. S., Cadman, D. T. et al. (1987). Ontario child health study. *Archives of General Psychiatry*, *44*, 832–836.
314. Angold, A., Messer, S. C., Stangl, D., & Burns, E. J. (1988). Perceived parental burden and service use for child and adolescent psychiatric disorders. *American Journal of Public Health*, *88*(1), 75–80.
315. Hoberman, H. M. (1992). Ethnic minority status and adolescent mental health services and utilization. *Journal of Mental Health Administration*, *19*(3), 246–267.
316. Garralda, M. E., & Bailey, D. (1988). Child and family factors associated with referral to child psychiatrists. *British Journal of Psychiatry*, *153*, 81–89.
317. Dulcan, M. K., Costello, E. J., Costello, A. J., Edelbrock, C., Brent, D., & Janiszewski, S. (1990). The pediatrician as gatekeeper to mental health care for children: Do parents' concerns open the gate? *Journal of the American Academy of Child and Adolescent Psychiatry*, *29*(3), 453–458.
318. Jensen, P. S., Bloedau, L., & Davis, H. (1990). Children at risk: II. Risk factors and clinic utilization. *Journal of the American Academy of Child and Adolescent Psychiatry*, *29*(5), 804–812.
319. Cohen, P., Kasen, S., Brook, J. S., & Struening, E. L. (1991). Diagnostic predictors of treatment patterns in a cohort of adolescents. *Journal of the American Academy of Child and Adolescent Psychiatry*, *30*(6), 989–993.

320. Hunter, S. C., Boyle, J. M. E., & Warden, D. (2004). Help seeking amongst child and adolescent victims of peer-aggression and bullying: The influence of school-stage, gender, victimization, appraisal, and emotion. *British Journal of Educational Psychology, 74*, 375–390.
321. Tingus, K. D., Heger, A. H., Foy, D. W., & Leskin, G. A. (1996). Factors associated with entry into therapy in children evaluated for sexual abuse. *Child Abuse and Neglect, 20*(1), 63–68.
322. Glied, S., Hoven, C. W., Moore, R. E., Garrett, A. B., & Regier, D. A. (1997). Children's access to mental health care: Does insurance matter? *Children's Mental Health, 16*(1), 167–174.
323. Horwitz, S. M., Leaf, P. J., Leventhal, J. M., Forsyth, B., & Speechley, K. N. (1992). Identification and management of psychosocial and developmental problems in community-based, primary care pediatric practices. *Pediatrics, 89*(3), 480–485.
324. Cohen, R., Parmelee, D. X., Irwin, L., Weisz, J. R., Howard, P., Purcell, P. et al. (1990). Characteristics of children and adolescents in a psychiatric hospital and a corrections facility. *Journal of the American Academy of Child and Adolescent Psychiatry, 29*(6), 909–913.
325. Zahner, G. E. P., Pawelkiewicz, W., DeFrancesco, J. J., & Adnopoz, J. (1992). Children's mental health service needs and utilization patterns in an urban community: An epidemiological assessment. *Journal of the American Academy of Child and Adolescent Psychiatry, 31*(5), 951–960.
326. Pottick, K. J., Lerman, P., & Micchelli, M. (1992). Of problems and perspectives: Predicting the use of mental health services by parents of urban youth. *Children and Youth Services Review, 14*, 363–378.
327. Roghmann, K. J., Babigian, H. M., Goldberg, I. D., & Zastowny, T. R. (1982). The increasing number of children using psychiatric services: Analysis of a cumulative psychiatric case register. *Pediatrics, 70*(5), 790–801.
328. Zahner, G. E. P., & Daskalakis, C. (1997). Factors associated with mental health, general health, and school-based service use for child psychopathology. *American Journal of Public Health, 87*(9), 1440–1448.
329. Marks, A., Malizio, J., Hoch, J., Brody, R., & Fisher, M. (1983). Assessment of health needs and willingness to utilize health care resources of adolescents in a suburban population. *Journal of Pediatrics, 102*, 456–460.
330. Balassone, M. L., Bell, M., & Peterfreund, N. (1991). A comparison of users and nonusers of a school-based health and mental health clinic. *Journal of Adolescent Health, 12*, 240–246.
331. Kaplan, D. W., Calonge, B. N., Guernsey, B. P., & Hanrahan, M. B. (1998). Managed care and school-based health centers: Use of health services. *Archives of Pediatric and Adolescent Medicine, 152*, 25–33.
332. Kuhl, J., Jarkon-Horlick, L., & Morrissey, R. F. (1997). Measuring barriers to help-seeking behavior in adolescents. *Journal of Youth and Adolescence, 26*(6), 637–650.
333. Black, B. M., & Weisz, A. N. (2003). Dating violence: Help-seeking behaviors of African American middle schoolers. *Violence Against Women, 9*(2), 187–206.
334. Ocampo, B. W., Shelley, G. A., & Jaycox, L. H. (2007). Latino teens talk about help seeking and help giving in relation to dating violence. *Violence Against Women, 13*(2), 172–189.

335. Pavuluri, M. N., Luk, S.-L., & McGee, R. (1996). Help-seeking for behavior problems by parents of preschool children: A community study. *Journal of the American Academy of Child and Adolescent Psychiatry*, *35*(2), 215–222.
336. Srebnik, D., Cauce, A. M., & Baydar, N. (1996). Help-seeking pathways for children and adolescents. *Journal of Emotional and Behavioral Disorders*, *4*(4), 210–221.
337. Haskett, M. E., Nowlan, N. P., Hutcheson, J. S., & Whitworth, J. M. (1991). Factors associated with successful entry into therapy in child sexual abuse cases. *Child Abuse & Neglect*, *15*, 467–476.
338. Finkelhor, D., & Berliner, L. (1995). Research on the treatment of sexually abused children: A review and recommendations. *Journal of the American Academy of Child and Adolescent Psychiatry*, *34*(11), 1408–1423.
339. March, J. S., Amaya-Jackson, L., Murray, M. C., & Schulte, A. (1998). Cognitive-Behavioral Psychopathology for children and adolescents with posttraumatic stress disorder after a single-incident stressor. *Journal of the American Academy of Child and Adolescent Psychiatry*, *37*(6), 585–593.
340. Sciarra, D. (1999). Assessment and treatment of adolescent sex offenders: A review from a cross-cultural perspective. *Journal of Offender Rehabilitation*, *28*(3/4), 103–118.
341. Ryan, G., Muyoshi, T., Metzner, J., Krugman, R., & Freyer, G. E. (1996). Trends in a national sample of sexually abusive youths. *Journal of the American Academy of Child and Adolescent Psychiatry*, *35*(1), 17–25.
342. Federal Bureau of Investigations. (1996). *Crime in the United States, 1994: Uniform crime reports*. Washington, DC: U.S. Department of Justice.
343. Rosenstock, I. M. (1966). Why people use health services. *Milbank Memorial Fund Quarterly*, *44*, 94–124.
344. Aday, L. A., & Andersen, R. (1974). A framework for the study of access to medical care. *Health Services Research*, *9*, 208–220.
345. Aday, L., Andersen, R., & Fleming, G. V. (1980). *Health care in the U.S.: Equitable for whom?* Beverly Hills, CA: Sage.
346. Prochaska, J. O., & Velicer, W. F. (1997). The Transtheoretical model of health behavior. *American Journal of Health Promotion*, *12*, 38–48.
347. Pescosolido, B. A. (1992). Beyond rational choice: The social dynamics of how people seek help. *American Journal of Sociology*, *97*(4), 1096–1138.
348. Rennison, C. M., & Welchans, S. (2000). *Intimate partner violence* (pp. 1–11). Washington, DC: U.S. Department of Justice, Bureau of Justice Statistics.
349. Jones, L. M., Finkelhor, D., & Kopiec, K. (2001). Why is sexual abuse declining? A survey of state child protection administration. *Child Abuse & Neglect*, *25*(9), 1139–1158.
350. Finkelhor, D., & Jones, L. M. (2004). *Explanations for the decline in child sexual abuse cases*. Washington, DC: Office of Juvenile Justice and Delinquency Prevention.
351. Minnesota Department of Children, Families & Learning, & Minnesota Department of Human Services (2001). *Minnesota student survey: Key trends through 2001*. Roseville, MN: Author.
352. Jones, L. M., Finkelhor, D., & Halter, S. (2006). Child maltreatment trends in the 1990s: Why does neglect differ from sexual and physical abuse? *Child Maltreatment*, *11*(2),107–120.
353. Moore, K. A., Manlove, J., Terry-Humen, E., Williams, S., Papillo, A. R., & Scarpa, J. (2001). *CTS facts at a glance* (pp. 1–6). Washington, DC: Child Trends.

354. Hammer, H., Finkelhor, D., & Sedlak, A. J. (2002). *Runaway/thrownaway children: National estimates and characteristics* (p. 12). Washington, DC: Office of Juvenile Justice & Delinquency Prevention.
355. Steffensmeier, D., & Harer, M. D. (1999). Making sense of recent US crime trends, 1980 to 1996/1998: Age composition effects and other explanations. *Journal of Research in Crime and Delinquency, 36*(3), 235–274.
356. Lynch, J. P. (2002). *Trends in juvenile violent offending: An analysis of victim survey data.* Washington DC: U.S. Department of Justice, pp. 1–19.
357. Blumstein, A., & Wallman, J. (2000). *The crime drop in America.* New York: Cambridge University Press.
358. Conklin, J. E. (2003). *Why crime rates fell.* (J. Jacobson, Ed.). Boston, MA: Allyn and Bacon.
359. Lanning, K. V. (2001). *Child molesters: A behavioral analysis* (pp. 1–160). Alexandria, VA: National Center for Missing & Exploited Children.
360. Trocme, N., Fallon, B., MacLaurin, B., Daciuk, J., Felstiner, C., Black, T. et al. (2005). *Canadian Incidence Study of Reported Child Abuse and Neglect—2003: Major findings.* Ottawa, Ontario, Canada: Ministry of Public Works and Government Services.
361. U.S. Department of Health and Human Services, Administration on Children Youth and Families (2002). *Child Maltreatment 2000: Reports from the states to the National Child Abuse & Neglect Data System.* Washington, DC: U.S. Government Printing Office.
362. Durfee, M., Tilton Durfee, D., & West, M. P. (2002). Child fatality review: An international movement. *Child Abuse & Neglect, 26,* 619–636.
363. Centers for Disease Control and Prevention, National Centers for Injury Prevention and Control (2005). *Web-based Injury Statistics Query and Reporting System (WISQARS).* Retrieved December 20, 2004, from http://webappa.cdc.gov/sasweb/ncipc/mortrate.html.
364. Romano-Papillo, A., Franzetta, K., Manlove, J., Anderson Moore, K., Terry-Humen, E., & Ryan, S. (2002). *Teen birth rates* (pp. 1–6). Washington, DC: Child Trends.
365. Ventura, S. J., Mathews, T. J., & Hamilton, B. E. (2001). Births to teenagers in the United States, 1940–2000. *CDC—National Vital Statistics Reports, 49*(10), 1–24.
366. Federal Interagency Forum on Child and Family Statistics. (2000). *America's children: Key national indicators of well-being, 2000.* Washington, DC: U.S. Government Printing Office.
367. U.S. Bureau of the Census. (2003). *State estimates for people under age 18 in poverty for US: 2000.* Washington, DC: Housing and Household Economic Statistics Division, Small Area Estimates Branch.
368. Federal Interagency Forum on Child and Family Statistics. (2005). *America's children: Key national indicators of well being—2004.* Washington, DC: U.S. Government Printing Office.
369. Achenbach, T. M., Deumenci, L., & Rescorla, L. A. (2003). Are American children's problems still getting worse? A 23-year comparison. *Journal of Abnormal Child Psychology, 31*(1), 1–11.
370. Johnston, L. D., O'Malley, P. M., Bachman, J. G., & Schulenberg, J. E. (2005). *Monitoring the future national survey results on drug use, 1975–2004: Volume 1, Secondary school students.* Bethesda, MD: National Institute on Drug Use.

371. Peddle, N., & Wang, C.-T. (2001). *Current trends in child abuse prevention, reporting, and fatalities: The 1999 fifty state survey* (pp. 1–25). Chicago: Prevent Child Abuse America.
372. Land, K. C., Lamb, V. L., & Kahler Mustillo, S. (2001). Child and youth well-being in the United States, 1975–1998: Some findings from a new index. *Social Indicators Research, 56*, 241–320.
373. Levitt, S. D. (2004). Understanding why crime fell in the 1990s: Four factors that explain the decline and six that do not. *Journal of Economic Perspectives, 18*(1), 163–190.
374. DiIulio, J. (1996). Help wanted: Economists, crime, and public policy. *Journal of Economic Perspectives, 10*, 3–24.
375. Fox, J. A. (1996). *Trends in juvenile violence: A report to the United States Attorney General on current and future rates of juvenile offending*. Washington, DC: Bureau of Justice Statistics.
376. Child Trends—Demographics (2005). *Number of children*. Retrieved November 4, 2005, from http://www.childtrendsdatabank.org/tables/53_Table_1.htm.
377. Child Trends—Demographics. (2005). *Family structure*. Retrieved November 4, 2005, from http://www.childtrendsdatabank.org/tables/59_Table_1.htm.
378. Child Trends—Demographics. (2005). *Racial and ethnic composition of the child population*. Retrieved November 4, 2005,from http://www.childtrends databank.org/tables/60_Table_1.htm.
379. Cameron, S. (1994). A review of the econometric evidence on the effect of capital punishment. *Journal of Socio-Economics, 23*, 197–214.
380. Ehrlich, I. (1975). The deterrent effect of capital punishment: A question of life and death. *American Economic Review, 65*(3), 397–417.
381. Ehrlich, I. (1977). Capital punishment and deterrence: Some further thoughts and evidence. *Journal of Political Economy, 85*(4), 741–788.
382. Dezhbakhsh, H., Rubin, P., & Shepherd, J. (2002). *Does capital punishment have a deterrent effect? New evidence from port-moratorium panel data*. Atlanta, GA: Emory University.
383. Mocan, H. N., & Gittings, R. K. (2003). Getting off death row: Commuted sentences and the deterrent effect of capital punishment. *Journal of Law and Economics, 46*, 453–478.
384. Shirk, M. (2005, October). The Meth epidemic: Hype vs. reality. *Youth Today*, pp. 42–43, 45.
385. Braga, A. A., Kennedy, D. M., Waring, E. J., & Morrison Piehl, A. (2001). Problem-oriented policing, deterrence, and youth violence: An evaluation of Boston's operation ceasefire. *Journal of Research in Crime and Delinquency, 38*, 195–225.
386. Donohue, J. J., & Levitt, S. D. (2001). The impact of legalized abortion on crime. *Quarterly Journal of Economics, 116*(2), 379–420.
387. Donohue, J. J., & Levitt, S. D. (2004). Further evidence that legalized abortion lowered crime: A reply to Joyce. *The Journal of Human Resources, 34*(1), 29–49.
388. Fryer, R. G., Heaton, P. S., Levitt, S. D., & Murphy, K. M. (2005). *Measuring the impact of crack cocaine*. Cambridge, MA: National Bureau of Economic Research.
389. Foote, C. L., & Goetz, C. F. (2005). *Testing economic hypotheses with state-level data: A comment on Donohue and Levitt (2001)*. Boston: Federal Reserve Bank of Boston.

390. Joyce, T. (2004). Did legalized abortion lower crime? *Journal of Human Resources, 39*(1), 1–28.
391. Lott, J. R., & Whitley, J. E. (2001). *Abortion and crime: Unwanted children and out-of-wedlock births*. Yale Law & Economics Research Paper No. 254. Retrieved September 18, 2007, from http://ssrn.com/abstract=270126.
392. Hernandez, D. J. (1993). *America's children: Resources from family, government, and the economy*. New York: Russell Sage Foundation.
393. Sorenson, S. B., Wiebe, D. J., & Berk, R. A. (2002). Legalized abortion and the homicide of young children: An empirical investigation. *Analyses of Social Issues and Public Policy, 2*(1), 239–256.
394. Finkelhor, D., & Ormrod, R. K. (2001). *Homicides of children and youth* (pp. 1–12). Washington, DC: Office of Juvenile Justice & Delinquency Prevention.
395. Gruber, J., Levine, P., & Staiger, D. (1999). Abortion legalization and child living circumstances: Who is the "Marginal Child"? *Quarterly Journal of Economics, 114*(1), 263–291.
396. Milner, J. S. (1993). Individual and family characteristics associated with intrafamilial child physical and sexual abuse. In P. K. Trickett & C. J. Schellenbach (Eds.), *Violence against children in the family and community* (pp. 141–170). Washington, DC: American Psychological Association.
397. Farley, R. (1998). *The new American reality: Who we are, how we got here, where we are going*. New York: Russell Sage Foundation.
398. Hirschi, T. (1969). *Causes of delinquency*. Los Angeles, CA: University of California Press.
399. Hanson, R. K., & Morton-Bourgon, K. E. (2005). The characteristics of persistent sexual offenders: A meta-analysis of recidivism studies. *Journal of Consulting and Clinical Psychology, 73*, 1154–1163.
400. Uggen, C. (2000). Work as a turning point in the life course of criminals: A duration model of age, employment, and recidivism. *American Sociological Review, 67*, 529–546.
401. Spelman, W. (2000). The limited importance of prison expansion. In A. Blumstein & J. Wallman (Eds.), *The crime drop in America* (pp. 97–129). Cambridge, UK: Cambridge University Press.
402. Finkelhor, D., & Ormrod, R. K. (2001). *Offenders incarcerated for crimes against juveniles* (pp. 1–12). Washington, DC: U.S. Department of Justice, Office of Juvenile Justice and Delinquency Prevention.
403. U.S. Bureau of the Census. (n.d.) *Employed civilians by occupation, sex, race, and Hispanic origin,* 1982–2006. Retrieved June 5, 2006, from http://www.census.gov/prod/www/statistical-abstract.html.
404. Martin, S. E., & Besharov, D. J. (1991). *Police and child abuse: New policies for expanded responsibilities*. Washington, DC: National Institute of Justice, pp. 1–23.
405. Glasscock, B., Bilchik, S., Chandler, N., Rosenblatt, D., Cromartie, G., & Needle, J. (2002). *Building partnerships that protect our children: Recommendations from the 2001 Child Protection Summit*. Washington, DC: International Association of Chiefs of Police, Child Welfare League of America, Office of Juvenile Justice & Delinquency Prevention, and National Children's Alliance.
406. U.S. Department of Justice. (1999). *A national assessment of school resource officer programs* (pp. 1–8). Washington, DC: National Institute of Justice.

407. Marans, S., Berkowitz, S. J., & Cohen, D. J. (1998). *Police and mental health professionals. Collaborative responses to the impact of violence on children and families. Child & Adolescent Psychiatric Clinics of North America*, *7*(3), pp. 635–651.

408. Dugan, L., Nagin, D., & Rosenfeld, R. (2003). Exposure reduction or retaliation? The effects of domestic violence resources on intimate partner homicide. *Law & Society Review*, *37*(1), pp. 169–198.

409. Snyder, H. N., & Sickmund, M. (1999). *Juvenile offenders and victims: 1999 national report*. Washington, DC: U.S. Department of Justice, Office of Juvenile Justice and Delinquency Prevention.

410. Finkelhor, D., Cross, T. P., & Cantor, E. (2005). The justice system for juvenile victims: A comprehensive model of case flow. *Trauma Violence & Abuse*, *6*(2), pp. 83–102.

411. Kessler, R. C., Demler, O., Frank, R. G., Olfson, M., Pincus, H.A., Walters, E.E. et al. (2005). Prevalence and treatment of mental disorders, 1990 to 2003. *New England Journal of Medicine*, *352*(24), 2515–2523.

412. Mechanic, D., & Bilder, S. (2004). Treatment of people with mental illness: A decade-long perspective. *Health Affairs*, *23*(4), 84–95.

413. Straus, M. A., & Gelles, R. J. (1986). Societal changes and change in family violence from 1975 to 1985 as revealed by two national surveys. *Journal of Marriage and the Family*, *48*, 465–480.

414. Lafree, G. (1999). Declining violent crime rates in the 1990's: Predicting crime booms and busts. *Annual Review of Sociology*, *25*(1), 145–169.

415. Lafree, G. (1998). *Losing legitimacy: Street crime and the decline of social institutions in America*. Boulder, CO: Westview.

416. John Jay College of Criminal Justice. (2003). *The nature and scope of the problem of sexual abuse of minors by Catholic priests and deacons in the United States*. Retrieved December 7, 2005, from http://www.usccb.org/nrb/johnjaystudy/index.htm.

417. Olfson, M., Marcus, S. C., Druss, B., Elinson, L., Tanielian, T., & Pincus, H. A. (2002). National trends in the outpatient treatment of depression. *Journal of the American Medical Association*, *287*(2), 203–209.

418. Zito, J. M., Safer, D. J., dosReis, S., Garner, J. F., Magder, L., Soeken, K. et al. (2003). Psychotropic practice patterns for youth: A 10-year perspective. *Archives of Pediatrics & Adolescent Medicine*, *157*,17–25.

419. Jensen, P. S., Edelman, A., & Nemeroff, R. (2003). *Pediatric psychopharmacoepidemiology: Who is prescribing, and for whom, how, and why?* In A. Martin, L. Scahill, D. Charney, & J. Leckman (Eds.), *Textbook of child adolescent psychopharmacology* (pp. 701–711). New York: Oxford University Press.

420. Olfson, M., Marcus, S. C., Weissman, M. M., & Jensen, P. S. (2002). National trends in the use of psychotropic medications by children. *Journal of the American Academy of Child and Adolescent Psychiatry*, *41*(5), 514–521.

421. Robison, L. M., Sclar, D. A., Skaer, T. L., & Galin, R. S. (1999). National trends in the prevalence of attention-deficit/hyperactivity disorder and the prescribing of methyphenidate among school-age children: 1990–1995. *Clinical Pediatrics*, *38*(4), 209–217.

422. Robison, L. M., Skaer, T. L., Sclar, D. A., & Galin, R. S. (2002). Is attention deficit hyperactivity disorder increasing among girls in the U.S.? *CNS Drugs*, *16*(2), 129–137.

423. Gibbons, R. D. (2005). The relationships between antidepressant medication use and rate of suicide. *Archives of General Psychiatry*, *62*(2),165–172.
424. Ouimet, M. (2005, November). *Oh Canada! The crime decline north of the border*. Presented at the American Society of Criminology Conference, Toronto, Ontario, Canada.
425. N. Trocme. (2006). Personal communication, May 17.
426. Gladwell, M. (2000). *The tipping point: How little things can make a big difference*. New York: Little, Brown.
427. Aber, L. J., Brooks-Gunn, J., & Maynard, R. (1995). The effects of welfare reform on teenage parents and their children. *The Future of Children*, *5*(2), 3–71.
428. Allen, M. (1996). *The implications of the Welfare Act for Child Protection*. Washington, DC: Children's Defense Fund.
429. Knitzer, J., & Bernard, S. (1997). *The new welfare law and vulnerable families: Implications for child welfare/child protection systems. Children and Welfare Reform Issue Brief 3*. New York: Columbia University Press.
430. Sengupta, S. (2000). No rise in child abuse seen in welfare shift. *New York Times*, August 10, p. A1.
431. Geen, R., Fender, L., Leos-Urbel, J., & Markowitz, T. (2001). *Welfare reform's effect on child welfare caseloads*. Washington, DC: The Urban Institute.
432. Winship, S., & Jencks, C. (2004). *How did the social policy changes of the 1990s affect material hardship among single mothers? Evidence from the CPS Food Security Supplement* (pp. 1–60). Cambridge, MA: Harvard University Kennedy School of Government.
433. Finkelhor, D., & Ormrod, R. K. (2000). *Juvenile victims of property crimes*. Washington, DC: U.S. Department of Justice, Office of Juvenile Justice and Delinquency Prevention.
434. Norris, F. H., & Kaniasty, K. (1994). Psychological distress following criminal victimization in the general population: Cross-sectional, longitudinal, and prospective analyses. *Journal of Consulting and Clinical Psychology*, *62*(1), 111–123.
435. U.S. Department of Health and Human Services, Administration on Children Youth and Families. (2001). *Child Maltreatment 1999*. Washington, DC: U.S. Government Printing Office.
436. Wells, S. J. (1998). *Responding to reports of child abuse and neglect*. Presented at the American Association for Protecting Children 112th Annual Conference, Washington, DC.
437. Karski, R. L. (1999). Key decisions in child protective services: Report investigation and court referral. *Children & Youth Services Review*, *21*(8), 643–656.
438. Schene, P. (2001). Meeting each family's needs: Differential response in reports of child abuse & neglect. In National Child Welfare Resource Center for Family-Centered Practice (Ed.), *Best practice/next practice: Family-centered child welfare* (pp. 1–14). Washington, DC: National Child Welfare Resource Center for Family-Centered Practice.
439. Cohen, B., Kinnevy, S., Huang, V., Gelles, R., Bae, H.-O., Fusco, R. et al. (2002). *Evaluation of the transfer of response for child protective investigations to the Broward County Sheriff's office*. Philadelphia: Center for the Study of Youth Policy, University of Pennsylvania.

440. Ormrod, R. K. (2002). *Data from National Survey of Child and Adolescent Welfare*. Durham, NH:University of New Hampshire.
441. Faller, K. C., & Henry, J. (2000). Child sexual abuse: A case study in community collaboration. *Child Abuse & Neglect*, *24*(9), 1215–1225.
442. Hibbard, R. A. (1998). Triage and referrals for child sexual abuse medical examinations from the sociolegal system. *Child Abuse & Neglect*, *22*(6), 503–513.
443. Whitcomb, D., Goodman, G. S., Runyan, D. K., & Hoak, S. (1994). *The emotional effects of testifying on sexually abused children*. Washington, DC: National Institute of Justice.
444. Jenny, C. (2002). Criminal investigation of sexual victimization of children. In J. E. B. Myers, L. Berliner, J. Briere, C. T. Hendrix, C. Jenny, & T. A. Reid (Eds.), *The APSAC handbook of child maltreatment* (pp. 235–247). Thousand Oaks, CA: Sage.
445. Britton, H. (1998). Emotional impact of the medical examination for child sexual abuse. *Child Abuse & Neglect*, *22*(6), 573–579.
446. Kerns, D. L. (1998). Triage and referrals for child sexual abuse medical examinations: Which children are likely to have positive medical findings. *Child Abuse & Neglect*, 22(6), 515–518.
447. Oates, R. K., Jones, D. P., Denson, D., Sirotnak, A., Gary, N., and Krugman, R. D. (2000). Erroneous concerns about child sexual abuse. *Child Abuse & Neglect,*. *24*(1), 149–157.
448. Jones, D. P., & McGraw, J. M. (1987). Reliable and fictitious accounts of sexual abuse to children. *Journal of Interpersonal Violence*, *2*, 27–45.
449. Everson, M., & Boat, B. (1989). False allegations of sexual abuse by children and adolescents. *Journal of the American Academy of Child and Adolescent Psychiatry*, 1 *28*(2), 230–235.
450. Children's Bureau. (2001). *The Adoption and Foster Care Analysis Reporting System Preliminary Report*. Washington, DC: U.S. Department of Health and Human Services, Administration on Children, Youth and Families.
451. Child Welfare Outcomes. (2001). *Technical report, 1999*. Arlington, VA: James Bell Associates.
452. Rezac, S., & Finkelhor, D. (2002). *Arrest patterns for offenders against juveniles*. Unpublished manuscript.
453. National Association of Crime Victim Compensation Boards (2003). *Homepage*. Retrieved February 23, 2003, from http://www.nacvcb.org/index.html.
454. Davis, N. S., & Wells, S. J. (1996). *Justice system processing of child abuse and neglect cases*. Washington, DC: American Bar Association Center on Children and the Law.
455. Stevens, G., Fischer, D. G., & Berg, L. (1992). *Review and monitoring of child sexual abuse cases in selected sites in Saskatchewan: Studies on the sexual abuse of children in Canada*., Ottawa, Ontario, Canada: Department of Justice.
456. Cross, T. P., Walsh, W., Jones, L. M., & Simone, M. (2002). Prosecution of child abuse: A meta-analysis of rates of criminal justice decisions. *Trauma Violence & Abuse*, *4*(4), 323–340.
457. Mennerich, A. L., Martell, D., Cross, T. P., & White, A. (2002). *Case and system predictors of prosecution of child abuse*. Washington, DC: Department of Sociology, American University.
458. Smith, B. E., & Elstein, S. G. (1993). *The prosecution of child sexual and physical abuse cases*. Washington, DC: National Center on Child Abuse and Neglect.

459. Runyan, D. (1998). Discussion: Emotional impact of the child sexual abuse medical examination. *Child Abuse & Neglect*, *22*(6), 585.

460. Cashmore, J., & Horsky, M. (1998). The prosecution of child sexual assault. *Australian and New Zealand Journal of Criminology*, *21*, 241–252.

461. Cross, T. P., Whitcomb, D., & De Vos, E. D. (1995). Criminal Justice outcomes of prosecution of child sexual abuse: A case flow analysis. *Child Abuse & Neglect*, *19*(12), 1431–1442.

462. Martone, M., Jaudes, P. K., & Cavins, M. (1996). Criminal prosecution of child sexual abuse cases. *Child Abuse & Neglect*, 20(5), 457–464.

463. Rogers, C. M. (1982). Child sexual abuse and the courts: Preliminary findings. *Social Work and Human Sexuality*, *1*(1),145–153.

464. Cohen, J. A., & Mannarino, A. P. (1997). A treatment study for sexually abused preschool children: Outcome during a one-year follow-up. *Journal of the American Academy of Child and Adolescent Psychiatry*, *36*(9), 1228–1235.

465. Deblinger, E., Stauffer, L. B., & Steer, R. A. (2001). Comparative efficacies of supportive and cognitive behavioral group therapies for young children who have been sexually abused and their non-offending mothers. *Child Maltreatment*, *6*, 332–343.

466. Whitcomb, D., & Hardin, M. (1996). *Coordinating criminal and juvenile court proceedings in child maltreatment cases* (pp. 1–3). Washington, DC: National Institute of Justice.

467. Taussig, H. N., Clyman, R. B., & Landsverk, J. (2001). Children who return home from foster care: A 6-year prospective study of behavioral health outcomes in adolescence. *Pediatrics*, *108*(1), 108–118.

468. U.S. Department of Health and Human Services. (2003). *National study of child protective services systems and reform efforts: Review of state CPS policy*. Retrieved July 31, 2006, from http://aspe.hhs.gov/hsp/cps%2Dstatus03/state%2Dpolicy03/.

469. Gelles, R. J. (2003). Florida sheriffs take on child abuse investigations. *NIJ Journal*, *250*, 36–38.

470. Marneffe, C. (1999). Alternative forms of intervention. In M. E. Helfer, R. S. Kempe, and R. D. Krugman (Eds.), *The battered child* (pp. 500–520). Chicago: University of Chicago Press.

471. Elder, R. W., Shults, R. A., Sleet, D. A., Nichols, J. L., Zaza, S., & Thompson, R. S. (2002). Effectiveness of sobriety checkpoints for reducing alcohol-involved crashes. *Traffic Injury Prevention*, *3*(4), 266–274.

472. Frey, K. S., Nolen, S. B., Van Schoiack Edstrom, L., & Hirschstein, M. K. (2001). Second step: Effects on social goals and behavior. Presented at the Annual Meeting of the Society for Prevention Research, Washington, DC.

473. Thornton, T. N., Craft, C. A., Dahlberg, L. L., Lynch, B. S., & Baer, K. (2000). *Best practices of youth violence prevention: A sourcebook for community action*. Atlanta, GA: Centers for Disease Control and Prevention.

474. Tremblay, R. E., Pagani-Kurtz, L., Masse, L. C., Vitaro, F., & Pihl, R. O. (1995). A bimodal preventive intervention for disruptive kindergarten boys: Its impact through mid-adolescence. *Journal of Consulting and Clinical Psychology*, *63*, 560–568.

475. Conduct Problems Prevention Research Group. (1999). Initial impact of the Fast Track prevention trial for conduct problems: I. The high-risk sample. *Journal of Consulting and Clinical Psychology*, *67*, 631–647.

476. Mytton, J., DiGuiseppi, C., Gough, D., Taylor, R., & Logan, S. (2005). School-based secondary prevention programmes for preventing violence. *Cochrane Database of Systematic Reviews*, *3*, CD004606.
477. Flannery, D. J., Vazsonyi, A. T., Liau, A. K., Guo, S., Powell, K. E., Atha, H., Vesterdal, W. et al. (2003). Initial behavior outcomes for the PeaceBuilders Universal School-Based Violence Prevention Program. *Developmental Psychology*, *39*(2), 292–308.
478. Foshee, V. A., Bauman, K. E., Ennett, S. T., Suchindran, C., Benefield, T., & Linder, F. G. (2005). Assessing the effects of the dating violence prevention program "Safe Dates" using random coefficient regression modeling. *Prevention Science*, *6*(3),245–258.
479. Grossman, D. C., Neckerman, H. J., Koepsell, T. D., Liu, P. Y., Asher, K. N., Beland, K., et al. (1997). Effectiveness of a violence prevention curriculum among children in elementary school. A randomized controlled trial. *Journal of the American Medical Association*, *277*, 1605–1611.
480. Melton, G. B. (1992). The improbability of prevention of sexual abuse. In D. Willis, E. Holden, & M. Rosenberg (Eds.), *Child abuse prevention* (pp. 168–189). New York: John Wiley.
481. Reppucci, N. D., & Haugaard, J. J. (1989). Prevention of child sexual abuse: Myth or reality. *American Psychologist*, *44*(10), 1266–1275.
482. Krivacska, J. J. (1990). *Designing child sexual abuse programs*. Springfield, IL: C. C. Thomas.
483. Budin, L., & Johnson, C. (1989). Sex abuse prevention programs: Offenders' attitudes about the efficacy. *Child Abuse & Neglect*, *13*, 77–87.
484. Finkelhor, D., & Baron, L. (1986). High-risk children. In D. Finkelhor (Ed.), *A sourcebook on child sexual abuse* (pp. 60–88). Beverly Hills, CA: Sage.
485. Daro, D. (1989). When should prevention education begin? *Journal of Interpersonal Violence*, *4*(2), 257–260.
486. MacIntyre, D., & Carr, A. (2000). Prevention of child sexual abuse: Implications of programme evaluation research. *Child Abuse Review*, *9*, 183–199.
487. Kaufman, K., Barber, M., Mosher, H., & Carter, M. (2002). New directions for prevention: Reconceptualizing child sexual abuse as a public health concern. In P. A. Schewe (Ed.), *Preventing violence in relationships: Developmentally appropriate intervention across the life span* (pp. 27–54). Washington, DC: APA Books.
488. Gibson, L. E., & Leitenberg, H. (2000). Child sexual abuse prevention programs: Do they decrease the occurrence of child sexual abuse? *Child Abuse & Neglect*, *24*(9), 1115–1125.
489. Finkelhor, D., Asdigian, N., & Dziuba-Leatherman, J. (1995). The effectiveness of victimization prevention instruction: An evaluation of children's responses to actual threats and assaults. *Child Abuse & Neglect*, *19*(2), 137–149.
490. Klein, A., & Tabachnick, J. (2002). Framing a new approach: Finding ways to effectively prevent sexual abuse by youth. *Prevention Researcher*, *9*(4), 8–10.
491. Tabachnick, J., & Blanchard, G. (2002). The prevention of sexual abuse: Psychology and public health perspectives. *Journal of Sexual Addiction and Compulsivity*, *9*, 1–14.
492. Saul, J., & Audage, N. C. (2007). *Preventing child sexual abuse within youth-serving organizations: Getting started on policies and procedures*. Atlanta, GA: Center for Disease Control and Prevention, National Center for Injury Prevention and Control.

Index

CPSIA information can be obtained
at www.ICGtesting.com
Printed in the USA
BVHW03s1119200918
528003BV00003B/61/P